Literary Theory:

For Naomi and Gareth,
Miriam and Olalekan,
Sam and Tim

Literary Theory:
A Reintroduction

David Ayers

Blackwell
Publishing

BLACKWELL PUBLISHING
350 Main Street, Malden, MA 02148–5020, USA
9600 Garsington Road, Oxford OX4 2DQ, UK
550 Swanston Street, Carlton, Victoria 3053, Australia

First published 2008 by Blackwell Publishing Ltd

1 2008

Library of Congress Cataloging-in-Publication Data

Ayers, David, 1960–
    Literary theory : a reintroduction / David Ayers.
        p. cm.
    Includes bibliographical references (p.) and index.
    ISBN 978-1-4051-3601-3 (pbk. : alk. paper)—ISBN 978-1-4051-3602-0 (hardcover : alk. paper) 1. English literature—History and criticism—Theory, etc. 2. Literature—History and criticism—Theory, etc. 3. American literature—History and criticism—Theory, etc. 4. Politics and literature—English-speaking countries. 5. Criticism—English-speaking countries. I. Title.

    PR21.A94 2008
    820.9—dc22
                                                                                    2007015776

A catalogue record for this title is available from the British Library.

Set in 10/12.5pt Galliard
by Graphicraft Limited, Hong Kong
Printed and bound in Singapore
by Markono Print Media Pte Ltd

The publisher's policy is to use permanent paper from mills that operate a sustainable forestry policy, and which has been manufactured from pulp processed using acid-free and elementary chlorine-free practices. Furthermore, the publisher ensures that the text paper and cover board used have met acceptable environmental accreditation standards.

For further information on
Blackwell Publishing, visit our website at
www.blackwellpublishing.com

Contents

Introduction

This study is a reintroduction to literary theory which has the aim of setting the arrival of 'theory' in the 1970s in a social and historical context. There is a lot of society and history that could have been brought in and I have been necessarily selective! Above all events, it is the Russian Revolution which stands over the creation of modern English studies, and developments in theory have always been defined in relation, however mediated, to the major events of decolonization, civil rights, women's liberation, strikes and wars, cold or otherwise. I interpret 'literary theory' very broadly, to include theories affecting the institutionalization of literary studies, and occasionally to allude to theoretical developments which lie outside the frame of the official university altogether. By way of reintroducing literary theory, I have gone back to Leavis (and to Arnold), and come up through I. A. Richards, John Crowe Ransom, Raymond Williams and others to the arrival of theory proper in the 1960s. These earlier phases of literary theory were often treated dismissively by the 'theory' of the 1970s, and are sometimes excluded from anthologies of theory, although they have all been the subject of important though mostly hostile critical study. Chapters 1, 2 and 3 effect this reintroduction, and I have given this period a relatively full exposition. Chapters 4 and 5 deal with the arrival of 'high theory' in what I have called the 'moment of theory' of the 1960s and 1970s. The usual names are here, mostly French – Louis Althusser, Roland Barthes, Jacques Derrida – but I shift focus from these theorists to the process of their reception and adaptation to British and American contexts. Chapter 6 charts the growing interest in anti-Enlightenment thought which culminates in the dominance of Foucault in the 1980s and the florescence of postmodernism. Chapter 7 is an interlude which examines the PC Wars in the United

States, a moment of intense interest for the unprecedented attack, orchestrated at the highest level, on university culture. Under the rubric of 'Ethics' in Chapter 8 I suggest that in a complicated fashion the ethical priority in literary theory has shifted to the United States, via a positionally ambiguous 'postcolonial' detour, which I discuss in relation to queer theory and ethnic studies. These developments of the 1990s are not so vulnerable that they cannot handle a little critique, and, while asserting the ethical centrality of these branches of theory, I have taken the opportunity to identify a few distortions. Finally, I present a short discussion of the nature of literature as seen by Alain Badiou, and ask whether the functionalist mode of literary theory from Arnold to Vizenor requires correction or supplementation by a return to literature 'as such', as some have started now openly to wonder.

One consequence of my approach is that elements of theory not origi-nating in the United States or Britain are discussed in terms of the moment and context of their adoption. This means, for example, that Ferdinand de Saussure, whose influential *Course in General Linguistics* was published in 1916, is discussed not in Chapter 1, as simple chrono-logy would appear to demand, but in Chapter 4, in the context of a discussion of the Anglo-American reception of French structuralist poetics in the 1970s. Although this structure may seem counter-intuitive, I have been keen to stress the moment of adoption of Saussure's work over its meaning for and in its original context, not least since it is evident that the later reception of Saussure's work, outside and even inside the context of linguistic study, has involved significant misprisions. These have been unpacked at length by Saussure scholars keen to rescue the original Saussure from what they consider to be the tainted contexts of anthropo-logy and semiology which I describe here.[1]

I am very aware of gaps in this study and have resisted the temptation to pile in too many names and references for the sake of completeness. I have discussed theory in both Britain and the United States, even though it would have been difficult in one volume to present either nation comprehensively. However, I feel that the difference between Britain and the United States is important for theory, although it is only occasionally acknowledged. Finally, I am aware that important figures are presented through selected key works, with the effect that changes in their thinking are not reflected in my accounts. This is because I am trying to give an account of certain moments in the development of theory, not of the whole careers of theorists.

Part of Chapter 1 condenses arguments and material which I have presented at length in 'Literary Criticism and Cultural Politics', in Laura

Marcus and Peter Nicholls, eds., *The Cambridge History of Twentieth-Century English Literature* (Cambridge University Press, 2005, pp. 379–95), and is reprinted with permission. A short section in Chapter 3 is drawn from a longer exposition in 'Materialism and the Book' published in *Poetics Today* 24: 4 (2004).

I would like to thank the School of English at the University of Kent for understanding treatment in respect of study leave. My present and former colleagues at Kent have always provided an environment of the highest calibre, and I have had many useful conversations in corridors and seminar rooms which have contributed to this study. For their particular help, I would like to thank David Stirrup for his guidance on Native American matters; Henry Claridge for help in tracking down 1930s texts; my former colleague Thomas Docherty for sharing his extensive knowledge of all matters French; Rod Edmond for innumerable useful exchanges. Thanks to my editors and readers at Blackwell for their impressive efficiency. Special thanks for all her support to Margaret. Finally I would like to recall a memorable conversation about beauty and form which I had with our late, talented and much missed colleague, Sasha Roberts.

Chapter 1

English as
a University Subject

Literature has always been an object of study. It is necessary to study literature and reflect on its processes in order to create it in the first place. The process of reflection on literature might be silently incorporated into the practice of creating it, or it might be formed into an explicit, extra-literary discourse designed to accompany literature, be set alongside it, in order to clarify and explain, or perhaps mask and appropriate literature or literary objects. Indeed, as an art of words, literature can include explicit verbalized theory within itself, modifying if not entirely upsetting the apparent opposition of literature as a concrete actuality and theory as the discourse which comments on that actuality – Hamlet's remarks to the Player are among the most famous examples, and the tradition goes back to Homer. These simple facts are worth keeping before us as we review the recent history of theory, since they remind us that any human practice is always implicitly theoretical, and that any theory is unavoidably involved in some kind of practice. Some commentators will proceed from this simple insight to question the ability of theory (discourse, language, the idea) to transcend physical and social realities, and will stress that all forms of organized language which make theoretical claims are reflective of social interests, 'discourses' which silently embody coercive institutional imperatives. Since this position is one of the common stances of contemporary theory, it cannot be the stance of a study, even a survey such as this, which aims to bring into view recent practices of theory on terms other than their own. However, for the purpose of this study it is desirable to qualify the use of the notion of 'literary theory' by specifying that 'theory' is not exclusively located in the key theoretical documents of official literary theory, but is found too in practices of literary criticism and commentary, and may be silently embodied in literary works, in the practice of their creation, distribution and reception, and – if we are to assume any relationship between 'literature' and 'life' at all – theory as discourse and as practice will reveal itself to belong in large part to the cultural, social and political discourses, institutions and practices of which it is part.

This study will focus on the last 100 years or so, and will predominantly examine theory as an element of the University study of English. That said, the notion of theory should not be limited to the University, not only because the study or reading of literature at a high level is not exclusively the domain of the University, but also because 'theory' is a key term in the University's appropriation of literature for and as literary studies. In this respect, literary studies themselves form part of a complex system of cultural capital in which the legitimacy of literature and of the various modalities of its pedagogic propagation are intimately tied to the labour market: a degree in English is a qualification with the potential to confer status and economic opportunity. The theory of literary studies is part of this system of legitimation, although literary study itself has mostly attempted to suppress this connection, and the present study is no exception. What this study does stress is the *immanence* of theory, its perpetual involvement with something which is *not* the University, and in a key respect the use of the term theory made here contradicts the form in which the term appeared. For there was certainly a moment, located broadly in the 1970s, in which a challenge to the established study of literature in English Departments in England and America was laid down by socialists and feminists who had become apprised of developments in French and German thought, particularly Marxism and linguistics, which seemed set to shatter the assumptions and methods of the discipline as it then stood. The term 'theory' was used as the catch-all phrase under which linguistic, psychoanalytic, feminist and Marxist criticism announced a war on established literary studies, which for the sake of convenience were labelled 'Leavisism' in Britain, due to the perceived influence of the Cambridge academic F. R. Leavis in the formation of the method and curriculum of literary studies. Leavisism came to be perceived as the root of an ideological blindness and almost willed ignorance within English studies which it was the job of 'theory' to sweep away. The need to 'theorize' a particular text or topic was announced on all hands by critics who called themselves 'theorists', and the markers were laid down in a war between 'theorists' and 'Leavisites' which was often bitter and resulted, in some British universities, in a divided English Department with the two sides barely on speaking terms. Those were interesting times indeed, which this study in part documents, but the term 'theory' cannot be taken on its own terms, even though those terms must be explained, and while it is certainly the case that the adoption by Anglo-American literary studies of numerous ideas new to the discipline marked a period of great change (mediated and disseminated by a succession of primers in, and anthologies of, 'literary theory'), it is also the case that the tendency of 'theory' to cast itself as the Renaissance and the Enlightenment combined and animated by a Romantic hatred for tyranny requires, with hindsight, a little modification.

The teaching of English, though sometimes thought of as a twentieth-century novelty building on precarious nineteenth-century origins, can be traced back to the ancient practice of teaching rhetoric, which survived through the Middle Ages and was a central element in education until the eighteenth century. The pre-eminence of rhetoric was threatened by rationalist criticisms, and the educational centrality of Greek and Latin literature began to give way to vernacular literature as early as the mid-seventeenth century. The growing importance of English studies was confirmed by the landmark appointment in 1828 of a Chair of English Language and Literature at University College, London. Shortly afterwards, the appointment of F. D. Maurice at the newly opened King's College, London, confirmed the beginnings of English literary studies in something like their modern form. Maurice's approach tended towards textual close reading, based on his own classical background. He believed that English literature and English history were linked in a consciousness of nationality and national destiny, and emphasized the importance of the function of English among the middle class. The middle class were to be targets of English literary education because he saw them as bearers of the national project and as a politically stabilizing force in a time of Chartist unrest. Maurice considered English to be an appropriate subject for women, and was able to implement his ideas on female education when he became the first principal of Queen's College in 1848.[1] Oxford and Cambridge developed English studies only later. The first Chair in English at Oxford came in 1904 and the Cambridge English Tripos originated in 1917.

It is usual to date the origins of modern English studies from its foundation at Cambridge, because it was at Cambridge that a version of the subject in which the reading of texts would be elevated above their history or philology was first heavily promoted. This form of English studies was plainly anticipated in the nineteenth century, as we have noted, but the version of English established at Cambridge by F. R. Leavis, Q. D. Leavis and I. A. Richards is generally considered to have provided the dominant model in Britain for at least three decades. The approach of the Leavises was fundamentally centred on the conditioning of the reader, and its keyword was 'sensibility', a term which subsequent theory has tended to dismiss as an anti-rational, ideological mask. Although the Leavises harked back to a lost condition of England in which class stratification was unalienated because each knew his or her place and all were linked by common linguistic intelligence, the Leavisite project was fundamentally futuristic, and in its way no less radical than the socialist and feminist projects which came bitterly to oppose it under the banner of theory.

It is customary to compare the project of the Leavises, in particular, to that of the poet and educationalist Matthew Arnold (1822–88). The validity of the comparison does not lie primarily in any detailed similarity of theoretical articulation. Indeed, the mapping of history in terms of dominant ideas ('Arnoldian' or 'Leavisite') can easily be pushed into a false idealism which finds something like an evil power (albeit a discursive power) at work behind history, moving it on in a sinister way. The use-fulness of establishing the connection between nineteenth-and twentieth-century versions of English studies lies in the comparison of contexts, and in the insight that modern literary studies have tended to be shaped as a response to social antagonism, whether as an attempt to meliorate or offset the conflict of social classes, or further to articulate and provoke such conflict in order to accelerate social change. It is certainly possible to view Arnold and Leavis as opponents of social change and defenders of the status quo,[2] and a Marxist reading of history which views com-munism as a teleological inevitability will tend to see them as little more than obstacles to change. The apparent conservatism of Arnold and Leavis can be given a different gloss, however, albeit one that a Marxist view of history might find hard to sustain. Both Arnold and Leavis are operating in the context of what they perceive to be rapid social change, and are interested in two ideals: the avoidance of unbridled social conflict and the preservation of the best values of existing society, even though the elements in society which created or sustained those values are now losing power. Arnold's lessons concern peace, the maintenance of differ-ence in unity, and the modernization of cultural identities in a process of historical change. This will seem like a contentious claim, but I suggest that Arnold's vision of the essential universality of culture is not worse than any contemporary claims about hybridization of the arts and of identity itself. The need for dominant powers to adopt subordinate cul-tures is an issue as much of our own time as Arnold's, and Arnold's very nineteenth-century assumptions about the identity of a people and its culture are not very different from those of liberal pluralists in our own times who share Arnold's agenda of diminishing the potential for social conflict through cultural convergence and enlightenment.

Arnold states that he wrote the lectures which appeared as *On the Study of Celtic Literature* (1867) in response to a piece in *The Times* which was itself a response to his own support for a Welsh Eisteddfod – a festival of Welsh-language literature and Welsh music and dance. Arnold had made measured comments in support of the Eisteddfod, in terms which endorsed cultural Welshness, but insisted on the need for people in Wales to embrace English. He compared what he took to be the people's culture as manifested at the Eisteddfod to the lack of culture among the commercial middle class of England – whom he termed 'Philistines':

> When I see the enthusiasm these Eisteddfods can awaken in your whole people, and then think of the tastes, the literature, the amusements, of our own lower and middle class, I am filled with admiration for you. It is a consoling thought, and one which history allows us to entertain, that nations disinherited of political success may yet leave their mark on the world's progress, and contribute powerfully to the civilisation of mankind. We in England [. . .] are imperilled by what I call the 'philistinism' of our middle class. On the side of beauty and taste, vulgarity; on the side of morals and feeling, coarseness; on the side of mind and spirit, unintelligence – this is Philistinism. Now, then, is the moment for the greater delicacy and spirituality of the Celtic peoples who are blended with us, if it be but wisely directed, to make itself prized and honoured. In a certain measure the children of Taliesin and Ossian have now an opportunity for renewing the famous feat of the Greeks, and conquering their conquerors.[3]

The Times' response to Arnold tackled the issue of the assimilation of Wales to England in a strident modernizing fashion, insisting that the Welsh look to their future with England and forget their cultural past. We should bear in mind when looking at this text that Wales was not a recent imperial addition but a long-standing and integral part of the English throne. Arnold quotes from *The Times*:

> The Welsh language is the curse of Wales. Its prevalence, and the ignorance of English have excluded, and even now exclude the Welsh people from the civilization of their English neighbours. An Eisteddfod is one of the most mischievous and selfish pieces of sentimentalism which could possibly be perpetrated. It is simply a foolish interference with the natural progress of civilization and prosperity. If it is desirable that the Welsh should talk English, it is a monstrous folly to encourage them in a loving

fondness for their old language. Not only the energy and power, but the intelligence and music of Europe, have come mainly from Teutonic sources, and this glorification of everything Celtic, if it were not pedantry, would be sheer ignorance. The sooner all Welsh specialities disappear from the face of the earth the better.[4]

Arnold opposes culture to progress. 'Improvement' and 'progress' had been bywords of the Industrial Revolution. As far as proponents of economic development were concerned, progress was to be led by changes in economic methods of production, and the past was to be unsentimentally discarded in the interest of whatever practices would increase the general wealth (and the particular wealth of property owners). Readers of Jane Austen will recall that one of the key moments of moral self-definition given to Fanny Price in *Mansfield Park* occurs when, with her customary reserve, she signals her dislike of the 'improvement' of the Sotherton estate by its modernizing owner, Rushworth. Modernization is driven by the capital surpluses generated by changes in the technology and organization of production, the process which Karl Marx had attempted to account for in *Capital* (1867). The very process of rapid change generated in some quarters an unsentimental attitude towards the past but, equally, rapid change made the historical nature of humanity far more visible than ever.

The growing awareness of history as a process of change, and not merely as a random selection of events dictated by destiny or chance, was accompanied by a rising tendency to equate culture, as an ensemble of objects and practices across arts and daily life, with the very stuff that defined a 'people' as a historical agent or entity. Johann Gottfried von Herder (1744–1803) argued in a series of publications that history was best grasped in terms of the culture of peoples rather than as the history of battles and conquest, and advanced a relativistic account of human cultures in which cultural difference came into view through analysis of the literature and other arts of a people. Herder's approach suggested that the contemporary shape of existence within one's own national culture might also be grasped as the product of a historical process that could in turn be understood through the analysis of the nation's past cultural products. In a similar vein, Giambattista Vico's *Principles of New Science* (1725) attempted to demonstrate the importance of poetic understanding for the development of modern society. Vico claimed that the history of a nation resembled the development from infancy to maturity. Knowledge in the earliest society was the domain of poet-theologians. This insight gives Vico the means to interpret the literary texts of

ancient societies as the symbolic encoding of the totality of their knowledge. The *New Science* was an early example of the growing tendency
to view human society as historical, not natural, and was original in its
attempt to grasp social evolution through the analysis of culture. Whether
presenting narratives of degeneration (Rousseau) or of progress (Vico,
Herder and Condorcet), eighteenth-century historicists took man's
historical progress from ancient to modern times as their subject.

Arnold's response to the article in *The Times* is an attempt to offset the
modernizing attitude to the past. This is not done from antiquarian
interest, but from the point of view of the dominant and, on Arnold's
terms, progressive state power as it stands in relation to subordinate
peoples. It is an early examination of the cultural problems attendant on
imperialism and on what is now called 'globalization', and of the potential consequences both for the dominant power and for the subaltern in
that process. Arnold does not map this in terms of the Western 'subject'
versus the colonized 'Other' – terms which would be given wide currency in this context only after 1945, in the tradition of de Beauvoir and
Sartre – but instead thinks in terms of race, following the assumptions of
that time that the English were basically Germanic and the Irish basically
Celtic. This racial categorization seems to creak more than a little from
our own contemporary point of view: the underlying assumption that
people are shaped by collective cultural unities has proved one that modern commentators have attempted to leave behind. The unity of a culture
is now seen more in terms of its formative social conflicts than in terms
of any prior, idealized unity of 'spirit'. Yet the problem is fundamentally
modern, and Arnold's intervention indicates the scope of claims that will
be made about literature in particular as a bearer of cultural identities
which have ever since haunted the theory of literature.

'Behold England's difficulty in governing Ireland!'[5] Arnold views *The
Times'* attack on Welsh-language culture as a problem of imperialism.

> There is nothing like love and admiration for bringing people to a likeness
> with what they love and admire; but the Englishman seems never to dream
> of employing these influences upon a race he wants to fuse with himself.
> [. . .] His Welsh and Irish fellow citizens are hardly more amalgamated
> with him now than they were when Wales and Ireland were first con-
> quered.[6]

Arnold's program is one of remarkable realism, even if the terms of
his study, which depends on the notion of racial 'genius', now seem
superseded. The realism, of course, might not be to all tastes. Political

subordination is accepted as a given and even a good; subaltern culture is encouraged in flattering terms. Celts are 'airy', 'quick', 'noble', 'indomitable', 'sensuous' and so on, while their poetry gains in style precisely because of their lack of technological domination of nature: 'Celtic poetry seems to make up to itself for being unable to master the world and give an adequate interpretation of it, by throwing all its force into style, by bending language at any rate to its will, and expressing the ideas it has with an unsurpassable intensity, elevation, and effect.'[7] Celtic poetry is closer to nature, because it does not share in the process of modernization which has made nature the object of language, and its very substance constitutes a kind of repressed element to which its opposite – in Arnold's account the 'Germanic spirit' – has limited access. Although Arnold's account is cast in racial terms, it is also plain that the opposition between the Celtic and the Germanic constitutes a kind of allegory of the trajectory of human spirit, from the pre-rational to the rational state, with Celtic literature coming to stand in some ways for the whole of literature, having the function of carrying the beauty of the magical and pre-scientific view of nature into the world of scientific rationalism which has made nature its object. Arnold does not explicitly express the matter in these terms but, as we review the vocabulary with which he refers to the Celts and laments the loss of their culture, it is hard to avoid the conclusion that for him literature is the expression not only of this or that people or culture, but also of the lost, pre-scientific world as such.

Arnold reflects other eighteenth- and nineteenth-century thinkers in seeing literature as what we might now call a collective cultural imaginary, finding whole attitudes and ways of being encoded or sedimented in a particular rhetorical flourish or stylistic preference. The teaching of literature, and of poetry in particular, must also ameliorate present conflict, a function examined by Arnold in *Culture and Anarchy* (1869). *Culture and Anarchy* classifies the aristocratic, established church, Conservative interests as 'Barbarian', the commercial, nonconformist, Liberal interests as 'Philistine', and the workers and socialists as 'the Populace'. As the Barbarians lose power with the rise of the Philistines, Arnold asserts that culture will offset the tendency to anarchy created by the one-sided 'Hebraism' of the individualist Philistines, and by the mass demonstrations and social unruliness of the Populace. Culture is 'the study of perfection' and 'goes beyond religion'.[8] Culture is identified with poetry. Arnold later wrote: 'The future of poetry is immense, because in poetry, where it is worthy of its highest destinies, our race, as time goes on, will find an ever surer and surer stay'.[9] The middle class will learn not to *produce* cultural artefacts but to *know* them. Hence the emphasis on *criticism* rather than *creativity*. Culture embodies a universality, a 'harmonious expansion of *all* the powers which make the beauty and worth of human nature', which 'goes beyond religion' and 'consists in becoming something rather than in having something', defending an 'idea of perfection as an *inward* condition of the mind and spirit' which 'is at variance with the mechanical and material civilisation' of England. Culture therefore stands for the greatest possible degree of universality and is not merely the vehicle of human progress but also its substance.

The influence of Arnold in the early twentieth century is found far more in the field of criticism than in that of poetic practice, and especially in the development of English as a university subject. On the one hand, Arnold situates literature in a key position as the expression of the identity of a nation or people, as the repository of a lost or eclipsed way of being, as a way to moderate what he perceives to be the materialism of the rising commercial class (and also of their upcoming socialist rivals), and as the bearer of the values of conquered or colonized peoples which can be preserved in the conquering imperial culture in a dialectical process which modifies the dominant power, thereby ensuring a secret triumph for the defeated, and at the same time pacifies the colonized and establishes the legitimacy of the conqueror. On the other hand, Arnold brings all of these grand narratives of cultural identity and change back down to the text as an object of criticism, in the idea that nuances of observation and judgement, rather then broad content, are at the very heart of the culture-bearing modality of texts, not peripheral questions of refinement of an effete 'taste'. Arnold's vision builds on views of race and culture developed during the previous hundred years, and is a synthesis of historicist views of culture. It is developed with a keen awareness that existing society is in a process of change, and with the intention of developing a strategy to manage that change. Criticism and pedagogy are the cornerstones of this complex social program, of such potential scope that Arnold's work can only partially suggest its future course. It is above all an administrative venture. It proceeds in the name of all that is true and beautiful, but there is a tension between the aesthetic refinement it advocates and the grand narrative of culture and change which it identifies as the metanarrative governing all human culture. It seeks to account for and manage what it terms 'culture' as part of a process of government (and therefore national and particular), but also to situate culture as the site in which an as yet unexpressed future of changed relations of class and race are being anticipated and negotiated (and therefore supranational and universal). Literary reading and scholarship are granted a massive legitimacy in this set of claims, and even though Marxist and postcolonial commentary of recent decades has tended to dismiss Arnold as authoritarian and imperialist, the kind of models he employs are not too far from those implicitly favoured by cultural administration today – certainly at the level of arts management, and especially in the framing assumptions of literary studies in the University.

In Arnold's work, literature can be seen in the process of coming to occupy a grand role, in part transcendent, in large part administrative, mediated by schools and universities, and by the official organs of criticism and taste. Literature at that time had not, however, subordinated itself to these grand institutional imperatives and grand narratives. *Culture and Anarchy* is certainly a seminal text for us, but was written against a background of hostility to culture, and literature in the later nineteenth century – to the extent it identified with art (poetry) and not with entertainment (fiction) – was a marginal activity in search of legitimation and a proper domain. That is not to say that practitioners of literature as art were socially marginal subjects – not exactly – although they were frequently at odds with the dominant elements in the privileged classes of which they formed a part. Arnold's own account, which proposes a connection between literature's domain of interiority and the outside world of practicality (commerce and science), articulates a distinction between the private and public worlds which is of growing structural importance for literature throughout the nineteenth century and into the twentieth – not least in the literary activities of modernism, which has a key role in the formation of literary studies, especially in the figure of T. S. Eliot.

The theoretical and philosophical material which has produced and analysed this splitting of a private, inner domain and a public and objective domain is a vast one and beyond the scope of this chapter. One dimension of this separation is produced by science, which reveals the objective world to be a mechanism, and indeed seems to imply that subjectivity too may be a mechanism. A key text on this topic is Kant's *Critique of Pure Reason* (1781), which proposes a rigorous separation of the mechanical world of nature and the subjective realm of moral freedom. Another dimension of the separation is brought about by the development of capitalism and the evolution of the 'interior' as a living space which increasingly replaces nature. This phenomenon – which includes such effects as the bourgeois living room, the arcade, and the closed illusionistic theatre of Wagner – is given theoretical substance in the work of Walter Benjamin and Theodor Adorno.[10] There are other possible routes to considering the separation of inner and outer worlds, but what should be noted at this point is that the separation is produced within history and is a social fact rather than an absolute fact of nature. The splitting of inner and outer is then a fact both for literature and for literature's own self-theorization, and its persistence as a guiding trope in literary-theoretical debate is central to the opposition between the 'sensibility' of Leavisism and the quasi-scientific and ruthlessly anti-subjective unmasking approach taken by the dominant strand of Althusserian Marxist theory in the 1970s.

In the English literature of the later nineteenth century, aestheticism and its successor movement, decadence, made an ideal of sensory subjectivity. Walter Pater's *Studies in the History of the Renaissance* (1873) celebrated 'perception', 'sensation', 'vision' – the apprehension of the vivid but fleeting moment – as the apex of subjective richness. The human spirit must 'be present always at the focus where the greatest number of vital forces unite in their purest energy. To burn always with this hard, gemlike flame, to maintain this ecstasy, is success in life.'[11] The work of the earlier Romantics usually had moral and political dimensions even if it celebrated subjective affect. In Pater, sensation and perception are not the means of approaching 'nature' as in Wordsworth or Shelley; indeed, cultural objects are preferred over natural ones. The notion of personal, moral 'development' found in Wordsworth's *Prelude* is present in Pater, but only in a form which suggests the refinement of mind for its own sake. The artist as aesthete is given expression in Oscar Wilde's *The Picture of Dorian Gray* (1891), a canonical exploration of the artist which expresses doubts about the moral and political character of the decadent, sensuous consumer. Literature is not necessarily central to the aesthete. Indeed, the appreciation of fine materials – cloths, gems, perfumes – might be quite as important to the aesthetic existence as the higher arts. Moreover, the aesthete is also likely to be a sexual decadent, preferring the sensuous adventure of same-sex and short-term relationships to the propriety of marriage. However, the aesthete need not be viewed as an amoral figure. On the one hand, certainly, the aesthete stands at the apex of capitalist and imperialist culture, the consumer of all that is finest. On the other, as an anti-pragmatic figure who refuses to subordinate the life of the senses and the body to the disciplines of materialist and imperialist British society, the aesthete stands for an alternative mode of existence, and the artist can be read as the anticipatory figure of a future human liberation.

On the one hand, in Arnold 'culture' and 'literature' are assigned major roles in the definition of a people and are harnessed by schools and universities into a pedagogic programme; on the other, the idea of the artist, as developed under French influence by aestheticism and constantly worked over by early twentieth-century modernism, made an entirely different claim on poetic and other writing as an avant-garde activity. The governing question of literary theory is not usually 'What is literature?' but, far more often, 'What is literature for?', and it is not given in advance that it will be the education system rather than the artist which will determine the answer to this question.

American poet Ezra Pound exemplifies the attempt to argue for a function of literature outside the academy which might rise to the challenges of the broadest cultural and pedagogic claims without surrendering the privileged aesthetic consciousness. His 1913 essay 'The Serious Artist' claims Sir Philip Sidney's *Defence of Poesie* (1581) as its model, and claims that it will defend the morality of art against the British socialist Sidney Webb, for whom, Pound falsely claims, 'the arts had better not exist at all'.[12] In the context of 1913 it is a significant detail that Pound identifies a socialist rather than a capitalist as the enemy of the arts. At this time socialism begins to take over from capitalism as the perceived enemy of the arts – at least in the eyes of those artists whose identification is still with the upper classes, the repository of patronage and of all good material things. Ezra Pound's essay speaks in part from the tradition of aestheticism, and in part from the European tradition of anti-bourgeois avant-gardism which was at that time reaching England in the dramatic form of Italian futurism. Although such developments are generally treated as part of the history of literature and the arts, and *not* as part of the history of literary theory, it is important to recognize that comment on literature and its functions – that is, criticism – was not at that time the subject of any kind of administratively agreed division of labour as it is in our own time. Ezra Pound, however, is far from being able to rest any case on the legitimacy of 'creativity' in its own right – the rubric under which artistic production of any kind and at whatever level of competence is routinely celebrated today. Rather, the feeling evident in this essay is that literature must be legitimized in terms of its quasi-scientific moral and historical functions, and that the refinement of perception in the arts (so beloved of the aesthete) must be harnessed to the project of social perfection.

The arts, literature, poesy, are a science, just as chemistry is a science. Their subject is man, mankind, and the individual.

Bad art is inaccurate art. It is art that makes false reports. [. . .] If an artist falsifies his report as to the nature of man, as to his own nature [. . .] he is responsible for future oppressions and future misconceptions.

[... T]he arts provide data for ethics. [...] The serious artist is scientific in that he presents the image of his desire, of his hate, of his indifference as precisely that [...].

The permanent property, the property given to the race at large is precisely these data of the serious scientist and the serious artist [...].[13]

These quotations only hint at the program of production that would eventually include not only Pound's poetic *Cantos*, but also a series of pedagogic works including *ABC of Economics* (1933), *ABC of Reading* (1933) and *Guide to Kulchur* (1938). The eventual outcome of Ezra Pound's career, which ended in support for Mussolini manifested in treasonous and anti-semitic broadcasts made for Rome Radio during the Second World War, are often viewed as the errors of an exceptional and eccentric individual. They can also be seen as the messy development of a theory of literature in the public sphere in which the artist is the principal protagonist, as aesthete, avant-gardist and autodidact, conducting a struggle against institutionalized culture from the outside.

Ezra Pound created an example of the artist as outsider, and of literature as an extra-institutional realm on the margins of the public sphere, even when, in the 1930s, he joined a general trend to harness writers to the public good by presenting readers with digests of facts. Pound was not alone in seeking to continue and reinforce the public-sphere function of literature in the 1920s and 1930s and in this sense became part of the background against which modern literary studies were formulated.

*

The period between the two world wars is marked by a progressive transition in literary circles from an emphasis on the idea of the writer as an artist, an individual operating at the borders of and sometimes against society, to an idea of the writer as a social agent addressing the needs of the people. The main influences on this transition are the growth of socialism, increasing literacy, and the rise of Nazism as both a national and a social threat. Successive Education Acts in England had increased literacy, leading to expectations in some quarters of a general rise in cultural level. However, increased literacy had also resulted in the development of new publication types, such as the carefully commercialized best-seller, and cultural pessimists saw in mass literacy not a phenomenon of mass acculturation, but a process of deliberate under-cultivation in which powerful newspapers pitched at the less educated could create a climate of manipulation and even mass hysteria to suit political ends.

While in the 1920s influential writers and critics, such as Eliot and Leavis, tend to perceive socialism and communism in terms of the threat of massification to culture and civilization, nevertheless, in the 1930s, newer voices, such as Stephen Spender and George Orwell, looked for models with which to identify the writer with the left and escape from the ghetto of being an independent 'artist' – a position that seemed morally indefensible as the threat of war increased in Europe. This period is the background to the formation of Cambridge English and helps to explain and situate its principal theories.

Key documents of the formation of modern English include F. R. Leavis's short pamphlet *Mass Civilisation and Minority Culture* (1930) and Q. D. Leavis's extended study *Fiction and the Reading Public* (1932). *Mass Civilisation and Minority Culture* develops the opposition of its title, making reference to Arnold but noting that Arnoldian certainties regarding 'the will of God' and 'our true selves' can no longer be straightforwardly asserted as the content of 'culture'.[14] Leavis devotes more space to the 'mass civilisation' than to the 'minority culture' which it threatens to usurp. The vocabulary of 'minority culture' has certainly raised questions in the minds of many modern readers, who find it elitist and mystifying. Since this apparently elitist project has informed the substance of modern literary studies it is as well to try to bear in mind, as we read Leavis, that his arguments are embodied in our own practices, and that, albeit couched in a different vocabulary, he expressed goals that might be endorsed by many subsequent practitioners of apparently different political outlook.

Mass Civilisation and Minority Culture argues that there is a 'small minority' capable of the 'discerning appreciation of art and literature'; there are said to be 'only a few' capable of 'unprompted, first-hand judgement'. This matters because the possibilities of life itself are said to be closely influenced by the 'valuations' of this minority. These 'valuations' are called by Leavis a 'currency based upon a very small proportion of gold': 'to the state of such a currency the possibilities of fine living at any time bear a close relation'.[15] The metaphors of value are awkward in the context of culture, which has as its dominant claim the ability to transcend the merely material and commercial, and the phrase 'fine living' has heavy connotations of class and seems to suggest the fine wines or fine dining enjoyed by the privileged minority. However, the vocabulary Leavis employs could be understood both as a rhetorical strategy and as the implicit acknowledgement of objective problems with the venture. No one should be held to their metaphors too closely, perhaps. The parallel with the famous 'gold standard' is highly topical. The theory of some economists at that time was that national and international economy was better regulated by attaching currency value to actual gold reserves held by the banks. Britain abandoned the gold standard to pay for the war and reintroduced it in 1925. Leavis wants to suggest that it is the literature which is of real cultural importance, and criticism which is the mode of circulation of that value, an analogy which suggests a materialist analysis of the processes in which texts are given value or possess it independently which is not finally clarifying (since the economic meaning of the terms is not in itself transparent). The central notion is that the limited amount of valuable literature is like gold and constitutes the real wealth on which the national circulation depends. The notion of 'literary value' has been strongly contested ever since. The mention of 'fine living' is in part strategic – it avoids the appearance of simple moralism that would be incurred by the phrase 'good living' – but also suggests that Leavis's project lacks a real social object even though it constantly gestures towards one. If the goal is social justice, or equality, or wealth redistribution, or even simply peace, this can be stated. Leavis's 'fine living' avoids any political or social commitment in terms of an alliance with socialism or conservatism, but only hazily suggests that a mode of living is at stake: Leavis will frequently use the term 'life' and suggest that the best literature constantly turns towards it. Is the term 'life' a nebulous mystification or does it authentically suggest that something in the very practice of living can only be accessed through the refined thinking of great literature, something which modern culture tends to suppress? Certainly, the term 'life' and the related vocabulary of 'experience' were subsequently criticized by Althusserian theory; yet feminism has celebrated women's writing not only as the repository of life and experience, but as the vehicle of a future life currently denied and as yet unlived. It is as if Leavis harnesses a utopian vocabulary but resists the available utopian content of his own time – socialism, feminism and communism – with the effect of marking out a space for his project which is politically non-committal.

Mass Civilisation and Minority Culture spends more time creating space by attacking contemporary civilization than by mapping out the project of criticism. As an authority for his sense of change and crisis, Leavis cites *Middletown: A Study in Modern American Culture* (1929), the famous study of the impact of cultural modernization on a town in the American Midwest by Robert Staughton Lynd and Helen Merrell Lynd, and claims that Britain is following America in terms of the growing rapidity of change driven by the machine and commerce. Lord Northcliffe's mass-market newspaper the *Daily Mail* is cited as an example of the 'mass-production and standardisation' which threaten civilization. Radio broadcasting and film are said to be 'mainly a means of passive diversion' which 'tend to make active recreation, especially active use of the mind, more difficult'. The developing industry of advertising is cited as the leading example of the use of 'applied psychology' towards the end of 'that deliberate exploitation of the cheap response which characterises our civilisation'.[16] The manipulation of language in advertising debases the currency, in Leavis's jargon, and the effects are felt in both the promotion and the substance of literary fiction, as exemplified by the reviewing activities of the novelist Arnold Bennett. Bennett, the accomplished author of *Anna of the Five Towns* (1902) and *Clayhanger* (1910), was a powerful reviewer whose regular column in the *Evening Standard* was able to make or break reputations. Ezra Pound had represented him in his poetic sequence 'Hugh Selwyn Mauberley' (1920) as dismissing poetry for being commercially unviable. Similarly, Leavis accuses Bennett of complete ignorance regarding poetry, and mocks the strong advocacy he has given to lesser novelists. Leavis's point is not about Bennett himself, but about the alliance of poor critical standards and the press which prevents the best criticism from shaping the tastes of the public. It might seem remarkable that such a central role is claimed for literary criticism, yet in the various mutations of literary theory since Leavis this sense of priority has remained in place in one or other form, even though it is now rarely claimed that literature itself has a dominant social role. If it is our own instinct to be hostile to what we might easily take to be Leavis's elitism, we should note that *Mass Civilisation and Minority Culture* sees this hostility as being already in place and already part of the problem: ' "High-brow" is an ominous addition to the English language. I have said earlier that culture has always been in minority keeping. But the minority now is made conscious, not merely of an uncongenial, but a hostile environment.'[17] Leavis's text projects the author himself as a tetchy essayist, lamenting the loss of influence of a 'minority' that is only hazily defined and which cannot be identified with the more modern category of the 'intellectual'. Yet this work contains the sketch of a sociological thesis about changes in the nature of the public sphere. The key element in this is that mass literacy has not led to an increase in influence of the most literate, as might be hoped, but has stimulated the opposite, a manufactured stratification of literacy in which manipulation, rather than participation in dialogue, has become the objective of capitalists and politicians, aided by the science of behavioural psychology and its adjunct, advertising.

Q. D. Leavis's more extended study, *Fiction and the Reading Public* (1932), replicates F. R. Leavis's claims about the failure of improvements in literacy to be reflected in the dissemination of an improved 'sensibility', and compares the fragmented readership of the modern period to the common linguistic and literary culture which is held to have existed in the Elizabethan period. *Fiction and the Reading Public* makes it plain that the emphasis on individual sensibility is not a reflection of the priorities of aestheticism, but is the form under which the loss of culture as a common binding force in society appears. The background to the Leavises' accounts is the extension of democracy in Britain, the related rise of socialism, and the Russian Revolution. The establishment of English as a University subject is closely linked to the desire to neutralize revolutionary social conflict. The preference for Elizabethan England eschews both the English Revolution and Civil War and the period of massive capitalist growth of the eighteenth and nineteenth centuries. The project is aligned neither with capitalism nor with communism, which it tends to view as simply different versions of the same undesirable phenomenon – mass society. Yet the idea of the 'armed minority' reflects the pre-revolutionary party organization of the Russian Bolsheviks, the communist group led by Lenin, whose strategy in the successful October Revolution of 1917, which brought about the creation of the world's first communist state, was based on the preparedness of a small, theoretically well-equipped, and well-disciplined cadre able to lead the mass of workers at a time of struggle. Although the Leavises' goals are of course very different, their strategy consciously mimics that of the Bolsheviks. Universities and schools are the institutions through which sensibility is to be spread. This is not simply an education policy, functionally conceived, and literature is not simply conceived as the institutional possession of the education system; the Leavises present a strategy for the subversion of mass society, or at least of certain tendencies within it, led by the march of the armed minority through the educational institutions.

The literary journal was an obvious route for cultivating a sensitized audience, hence Leavis's criticism of the *Times Literary Supplement*, and the importance of his own journal, *Scrutiny*. Journals had potential importance in shaping a shared sensibility as an organ of criticism, rather than of scholarship, and were more likely to originate outside the University than within it. Leavis mentions T. S. Eliot's *The Criterion*, John Middleton Murry's *The Adelphi* and Edgell Rickword and Douglas Garman's *The Calendar of Modern Letters* as the most eminent 'highbrow' journals of the period. Each of these journals adopted a different stance towards the social purpose of literature. *The Calendar of Modern Letters* continued to uphold the independence of art and the artist, adopting a kind of pessimistic neutrality which resembled that of the modernist artist and writer Wyndham Lewis, whose critique of modernity in *The Art of Being Ruled* (1926) was compared by Rickword to Matthew Arnold's *Culture and Anarchy*.[18] The *Calendar* generally adopted a negative tone and accepted that literature was being forced out of the public sphere. Wyndham Lewis, who later entitled a book *Men Without Art* (1934), made this blunt assessment in the journal: 'The only *rationale* of the professional artist to-day is to provide the critic with material for criticism.'[19] The editor reflected this pessimism: 'verse [now] offers less nourishment to the sophisticated adult than it has done at any time in the last three hundred and thirty years.'[20]

Independent writers and artists such as Rickword and Lewis struggled to identify an independent role for art. The stance of the isolated artist had been undermined by the grimness of the First World War and the example of the Russian Revolution, which made it very difficult for artists to adopt the energetic and confrontational stance of pre-war avant-gardes such as futurism. Fascism in Italy and, subsequently, Nazism in Germany appeared to have a broader social base than traditional conservatism, and promised resistance to communism and socialism. They seemed to offer an alternative to the class politics of socialism and conservatism which attracted a small number of writers who persisted in seeing themselves as artists. However, as the decade of the 1930s progressed and the likelihood of war increased, writers and artists tended to identify with the left against Franco in Spain, Mussolini in Italy and Hitler in Germany, although Ezra Pound became a supporter of Mussolini and Wyndham Lewis became a defender of Hitler.

Unlike Pound and Lewis, of whom he was a friend and collaborator, T. S. Eliot was highly influential on the formation of the discipline of English even though he was not an academic and did not have a University position. His journal *The Criterion*, which began publication in 1922, had a distinct literary program organized around the term 'classicism', and aligned itself with French Catholic intellectuals and the right-wing Action Française. Eliot had been a productive essayist before he founded *The Criterion*, and some of these essays were gathered together in *The Sacred Wood* (1920), which had lasting influence on English studies. The most famous of these essays, 'Tradition and the Individual Talent' (1919),[21] claimed a centrality and seriousness for poetry and criticism. It asserted that critical attention should focus on poetry rather than on the biographies of poets, that the poet should be regarded as the impersonal catalyst for poetic activity, and that the poem should be assessed in terms of its relation to tradition, not in terms of its novelty. The principle of attending to the work rather than the author was to gain massive influence among one or other variety of formalist critic throughout the century, and the emphasis on the importance of criticism and the critic renewed the Arnoldian vision of the role of criticism.

The codification of Eliot's position of impersonality as a textual formalism was widely taken up in Britain and America, in contrast to the social and political program of which it was a part. Eliot's theory of impersonality was a cornerstone of his opposition to romanticism in both politics and the arts, and his journal *The Criterion* was the main organ of his anti-romantic, 'classicist' program. Eliot's classicist position was set out in a review of T. E. Hulme's *Speculations* (1924). Hulme influenced the aesthetics and politics of Pound and Lewis as well as Eliot, supplying each with a version of 'classicist', anti-romantic theory. The aesthetic element of Romanticism which Hulme opposed was the Romantic emphasis on subjectivity; in the realm of politics, classicism was opposed to the belief in progress, said to be Romantic, and linked in these accounts to unbridled Romantic subjectivity. Eliot refers to Hulme's collection of essays in setting out his own classicism:

> In this volume he appears as the forerunner of a new attitude of mind which should be the twentieth-century mind [. . .]. Hulme is classical, reactionary and revolutionary; he is the antipodes of the eclectic, tolerant and democratic mind of the end of the last century. [. . .] Classicism is in some sense reactionary, but it must be in a profounder sense revolutionary.[22]

Eliot's theory of textuality, which emphasizes the text as an autonomous object, is rooted in this opposition to Romantic subjectivism. For Eliot, art is on the side of order, while subjectivity and revolution are on the side of anarchy. Eliot shared with Wyndham Lewis the belief that the emphasis on subjectivity of the aestheticist movement had resulted in a catastrophic withdrawal of the artist from the public sphere. That said, Eliot and Lewis struggled to supply an alternative. In his article 'The Values of the Doctrine Behind Subjective Art', published in Eliot's *Criterion*, Wyndham Lewis called for 'a new, and if necessary shattering critique of modernity', and claimed that all artistic tradition had been destroyed, leaving modern artists as 'the cave-men of the new mental wilderness'. In this dramatic analysis, which refuses the soothing notion of artistic tradition as a comfortable continuity, it is revolutionary change in society which has shattered the possibility of a viable public sphere, and artists have failed to create a public art and public language by retreating into subjectivism.[23] *The Criterion* found little in contemporary literature to support, and in its emphasis on commentary predicted the theory journal of the later part of the century. Speaking of Wyndham Lewis, but perhaps also of himself, Eliot wrote: 'Mr. Lewis is the most remarkable example in England of the actual mutation of the artist into a philosopher of a type hitherto unknown.'[24] Eliot casts Lewis as what we might call a 'theorist', responsible not simply for producing art on which others might supply a secondary commentary, but also for creating an account of the social situation of art, by attending to philosophy, political theory, and the nebulous condition of public opinion.

The key to the success of Leavisism was its institutional strategy. While it had roots in the same kind of search for authentic being that was reflected in the modernist art movements, its strategy was democratic in tendency even where anti-socialist in intention. Yet in its time the kind of institutional dominance which it has achieved for English studies in general could only be projected. Literary theory still had an important extra-institutional dimension, especially concerning the negotiation made by writers regarding their role as artists and the relationship to their public – the growing, literate public which was increasingly seeking to understand its political role in the context of the menacing developments of the 1930s.

Although only a handful of her critical essays are frequently referenced, the significance of Virginia Woolf as a critic has been highlighted since the 1970s by feminist criticism which sees her arguments against the neglect of women writers as a benchmark for future activity. This has been especially true in the context of the United States, where Emily Dickinson and Gertrude Stein fail to yield the kind of politicized figure which feminist criticism calls for (in the case of Stein, the politics run the wrong way in terms of her support for the puppet Vichy regime in France, despite her importance as a lesbian writer). Woolf was widely recognized as a novelist in her own time, and aspects of her criticism topically related to the widely shared concern with the effects of mass literacy (two volumes of essays were titled *The Common Reader*). In *A Room of One's Own* (1929) she protested against the exclusion of women from higher education and from the pantheon of officially sanctioned great literature. Yet the influence of Woolf's criticism only came later, and came as much in its example as its content, which was not an attempt at a systematic treatment of women as writers, or indeed of patriarchy, although her fiction as well as her criticism contain many elements of such a critique. I have argued elsewhere that the symbolic system which can be read off from Woolf's work is, contrary to the role she has been called to play in socially progressive thought, basically

pessimistic about social progress and governed by a static set of oppositions that do not permit the kind of development sought by later feminist thought.[25] What I would like to emphasize here, however, is not so
much the content of Woolf's literary theory but its location and institutional strategy. Woolf continued to adhere to the view of the writer as an
isolated figure and private producer. Her famous notion that a woman
writer required 'a room of her own' and a guaranteed income stresses
artistic isolation and the privilege of the producer without offering any
reflection on the division of labour in which authorship participates.
Woolf's method of reaching and constructing a readership was through
the Hogarth Press which she ran with her husband, and her way of disseminating ideas was in the end more by coding them in her fiction than
by explaining them in prose. Woolf's case should remind us that literary
theory – not least because it is addressed to practice as well as product
and can therefore be implicit in the literary work itself – is not the
exclusive preserve of the University, however dominant a force that has
now become. Woolf uses essays and fiction to intervene in the public
discourse of literature; like other writers of the 1920s, she struggled to
define and effectively project a viable social role for the artist.

Created as journals more intended to advance a theory of literature,
culture and society, *The Calendar of Modern Letters* and *The Criterion*
struggled to define a viable role for the artist or make sense of the
function of culture in a society defined by rapid, economically and tech-
nologically driven change. Journals were of course in themselves a way to
enter the public sphere and connect artists to audiences. However, a
journal in itself was not a sufficient institutional base, not least when the
premise appeared to be that audiences could not in any case be reached.
It was the Leavises and their allies at Cambridge who developed an
institutional practice which was both revolutionary and reactionary, as
Eliot had called for. Following the example of *The Criterion*, their movement focused around a journal, *Scrutiny*. The social background of the
Scrutiny group tended to be urban and industrial, and this in part accounts
for their independence from the norms of the gentleman scholar, while
their middle-class, grammar-school work ethic lies behind their hostility
to mass politics.[26] *Scrutiny* began publication in 1932 under the editorship
of Leavis and others. The object of the journal was to project its critical
program beyond Cambridge and beyond the University in general. Anticipating the general development of literary studies to this day, *Scrutiny*
broadened the remit of literary criticism into the general criticism of
society. The tone of *Scrutiny* was pessimistic, in the manner of *The
Calendar of Modern Letters* and Wyndham Lewis's journal *The Enemy*,

but differed in attempting to formulate a positive alternative to artistic isolation.

A key difference between the 1920s and the 1930s is the rise of Nazism, its confrontation with German communism, and a corresponding tendency of British writers to identify with the political left. The *Scrutiny* group did not believe that socialism or communism was an alternative to capitalism and continued to celebrate the organic community of Elizabethan England as an alternative. They did this not in a fascistic or nationalistic way, but strategically sought to present their group as a radical alternative to communism. Leavis gave a lively defence of the political independence of the journal in his 1932 contribution, 'Under which King, Bezonian?',[27] which is framed as a discussion of Leon Trotsky's *Literature and Revolution* (1924). Leavis rejects the 'frequent' calls on *Scrutiny* to state its political affiliation on the ground that 'to identify *Scrutiny* with a social, economic or political creed or platform would be to compromise and impede its special function', but goes on to reject 'the dogma of the priority of economic conditions'. Leavis shrewdly points out that Trotsky defends bourgeois culture against other revolutionaries who sought the creation of an entirely new, post-revolutionary proletarian culture, thereby acknowledging that culture transcends economic conditions, in contrast to the claim of the earliest British Marxist criticism (such as that of Granville-Barker) that literary production was class-bound. *Scrutiny* attacked Marxism – at that time a relatively unsophisticated discourse in Britain – while acknowledging and engaging the dynamism and intelligence of figures such as Trotsky. It also avoided the right-wing defence of 'order' and 'the West' found in Eliot's *Criterion*. In doing so, throughout a period when political neutrality increasingly risked the appearance of irresponsibility, *Scrutiny* succeeded in its long-term goal of creating the notion of a criticism which was socially concerned but politically independent.

Scrutiny had responded to the growth of interest in and commitment to Marxism among writers and even some critics. Marxist cultural thought remained comparatively under-developed in Britain at this time, but the converts to fellow-travelling with communism in literary circles were numerous and notable. Literary journals connected with the left never acquired the impetus and gravity of *Scrutiny*, not least because they continued to operate in the general public sphere rather than within the confines of the University. Geoffrey Grigson's *New Verse* featured contributions from leftist authors such as W. H. Auden and Cecil Day Lewis, but its editor maintained a wavering posture of political independence, until the last edition of 1938, when, with European war imminent, the issue was entitled 'Commitments' and included no poetry, on the grounds that 'the aesthetic attitude is now out of place'. A 'memorial' to Eliot in the same issue claimed that he was '*malgré lui* a revolutionary poet'.[28]

The journal *New Verse* had attempted to connect political commitment to the well-rehearsed stance of the independence of the artist. What was needed was a Marxist theory of culture which could inform not only criticism but artistic practice. The nearest that *New Verse* came to supplying this was in its publication of British surrealist writers such as Charles Madge, Kathleen Raine and David Gascoyne. A major difference between the trajectory of French and British literary theory hinges on the development of surrealism in France and its comparative failure to become seeded in Britain. Surrealism as a literary movement was an avant-garde on the model of the pre-war avant-gardes such as futurism. The strange position of English-language modernism is that its avant-garde quality was muted, so that Eliot was an establishment figure whose theories seemed little to reflect the textual radicalism of his poetry, while the politics of both Pound and Eliot ran to the right and had more emphasis on the ordering or clarifying functions of literature rather than on its transgressive potentials. There were certainly alternatives to Eliot and Pound, but in the British context the poetic mainstream did not go in the direction of wild avant-gardism. In France, surrealist literature not only presented itself as anti-bourgeois and anti-normative, but in André Breton had a skilled theorist whose *Manifestos* (1924, 1930) developed a model of artistic practice which drew on the notion of the unconscious in psychoanalysis and the challenge of Marxism to the constitution of everyday life under capitalism. The idea that a literature which tapped the unconscious in the form of dream writing or automatic writing and thereby challenged the norms of consciousness imposed by bourgeois society conditioned assumptions about the role of literature in France. Indeed, the radical psychoanalytic theorist Jacques Lacan had extensive early association with the surrealist movement. One of the lasting effects of surrealism was that it conditioned French theory to think of literature as a disruptive and transgressive force. It is notable, for example, in the work of Michel Foucault, that while many other forms of discourse are considered as modes of the exercise of power, literature is usually assumed to represent a transgressive, rather than normative, force. Surrealism did not represent a thorough working-out of the cultural implications of psychoanalysis or Marxism, and remained rooted in a relatively individualistic and romantic artistic practice, but it set a contrasting model to the discourse of criticism and commitment which was dominant in Britain in the 1930s.

The journal remained an important mode of cultural-theoretical struggle at this time, and the journal *Left Review* (1934–8) was set up by the British section of the Communist Writers' International. An important achievement of the journal was its introduction of articulate Marxist cultural theory into Britain, in contributions from Alick West, Winifred Holtby and Edgell Rickword. This journal was addressed not to the University, but to the literary public sphere, where it perceived its main obstacle to be the continued adoption by writers of the posture of the 'artist'. *Left Review* rejected the 'exasperated or plaintive individualism' of the modernist artist, the preference for religion over politics found in Eliot, the absence of a political aesthetic in the work of key poets such as Auden. Following the then current Soviet strategy of the Popular Front which called for an alliance of communists and liberals against fascism, *Left Review* set out a call to the 'bourgeois intellectual' to join the fight against fascism. There had been 'forty years of stoppage of Marxist theory in England' which the *Left Review* set out to make up.[29] *Left Review* laid the grounds for the subsequent development of a Marxist cultural theory – this time in an institutional context.

Chapter 2

The New Criticism and Beyond

I. A. Richards had a background in philosophy rather than literary studies, and was well read in aesthetics, linguistics and psychology. This disciplinary range is perhaps typical of the kind of English studies we find practised today, and Richards was an important instigator of the multidisciplinary approach. He provided a theoretical basis for the development of English studies at Cambridge, albeit from only a semi-official position, and had a huge influence on the development of New Criticism in the United States. Richards brings perspectives to bear on literary studies which are unusual among his contemporaries, although his assessment of the social situation of literature and of art has elements in common with the aestheticism of Pater or Pound and the pessimism of Leavis or Lewis. Richards is best known for promoting a form of close reading of literary texts known as 'practical criticism', in one version of which texts are approached by a reader with no knowledge of context or authorship. Although practical criticism turned into the backbone of a certain kind of literary formalism, it is only one, illustrative element in Richards' work, which in fact has a wider orientation towards questions of the social role of literature, the legitimacy of literary studies and the possible modes of teaching literature. Richards' influential early studies include *Principles of Literary Criticism* (1924) and its short sequel, *Science and Poetry* (1926), which conveniently condenses some of the claims of the former volume. *Science and Poetry* begins with an epigraph from Arnold which suggests that this work will follow the implications of Arnold in promoting poetry as a kind of secularized substitute for religion. However, Richards notes that Arnold's claim that 'The future of poetry is immense',[1] while widely quoted, is generally disbelieved. He goes on: 'Indeed a more representative modern view would be that the future of poetry is *nil*', and quotes

Thomas Love Peacock in *The Four Ages of Poetry* (1820): 'A poet in our times is a semi-barbarian in a civilized community.' According to Peacock, the poet lives in the past and it is 'lamentable' to see minds 'capable of better things, running to seed in the specious indolence of these empty aimless mockeries of intellectual exertion'.[2] Richards does not raise these doubts about the value of poetry (and of literature and culture in general) in order breezily to dismiss them as philistinism and restore a status quo in which 'culture' occupies a central place. Rather, the doubts are shown to be legitimate and arise for the simple reason that poetry as a mode of knowing the world arose in pre-scientific society and has lost its priority. Like Arnold, Richards sees poetry as a relic of the age of magic. 'There is some evidence that Poetry, together with the other arts, arose with this Magical View. It is a possibility seriously to be considered that Poetry may pass away with it.'[3] It might seem remarkable that this doubt about the purpose and validity of poetry in the modern age is so strongly entertained by the founding figures of modern English, but in fact this doubt accounts in large part for the character and substance of English literary studies, even though the practice of English rarely acknowledges such fundamental doubts (so we are more often asked to question the canon than to question literature as such).

In response to this analysis of the domination of science, Richards developed a model of literature that privileged the reading process and was based on an assertion of the category of experience. From our perspective, the notion of experience is problematic, because it seems to imply the existence of a simple self as a self-knowing unity undergoing a temporally linear sensory process. Although subsequent thought has queried the notion of experience, not least as it is found in the work of Heidegger, Richards deploys it as a strategically important negation and extension of aestheticism. Making well-grounded but nevertheless generalized reference to psychology, Richards tried to establish the category of experience as the basis on which literary purpose could be restored. The essence of poetry lay in its appeal to experience as opposed to thinking, and this difference was coded in the modality of its language. This approach has the risk of leading into a kind of formalism, in which the way in which something is said is privileged over the content, but this risk is moderated by the claim that form corresponds to a felt 'experience'. Richards extrapolates from ideas set out in the poetic theories of Ezra Pound and T. S. Eliot which emphasize the correspondence of poetic or artistic form to an emotion or mood, ideas which themselves rewrite the post-impressionist emphasis on the artist as a kind of formal organizer presiding over his materials as a superior will.[4]

Misunderstanding and under-estimation of poetry is mainly due to over-estimation of the thought in it. [. . .] It is never what a poem *says* which matters, but what it *is*. The poet is not writing as a scientist. He uses these words because the interests which the situation calls into play combine to bring them, just in this form, into his consciousness *as a means of ordering, controlling and consolidating* the whole experience. The experience itself, the tide of impulses sweeping through the mind, is the source and the sanction of the words. They represent the experience itself, not any set of perceptions or reflections [. . .]. [The words] will reproduce in [the reader's] mind a similar play of interests putting him for the while into a similar situation and leading to the same response.

Richards asserts that 'experience is its own justification',[5] reproducing the distinction found in aestheticism between the aesthetic experience of sensory impression and the objective world of science. However, his use of experience implies both the moment of sensory experience and the more extended process of 'life experience': sensory experience is more than immediate sensory pleasure, and Richards insists that art is a communication of experience between artist and reader, not merely a 'pleasure'. This idea of art maintains an aesthetic basis (Richards refers to 'coenesthesia' [*sic*][6]) and, like aestheticism, rejects the simply moralistic reading of literature, but nevertheless retains familiar canons of mimesis and ethical responsibility which make art social and not private.

One element in Richards' thought is relatively eclipsed by our hazy modern recollection of him: the claim that literature has an adaptive psychological function. Although sometimes thought of as a later and exotic introduction into literary studies, psychoanalysis makes an important appearance at this early, critical juncture, albeit with the strongly practical, behaviourist inflection of the 1920s. According to Richards, psychoanalysis shows that 'persistent mental imbalances are the source of nearly all our troubles'. Most individuals are unable to escape from inner 'chaos', claims Richards, following Eliot in curiously running together the realms of psychological and social order:

> We are in need of something to take the place of the old order. [. . .] Only the rarest individuals hitherto have achieved this new order, and never yet perhaps completely. But many have achieved it for a brief while, for a particular phase of experience, and many have recorded it for these phases.
> Of these records poetry consists.

Richards frames his discussion in terms of impulses (psychological drives), and in doing so moves away from the traditional Kantian aesthetics which see engagement with the artwork as disinterested in any material or psychological sense. In Richards' account here, the artwork is still a formal unity, but engages the interests of the reader or spectator by involving 'as many of his impulses as possible'. These impulses can achieve a kind of ordered balance which allow for the best life possible for the individual – an essential task, since 'conflicts between different impulses are the greatest evils which afflict mankind'.[7] Richards does not supply a detailed model showing how this might work. For us now, this speculative framework reads as a symptom of structural problems which we have already signposted. Literature requires a social function, but can no longer be credited as a bearer of ideas. Nor can it be validated in terms of claims about its objective, disengaged formal qualities. Psychoanalysis appears to offer the ground on which these two imperatives can be met, supplying a meaningful function (social adaptation of impulses) and giving purpose to form. Moreover, conflating the new concept of psychological adaptation and the older and looser concept of 'experience' serves to validate the otherwise selfish and subjective appearance of the idea of a pre-dominantly sensory 'aesthetic experience'. Finally, these ideas all have a convenient convergence with the object aesthetics of Pound and Eliot.

Richards tackles the claim that scientific truth has superseded poetic truth by coining the term 'pseudo-statement':

> Countless pseudo-statements – about God, about the universe, about human nature [...] – pseudo-statements which are pivotal points in the organization of the mind, vital to its well-being, have suddenly become, for sincere, honest, and informed minds, impossible to believe. For centuries they have been believed; and now they are gone, irrecoverably; and the knowledge which has killed them is not of a kind upon which an equally fine organization of the mind can be based.

Science cannot supply the basis for culture, so the statements offered by poetry as once-true interpretations of the world must be retained but not believed: we must 'cut our pseudo-statements free from belief, and yet retain them, in this released state, as the main instruments by which we order our attitudes to one another and to the world'. Eliot's *The Waste Land* is credited as the poem which shows how the poetry of pseudo-statement must now look: 'by effecting a complete severance between his poetry and *all* beliefs, and this without any weakening of the poetry, he has realised what might otherwise have remained a largely speculative possibility, and has shown the way to the only solution of these difficulties.'[8]

Richards is perhaps most often thought of in terms of his work in *Practical Criticism* (1929), in particular its exercise in close reading in which poems without any contextualizing information are presented to student readers who are asked to respond. This was no more than an experiment, and does not mean that Richards supported the notion that literature must be thought of as without context. Rather, it is clear that Richards' inquiry is ethical in nature. It is not historical in the sense that it calls for a restoration of literature to context, although the historicism of his approach does extend to reiterated demands that literary theory be viewed historically and critically. It is clear, though, that Richards' attempt to find a legitimating frame for literature which would respond to scientific understanding resorts to unsatisfactory models, and for this reason the aspects of Richards' work I have concentrated on are rarely evoked, except for the purpose of dismissing his ideology. The emphasis on readerly processes is profoundly modern, however, and most certainly prepared the way for the later rapid acceptance of Barthes and Derrida who seemed, to New Critics in particular, to be pushing at the same door. However, the suggestion that 'the critic is as closely occupied with the health of the mind as the doctor with the health of the body'[9] reveals an ethics in crisis, one unable to ground itself in an idealized 'science'. The desire in these texts to establish literature as a 'value' and experience as 'its own justification'[10] fail to arrive at the objectivity they seek. Richards' use of the term 'value' reflects Wordsworth: 'The arts are our storehouse of recorded values. They spring from and perpetuate hours in the lives of exceptional people when their control and command of experience is at its highest [. . .].'[11] The emphasis on experience is certainly romantic in one of its elements, although the economic aspect of the term 'value' also invokes the desire of a quasi-scientific economics to account for the value of commodities. That 'the healthiest mind is that capable of securing the greatest amount of value'[12] rests on unargued notions of value and health that broadly reflect the intellectual ethos of the 1920s but do not establish the authority towards which they gesture. Notwithstanding these evident problems, Richards' desire to ground reading in an ethics in which experience is communicated in a holistic way that might exceed the contingency of reason, alongside his rejection of 'conformity to abstract prescriptions and general rules' in the interest of 'the "minute particulars" of response and attitude' in reading, confirmed the character of literary study as an ethical activity of the kind it recognizably remains today.

*

In 1922, the same year that Eliot launched *The Criterion* in London, John Crowe Ransom, Allen Tate and Robert Penn Warren were part of a group of poets who launched their own journal, *The Fugitive*, in Nashville, Tennessee. In doing so they were imitating the tradition of the little magazine which was already well founded in New York, Boston and Chicago. What is remarkable about this group is that it formed the nucleus of what was to become called the New Criticism, and that its influence grew out of a position of apparent political recidivism – a romantic anti-capitalism based on a morally ambiguous defence of pre-capitalist social relations in the South, a project which was embodied in two key collections of essays, *I'll Take My Stand: The South and Agrarian Tradition* (1930), authored by 'Twelve Southerners', and *Who Owns America? A New Declaration of Independence* (1936). The strategy of this group altered, in the mid-1930s, from being an extra-institutional, political-cultural program to the institutional cultural program of transforming English literary studies of the United States. That this is not a surprising change of strategy is apparent from the parallels with England. Certainly, Leavisism was differently founded, and always conceived its program as more cultural than political, but Leavis shares with the New Critics the emphasis on literary sensibility as a form of cultural resistance to modernity. The substantial difference between the two is that the Leavises developed the idea of Elizabethan England as an ideal hierarchical society somewhere between feudalism and modernity, in which culture and production were fused, while the Fugitives, restyling themselves 'Agrarians', adopted the more immediate past of the pre-Civil War South as the model for the ideal way of life, an agricultural utopia opposed to the anti-social economic priorities of the industrial North. Moreover, like Eliot and Wyndham Lewis, some of the Fugitives looked to Catholicism for order and an expression of human limitations of a kind not found in Protestantism. New Criticism is, as a consequence, seen in terms of two narratives which in a sense negate each other. On the one hand, it is uneasily linked in its earliest phase to the politics of slavery and Southern resurgence; on the other, its emphasis on close, textual criticism is frequently labelled as a formalism designed to repress social and political realities. It can more accurately be regarded as a form of anti-capitalist utopianism which accepted the view, common, say, to Marx and Eliot, that the modern subjectivity or sensibility had become divided, and which saw the practice of reading certain types of literature as the ground of a partial or fleeting restoration of lost aspects of the human. As in the case of Leavisism, New Criticism advocated a practice of reading with a strong element of pseudo-scientific rigour that did not simply bring about the political goals of its advocates; indeed, New Critics followed Richards in resisting the explicit political claims of literature – perhaps not least because so much of the Romantic literature favoured by close textual critics has a basis in the French Revolutionary politics which they regard as anathema.

Robert Penn Warren proposed that *I'll Take My Stand* be called *Tracts Against Communism*.[13] The title adopted is taken from the well-known song of 1859, 'Dixie': 'In Dixie land, I'll take my stand to live and die in Dixie.' Quoted here in standard English, the song was in fact written in an exaggerated African American vernacular idiom and expresses the sentiments of an escaped slave nostalgic for the South, although it was (probably) written by a white, 'blackface' performer, Daniel Decatur Emmett. Its use suggests an ardent and backward-looking loyalty to the Southern cause, as well as a romanticized, defensive posture. To have used Warren's suggested title would have clarified the non-regional aspirations of the group, and emphasized their anti-communist aims. At this time, it was common to see communism, not as the opposition to capitalism (as it appeared in the Cold War), but as its extension. The Agrarians shared this view:

> [. . .] the true Sovietists or Communists – if the term may be used here in the European sense – are the Industrialists themselves. They would have the government set up an economic super-organization, which in turn would become the government. We therefore look upon the Communist menace as a menace indeed, but not as a Red one; because it is simply according to the blind drift of our industrial development to expect in America at last much the same economic system as that imposed by violence upon Russia in 1917.

Warren identified the South as the preserver of European principles, analogous to England. 'European opinion does not make too much of the intense practical enterprises, but is at pains to define rather narrowly the practical effort which is prerequisite to the reflective and aesthetic life.' Warren shares with the Frankfurt School the vision of a capitalized 'Progress' as 'the concept of man's increasing command, and eventually perfect command, over the forces of nature'. Warren defends the culture of 'leisure' of the 'squirearchy' of the Old South, in which he claims that, as in Europe, the 'life of the spirit' and the 'arts of life' can be cultivated. Slavery is quietly sidelined as 'monstrous enough in theory, but, more often than not, humane in practice'. Agriculture, which calls for labour measured in intensity by nature itself, is opposed to the increased speed of work of industrialism. The implications for a theory of culture of the broad oppositions which Warren develops are set out by Donald Davidson in his contribution to *I'll Take My Stand*. The modern artist is a romantic, alienated from industrial society but also its product. What is needed is not the romantic artist as a producer of great art, but the regional artist and the arts which are integrated with the agricultural community. 'Harmony between the artist and society must be regained' by commitment to the agrarian program. The practical politics of this artistic agenda are not worked out in detail, but the general tenets are once again anti-industrial and anti-progressive. Other essays in the volume confirm parallels with the anti-romantic philosophy of T. E. Hulme in *Speculations* (1924) and developed in the work of his followers, Eliot and Wyndham Lewis, as well as parallels with Charles Maurras and other of the anti-communist thinkers of the Action Française favoured by Eliot's *Criterion*, although with an American inflection: so Lyle H. Lanier's 'A Critique of the Philosophy of Progress' criticizes Dewey alongside Hegel as advocates of the notion that change in society represents progress, while Allen Tate's 'Remarks on the Southern Religion' finds the old South to have been 'a feudal society without a feudal religion', its people simple and traditional in outlook, but disconnected from necessary theological tradition.[14]

The Agrarian group went beyond the figures who were to found the New Criticism – Ransom, Tate and Warren – but along with Donald Davidson these were the principal figures of a movement defined by cultural mission; they were not merely the poetic reflection of a political movement but central to it. The Agrarians had no practical success in the South or in the United States in general. Their defence of slavery as a quasi-medieval institution was quickly identified by Northern commentators; anti-semitism was barely disguised by negative references to 'cosmopolitanism'; the symbolic and impractical nature of their mythified account of the South was no less apparent to liberal commentators of the day than it is now.[15] In Britain, the World War was the overwhelming catastrophe which shaped a national consciousness; in the South it was defeat and reconstruction which shaped a more deep-seated sense of tragedy. To conservatives and pessimists in Britain, communism was a more immediate threat than to anyone in the South, as the state of industry and consequently the organization of labour were far more advanced in Britain. Yet the 1930s were shaped in both Europe and America by the recession and the sense of a looming threat as Stalin consolidated his power in the Soviet Union and European governments appeared increasingly unstable in the wake of mass unemployment and confrontation with communists and fascists. Against this background, the Agrarians' vision of a hierarchical society based on subsistence farming had very little appeal, rooted as it was in a binary myth of society designed to appeal to the culturally educated rather than to any of the yeoman farmers of whom it spoke. Liberals rejected the Agrarians not just as conservatives, but as racists and fascists, and their anti-communism, though topical, came with an unappealing baggage of metaphysical theory and European reference. Yet it is the anti-communism of the Agrarians, in its appearance as a literary theory allied to a conscious strategy of entry into University English Departments, which is the central thread in the transformation of this group into an influential cultural force.

*

Among the important documents of the New Criticism are the essays of John Crowe Ransom collected in *The World's Body* (1938) and *The New Criticism* (1941). Although the exercises in practical criticism of I. A. Richards seem to provide the model for all close reading to follow, Ransom sets out a position quite different from that of Richards. Ransom demands that a poem must be seen not in terms of its subjective affect, nor in terms of its moral or other content, but as an objective particular which bonds the imagination to nature. This is a loose paraphrase, since Ransom uses various formulations and does not attempt to be philosophically rigorous. Although his approach is essayistic rather than definitive, Ransom constantly orbits the conceptual frame of classical German philosophy, making reference in particular to Kant's substantiation of the separation between nature and morality, that is, between the laws of physics and the moral law, or, in Kant's vocabulary, the 'phenomenal' and the 'noumenal'. Ransom claims that science gives us the world through laws, but that poetry can restore the particulars of nature by using a different mode of language. It is not then a matter of explaining poetry in terms of science, but of establishing poetry – that is, the highest form of literary language – as an alternative to science which can partially or temporarily reground authentic human being. Ransom refers to this as ontology – the Greek word for being is *on* and ontology is the knowledge of human being. Ransom does not make reference to Heidegger, whose philosophy constantly pressed against the world of technology and attempted to ask what he called the 'question of being'. Nor does Ransom acknowledge the tradition of Marxism, which at the time appeared more as a theory of economics and politics than of being. Later commentators on Marx have discerned a different emphasis. For example, Michel Henry argues that 'the determination of reality is the central theme of Marx' and describes his emphasis on praxis as fundamentally ontological.[16] There are striking parallels, too, with Walter Benjamin's emphasis on the restoration of the particularity of nature in 'The Work of Art in the Age of its Techno-logical Reproducibility' (1936).[17] The notion of an inquiry or practice which will restore a reality alienated by science, technology or economy is common to thought after Kant, and depends on models found in the work of Hegel. What is remarkable is not that Ransom arrived at his own versions of these problems, but that this line of thinking is fundamental to the motivation for the creation of New Criticism, which is often thought of as being an empirical and anti-theoretical practice.

To create the space in which he can argue for an ontological criticism, Ransom defines himself against Richards. 'A Psychologist Looks at Poetry' (1935) labels Richards a 'behaviorist', criticizing his representa-tion of the human mind as a 'system of interests' rather than using the word 'thought'. Ransom argues that a poem must be considered as an object, and that Richards errs in explaining the poem simply in terms of its function in the mind of the reader. Imagination needs to be treated as the faculty in which mind and world encounter each other: specifically, it is where the mind encounters nature as direct perception and particular object, not in terms of ideas or understanding: 'I should say that the imagination is the organ of knowledge whose technique is images. It presents to the reflective mind the particularity of nature; whereas there is quite another organ, working by a technique of universals, which gives us science.'[18] Ransom's critical theory is continuously informed by this explanation of the mind's encounter with the world in terms of two distinct forms of practice: science and poetry. These are not simply aspects of understanding referred only to the mind, but representational practices which generate their own objects and participate in both the mental and physical realms. Ransom notes that, in his later work, Richards returns to the theory of the imagination in Coleridge, who is immersed in the problems of German philosophy, and whose work is characterized by the problem of conceptualizing the mind's encounter with nature. Although I am simplifying and compressing the different vocabularies used to approach this theoretical problem, and although Ransom's version of it is itself a simplified, wooden and excessively binary one, the striking point to note it is that this substantially theoretical motiva-tion appears at the root of the supposedly practical activity of the New Criticism as it spread though universities in the United States and, in inexact parallel, in Britain.

Ransom also discusses Richards in the book which gave the movement its name, *The New Criticism* (1941). In this passage Ransom names the two kinds of criticism against which New Criticism is defined and contrasted:

> Briefly, the new criticism is damaged by at least two specific errors of theory, which are widespread. One is the idea of using the psychological affective vocabulary in the hope of making literary judgements in terms of the feelings, emotions and attitudes of poems instead of in terms of their objects. The other is plain moralism which in the new criticism would indicate that it has not emancipated itself from the old criticism.[19]

These errors are said to go all the way back to classical literary theory. Aristotle's theory of catharsis refers tragedy to its effect on the spectator in much the same way that Richards refers to literature's adaptive function in balancing the psychological 'interests' of the mind (Aristotle 'seems to have been almost as romantic as Richards in devoting so much attention to the affections of the witnesses, instead of the objective situation which they witnessed'[20]). Ransom also identifies the danger of another strand of classical literary criticism, which he calls moralism. Ransom sees moral criticism of his own time as being excessively focused on the moral content of the literature it discusses, without reference to the virtues or otherwise of the literary object with which it deals. Such commentary on the actions of characters in fiction distracts attention from the objectivity of the literary form itself, claims Ransom, and indeed this emphasis goes all the way back to classical literary criticism, notably the assertion of Horace that poetry should 'profit' (i.e. morally benefit) or 'delight' (i.e. create pleasurable subjective affect). Richards had similarly argued that modern critical theory was still mired in the dogmatic critical vocabulary of the past: 'we think very much as our ancestors thought a hundred or two hundred generations ago.'[21] Ransom and Richards share the objective of dissolving a false distinction central to ancient and recent critical theory, which splits the literary object into an objective moral (i.e. social world) content and a subjective (i.e. psychological or emotional) affect. Ransom's criticism of Richards is that he fails to dissolve this opposition, not that he is incorrect in taking it as his object. Richards' slogan – 'It is never what a poem *says* which matters, but what it *is*'[22] – might well have been Ransom's own. We should recognize that the attention to the text which New Criticism proposes is not a merely socially decadent or intellectually reduced version of 'art for art's sake' but a serious attempt to waken criticism from its dogmatic slumbers. Indeed, it is striking that the deconstruction of Jacques Derrida, which found such favour among critics schooled in New Criticism, has as one of its principal interests the manner in which language, neither properly objective nor subjective, transgresses the philosophically sedimented opposition of 'outside' world and 'inside' mind.[23] It is notable that although the theory of the 1970s represented itself as a kind of enlightenment sweeping away the New Criticism, the New Critics had already themselves adopted a similar anti-dogmatic stance in their own call for theoretical renovation.

Theoretically modernizing it may have been, but New Criticism's emphasis on the text as an object tended to deflect attention from the reality of the referent, which is not merely nature but society. The attack on critical moralism does not only serve to displace that form of criticism which commentates on the moral attitudes and decisions of fictional characters, but also serves to force attention away from the political and social contents of texts. One effect of this is that texts of less than absolute literary merit but of intense social interest tend to be excluded from literary studies; another effect is that even those texts which respond to this kind of critical attention are likely to have their social or political implications repressed in the commentary they receive. It would be correct to find the roots of this in the New Critics' own politics, and particularly their resistance to the notion of historical progress, but at the same time, in terms of the general effects of the dissemination of the New Criticism, it would probably also be fair to say that many versions of the classroom practice of New Criticism were not heavily informed by its governing theories, but simply aimed at a kind of enjoyable and worthwhile pedagogy. When the theory of the 1970s directed its anger at practices of reading which it labelled apolitical, and curriculum formations which it deemed socially repressive, many teachers of literature caught in the onslaught seem to have been hurt by the implication that their politics were consciously reactionary: they had no more set about fulfilling the ontological remit of Ransom's theory than they had consciously decided to suppress history and politics.

Ransom writes of *The Meaning of Meaning* (1923), an early Richards work, co-authored with C. K. Ogden:

> Its bias is deeply *nominalist*, and by that I mean that it is very alert to the possibility that a word which seems to refer to the objective world, or to have an objective 'referent', really refers to a psychological context and has no objective referent; this bias has governed Richards' conception of poetry, for one thing, from almost that day to this. And with that bias

goes – and the combination is a very common one nowadays though almost paradoxical – a *positivist* bias through which the thinker is led to take the referential capacity of science as perfect, in spite of his nominal scepticism; and by comparison to judge all other kinds of discourse as falling short.[24]

Ontological criticism will reject this division of the nominalist and positivist:

> We have elected to know the world through our science [. . .] and by it know the world only as a scheme of abstract consciousness. [. . .] What we cannot know constitutionally as scientists is the world which is made of whole and indefeasible objects, and this is the world which poetry recovers for us.[25]

The strategy for this recovery of the world via a 'more scientific' criticism will be carried though the universities, in imitation of the institutionally centralizing processes of capitalism although to different ends. The historical scholarship which Ransom takes to govern the teaching of literature in universities is challenged. The university professor can 'spend a lifetime compiling the data of literature and yet rarely or never commit himself to a literary judgement [. . .]. Rather than occasional criticism by amateurs [. . .] I have the idea that what we need is Criticism, Inc., or Criticism, Ltd.'[26] This activity will be focused on poetry, which distinguishes itself on the technical side by the devices which are, precisely, its means of escaping from time, and 'the critic should regard the poem as nothing short of a desperate ontological or metaphysical manoeuvre'.[27]

*

Although he takes much theoretical impetus from him, Ransom credits Richards' *Practical Criticism* for 'his most incontestable contribution to poetic discussion [. . .] in developing the ideal or exemplary readings, and in provoking such readings from other scholars'. Richards and his pupil William Empson, whose *Seven Types of Ambiguity* (1930) set the standard for detailed rhetorical criticism of poetry, are credited as foundational figures:

> Writing as acute and at the same time as patient and consecutive as this have not existed in English criticism, I think, before Richards and Empson. They become frequent now; Richards and Empson have spread quickly. That is a principal reason why I think it is time to identify a powerful intellectual movement that deserves to be called a new criticism.[28]

It is the *practice* of New Criticism which has been its principal legacy, while its theoretical reappraisal of the romantic and classical theoretical heritage has remained the domain of specialists. *Understanding Poetry* (1938) was a teaching anthology edited by Cleanth Brooks and Robert Penn Warren which had a massive influence on the propagation of New Critical practice. The introductory 'Letter to the Teacher' warns against those forms of criticism which it is tempting to substitute for study of the poem as object: 'paraphrase of logical and narrative content [. . .] study of biographical and historical materials [. . .] inspirational and didactic interpretation'.[29] By contrast,

> a satisfactory method of teaching poetry should embody the following principles.
> 1. Emphasis should be kept on the poem as poem.
> 2. The treatment should be concrete and inductive.
> 3. A poem should always be treated as an organic system of relationships, and the poetic quality should never be understood as inhering in one or more factors taken in isolation.[30]

This set of principles certainly coincides with the more elaborated theories produced by Ransom and Tate among others, and the emphasis on organic unity which is indebted to Coleridge indeed became a byword for the insistence on studying a work in terms of the interrelationship of its parts rather than in terms of any detail of effect or any particularity of referent. Yet as set out here, it is easy to see how the New Critical position came to be viewed as a resistance to theory rather than its realization.[31] These clearly stated rules already constitute a kind of dogma. The sense of theoretical inquiry is repressed, as might be expected in a student textbook, but there is confirmation, in this theoretical muteness, of a sense of closure in the governing theoretical process from which the exercise of criticism is to proceed. Already the sense of Ransom's work is often of movement towards a position, rather than the opening of a theoretical inquiry, and this is even more the case in *Understanding Poetry*. This can be seen in Brooks' and Warren's discussion of the distinction between scientific and poetic language. The discussion is fairly elementary, as might be expected in this context, yet it is clear in its establishment of the basic distinction repeatedly asserted by New Critics. At the same time, the position is already formulaic – indeed, it is reminiscent of the binary fixations of the Agrarians. Many questions remain unasked and unanswered. How does it come about that there are two distinct modalities of language? Are there other modes? Can the social process which has befallen language really have split it in two in this way? What description of that process do we require in order both to understand this outcome and to overcome its (evidently deleterious) consequences? By insisting on one side of this language divide do we not simply consolidate its terms into a kind of cosmic balance, rather than look to move beyond them by grasping and superseding the division in consciousness into which we have fallen? These sorts of question are the substance of other, parallel traditions, especially the continual process of inquiry and discovery of questions found in the work of Heidegger, and the parallel aesthetic inquiries of Adorno and Benjamin, both strands which abut onto an inquiry into the nature of poetic language. In the moment of *Understanding Poetry* the overwhelming pressure of creating the business of University criticism overwhelms the inquiry. Scientific and poetic language, Brooks and Warren assert, are both modes of 'communication'. This notion of communication appears to slip back into the psychologism of Richards and away from the ontologism of Ransom. This is not, however, a calculated theoretical departure, but a sign of limitation in the theoretical process of New Criticism. The concept of 'communication' already assumes a model in which transmissible contents are transferred from one communicating entity to another. It consolidates a distinction between experiencing subjective mind and objective code of transmission which Richards and Ransom have already acknowledged is not sufficiently holistic – a reinforcement of the subject–object divide which it was supposed to be the objective of an ontological criticism to overcome. Moreover, the goal of producing 'criticism' which is to be spread among students is never really explained as an end. This criticism does not look outward at the forms of society; it seeks only the influence of agreed judgements. While it clearly does offer a route into some of the more involving aspects of a certain kind of text, it does not promise the liberation of 'being', whether as a concept or as an actual human liberation, towards which it might be thought to tend.

In a sense, this practice reproduces at the level of criticism the disinterestedness of the artwork advocated in Kant's aesthetics. Ransom had followed Kant in distancing art from appetite. In Kant's famous expression, art is characterized by 'purposeless purpose', that is, it is purposely shaped as if towards an end but in fact has no intended functional outcome (i.e. any material effect in the world). Although political criticism has found the New Critical emphasis on the autonomy of art to be politically suspect, it is worth noting that the autonomy of the artwork has received vigorous defence within the tradition of political criticism itself – notably in the work of Adorno, who defended the autonomy of the complex modernist artwork against demands for political commitment.[32] In the later 1930s, as the program of the New Critics took hold, the demand for political commitment was felt as strongly in the United States as it was in Europe, and it is easy to see why critics or theorists interested in the complicated internal processes of art might have felt reinforced in their resistance to demands for art to be read in terms of its broad political orientation. At the same time, the right had more to gain than the left from insisting that an artwork is only indirectly political, if it is political at all. However, despite the lines connecting the project of an ontological criticism to conservative politics, it is probably incorrect to view New Criticism as a pursuit of politics by other means – and not only because the right had no monopoly on the argument concerning the autonomy of the artwork.

*

New Critical theory and practice are not the same thing. We have already noted that the theory of Ransom and others tends towards the consolidation of certain positions – positions which, in fact, are only ever set out approximately. As in the case of Leavisism, New Criticism had to tread a fairly careful institutional path. Unlike the *Scrutiny* group, which found English studies relatively undeveloped at Cambridge and therefore open to intervention, the New Critics had to proceed with caution against existing scholars of English, many of whom pursued literary studies according to a philological model – that is, as a historical and linguistic study. These are the professors who Ransom roundly derided as able to pursue a career without ever making a literary judgment.[33] In the context of a university, however, scholarship is likely to win the upper hand in terms of its methodology and rigour, as against 'criticism', which may amount to no more than amateurish opinion better consigned to newspaper columns. Why pay a professorial salary to someone whose job is to decide whether they find *Middlemarch* a good read or not? The critics needed to give an impression of methodological rigour and of scientific foundation in order to compete with scholars for legitimacy. This perhaps explains why the theory of New Criticism does not have the appearance of a genuine theoretical inquiry. Its point seems to be to establish positions. Ransom appears more interested in metacritical commentary than in the practice of criticism which he argues for. It often seems to be the nature of theory in cultural studies that its role is more to legitimate and set the pattern for investigation than it is to further theory as a process of inquiry. The relationship between practical criticism and critical theory does not resemble that between applied and theoretical physics (Richards' use of applied reading in the context of theoretical inquiry in *Practical Criticism* is an unusual exception). Legitimation, and the dissemination of New Critical practice, were effected by the establishment of three journals: *The Kenyon Review*, *The Southern Review* and *The Sewanee Review*. Like *Scrutiny*, these journals sought to set standards for criticism; they also sought to provide ballast for the increasing professionalization of criticism in its confrontation with scholarship.

The strangest feature of New Criticism is not unique to it. Perhaps it is readers outside the United States who are more constantly struck by the incongruity that literary studies in the United States have been for so long focused on English literature. Discussions of literary canon formation in England will understandably dwell on works of English literature. It seems remarkable, just to take one example, that the discussion of the New Critical canon in John Guillory's *Cultural Capital: The Problem of Literary Canon Formation* (1993) analyses Cleanth Brooks' attitude to canonical poetry in terms of a preference for the difficult (English) over the popular (American).[34] This certainly is a question of 'cultural capital', but the question of the national origin of this cultural capital, as opposed to its level of difficulty, is not discussed by Guillory. The New Critics' own discussion of tradition slipped from the regional Southern to the English with an unargued assumption of continuity. English literature has of course proved of intense interest in many parts of the world, and in Guillory's terms proved to be an international form of 'cultural capital' which has added status to its students and teachers, and to the education systems and ultimately the nations to which they belong. Yet it seems surprising that the unconscious sense of possession of English literature by people outside England – as welcomed as it always has been by bodies such as the British Council – can be found not only in the New Critics themselves, but in a hostile discussion which aims to expose the flaws in their assumptions. Guillory follows Pierre Bourdieu in analysing the canon as a 'discourse of value', and registers the role of canon formation in placing America at the apex of Western culture. Indeed, Guillory perceives a general lack of critical clarity in the canon debate as it is conducted in the United States, for example in the use of the term 'Western' to supply a consolidated centre against which supposed margins can be defined. Guillory is excellent too on the suppression of class in debates about the canon (he seems to be referring to the US context). Yet he can write the following: 'The name "D. H. Lawrence," for example, may signify in the discourse of canonical critique a white author or a

European author, but it does not usually signify a writer whose origins are working class.'[35] Even more rarely, it might seem, does it signify an author who is English. The resolute generalization of the 'English' in 'English literature', whether to appropriate English literary products into a US canon or to vilify them as Western, is a remarkably neglected topic. This appropriation extends into the acquisition of major archives of the great authors of English literature, a process that will one day no doubt be challenged on the same terms that holdings of ancient antiquities or the remains of native people now are. Of course, this is not to say that members of one nation should not take an interest in the literary production of another nation. Nor is it to say that a nationhood or an ethnicity is a bounded integer. Yet it is surely surprising that the Englishness of English literature has such a low theoretical profile in the United States. There are, certainly, factors that work against the notion of the Englishness of English literature. Not only is much of it Irish, some Scottish and even a little Welsh, but one of the key figures in the redefinition of the English literary canon – T. S. Eliot – was an American. Yet there is surely some connection between the rush to purchase English furniture after the First World War, when many landed families were forced to sell up, and the intense appropriation of English literature at the service of the American teaching of literature. The topic of literature as cultural capital, and the sense of cultural stake-holding in English literature, invites broader study.

It was New Criticism which made possible this extrapolation of English literature to the American context by its resolute Platonic insistence on literary form over the extrinsic accidents of history. As a perhaps less intended consequence, it also created the basis for the construction of an American canon. Canon formation is one of the principal topics of literary theory, and it is an area where the situations of Britain and the United States are remarkably different. The canon of English literature had a long gestation, and a series of recent studies has unpacked many of the processes which contributed to it, dating its inception to the fifteenth century.[36] Without wishing to review all the obvious arguments concerning the non-absolute nature of canons, it is basically accurate to state that the English literary canon goes back several centuries not only in terms of its shifting formation as a canon, but in terms of the increased accumulation of works which have been by consensus found worthy of attention. American literature of course goes back a long way too, but in the early decades of the twentieth century there was no agreed American canon, even though American literature was an occasional component of literature courses in universities.[37] The consolidation of a canon of

American literature in its early formation during the 1940s and 1950s is generally seen as an unconscionable narrowing, and this it is. William C. Spengemann's 'What is American Literature?' (1978) is only one, early, example of the fundamental criticism of the contrivance of a notion of American literature that has run now for several decades:

> In 1934, Arthur Hobson Quinn's *American Fiction* traced the historical rise of realism through the artistically uneven work of 113 American novelists. Twenty-three years later, Richard Chase [in *The American Novel and its Tradition*] could feel perfectly justified in resting his counterproposition – that the American novel is not realistic at all but a romance – upon a detailed analysis of less than a dozen novels of demonstrable literary merit. There is no denying that the naïve historicism of Quinn's encyclopedic survey make Chase's close and imaginative readings seem serious and even scholarly in comparison.[38]

Spengemann's qualification seems important. On the one hand, a selection of American literature was being made based on quality – that is, on the basis of New Critical criteria which preferred symbolic and intensely self-reflexive works – and had little time for the social claims of realist works and their authors. On the other hand, this selection process made something called 'American literature' teachable and interesting. Spengemann was critical too of the tendency to project American literature as inhabiting an entirely different realm than that of British literature (a term rarely used in Britain: indeed, Spengemann's text oscillates uneasily around the usages of the terms 'British' and 'English'). He points out that American and British/English literature have close interrelationships, and claims even that 'when the history of English literature is described in terms of Anglo-American rather than British events, not only its overall shape and direction but those of its component periods take on an unwonted coherence and clarity'.[39] There is a lot of truth in this, but the radicalism of the notion of mapping as English the literature of both Britain and America would require many qualifications – aren't, say, Poe and Eliot part of French literature? Melville and Hawthorne part of Hebrew? Richard Wright and Toni Morrison part of African oral tradition? – so many qualifications, in fact, that the assumption of a possible English-language identity seems from one perspective simply to repeat the American appropriation of English literature in an even more expansive way.

*

What happened to the New Criticism? At the height of the period of dominance of high theory, Frank Lentricchia's *After the New Criticism* (1980) dates the end of New Criticism to the publication of Northrop Frye's *Anatomy of Criticism* (1957). The New Criticism is 'dead in the way that an imposing and repressive father figure is dead', claims Lentricchia, substituting the psychoanalytic model of influence preferred by Harold Bloom[40] (and a hint of the Nietzschean notion of the death of God) to try to claim for modern critical theory something of the pathos of struggle in a perpetual aftermath which it has made one of its recurrent gestures, forever post-this or post-that. Yet Lentricchia qualifies this temporal narrative by asserting that 'Frye's poetics is, from one perspective, contrary to the New Criticism, and, from another, yet one more (this time fantastical) document in the history of symbolist thought.'[41]

Northrop Frye's myth criticism was temporarily but widely adopted among critics in the United States. From one perspective it can be seen as an episode in the professionalization of the discipline of literary studies; from another, as a peculiar transitional stage between New Criticism and the arrival of structuralism. The need for literary criticism to appear as professional as possible had not subsided but increased, and in describing the place of his theoretical enterprise Frye makes comparisons between criticism and science which go further than ever. The essence of Frye's methodology is the claim that particular works of literature should be understood not in terms of their absolute uniqueness and originality, but as belonging to and drawing on a body of archetypal forms which remain permanent throughout the history of literature. The role of the critic is, like a scientist, to uncover the pattern of these forms in the same way that the physicist discovers the laws which determine the shape of the particulars of nature. Ransom claimed that while science discovered regularities, literature revealed particularities. Frye's claim is that the whole of literature should be treated as a rule-governed object. Ransom argued that poetry conveyed the subtlety of experience through departures from rhetorical norms; Frye argues that experience is no more a matter for criticism than the vision of redness or the sensation of heat or cold is a matter for the physicist. Ransom endorsed the Kantian notion of the autonomy of the artwork, and argued for a quasi-scientific rigorous criticism aimed at assessing the merits and demerits of individual literary objects; Frye argues that criticism too is autonomous, and that this autonomy is constituted both by its absolute relationship to literature (rather than to any extraneous discipline) and by its absolute independence from literature (which is the mute and non-discursive object of a scientific discourse): 'Art like nature has to be distinguished from the systematic study of it, which is criticism'.[42]

Frye taunts the New Critics, making them out to be elitists whose selection of preferred literary works and ranking of the same has parallels with social hierarchy. His alternative is an 'ethical criticism' which will avoid 'odious comparisons of greatness' but instead involve 'the consciousness of the presence of society [. . .] a sense of the real presence of culture in the community'. Recalling Eliot's model of tradition as a series of monuments, which he strongly approves, Frye claims that 'ethical criticism, then, deals with art as a communication from the past to the present, and is based on the conception of the total and simultaneous possession of past culture [. . .]. As a counterweight to historical criticism, it is designed to express the contemporary impact of all art, without selecting a tradition.'[43] Frye's desire to remove the element of judgment from literary criticism has both a cultural and an intellectual basis. While following the theoretical arguments of the principal New Critics is a matter of considerable interest, the very program of creating innumerable professional critics in University departments could only ever have led to an over-production of criticism, with every professor handing out judgements on all sides. The professional product required improvement, therefore, and Frye's approach offers to provide *even more science* than Ransom or even Richards had done. The critic, now as disinterested as the Kantian artwork itself, will rise above the contingencies of judgement and will supply something more systematic to the world: a theory of all literature. This theory is to be developed by treating literary works not as 'a miscellaneous pile of discrete "works"' but as a single entity. The model currently used to account for the relationship between literary works is 'tradition'; this is inadequate, Frye claims, as it overemphasizes the linear model of influence and the originality of the individual work, while disregarding literature as such; another model is needed.[44]

In some ways, Frye's approach is an extension of New Critical tastes and methods. While the New Critic treated the 'work' as a unit, Frye treats the whole of literature as a colossal single work. However, where before the New Critic looked for the relationship between the elements of a work which gave it its nuanced particularity, Frye's formalist approach, whether applied to narrative (mythos), symbol or genre, will identify the recurrent elements – 'archetypes' – which reveal the structure of all literature, to which the individual work belongs. Frye seems to extend New Criticism at the same time that he completely contradicts it. The social aspect of this is worth commenting on. Frye draws on Eliot's remarks on tradition. 'Tradition and the Individual Talent' represents tradition as a series of fixed monuments (great works) to which periodically another is added, altering the perspective on the whole. Eliot's motive in suggesting this model is to repudiate the notion of progress in the arts, just as he rejected the notion of progress in society, in line with the anti-romanticism of T. E. Hulme and Irving Babbitt which Eliot shared. Wyndham Lewis's *The Demon of Progress in the Arts* (1954) is a modernist artist's condemnation of the romantic emphasis on novelty which is contemporaneous with Frye. Yet there is a stark contrast between Frye's attempts to represent his approach as democratic and the plainly anti-democratic, anti-modern stance of Eliot and Lewis. The political implications of Frye's approach seem not to be democratic, however. Certainly, Frye's non-judgmental system opens the doors to all literary works, although in fact Frye tends to concentrate on works in languages that might already be known to a New Critic. However, the formalist system which treats all work as simultaneous, while it responds to a powerful truth articulated by Eliot, seems unable to register historical change of any variety, and, repeating errors denounced by the philosopher Henri Bergson (with whose work Frye was familiar), tends to spatialize time by deploying the metaphor of the 'level'. Some works are primitive, some more developed, but this is not a matter of progressive sophistication of the arts, nor are the different 'levels' to be understood as elements in a hierarchy going from good to better. There is therefore very little room for change or development in Frye's systematizing view. In particular, the view which can be found in figures as diverse as Vico, Hegel and Richards, that science has moved the world irreversibly out of the realm of myth and magic, finds no place here. Moreover, the attempt to discover a cognitive or other function for literature – its place in the unfolding of human understanding (Vico, Hegel), its ability to disrupt normative consciousness (surrealism, Ransom), or even its healing qualities (Richards) – seems to have no place in Frye's approach. Although Frye did not consider himself a Jungian, his interest in mythical archetypes is very compatible with Jung, whose theory of collective unconscious predicated that human subjects share a common collective unconscious. Jung's psychoanalysis is often considered to be the reactionary alternative to Freud – 'reactionary' in the sense that it precludes the possibility of a change in human nature of the kind predicted by theorists of progress. However Jungian he is often said to be, Frye rejects Jung because his own emphasis on literature as an autonomous system does not permit any causal connection between the unconscious and the literary work, nor does the autonomy of the critic permit any interaction with other equally autonomous disciplines.

The list of defects and limitations of Frye's formalism could be extended. Indeed, the manner of his own approach is to create typological lists which can be ingeniously elaborated. Frye's approach is in this sense of its time. Behavioural psychology and an administratively geared psychoanalysis at that time used similar typologies to categorize human types and assign individuals to the categories (a tendency in our own time to refer to an 'anal type' is a residue of this way of thinking). Business books to this day commonly market themselves on the basis of a new schema which is claimed can account for all possible permutations of a certain management strategy or employee type. These business manuals are not only examples of the scientific impulse to find predictable models of human behaviour, but examples of the author's skill in devising the typology in the first place, and in then persuading us that individual cases must inevitably come under one of the types established. One problem of Frye's formalism is that, far from challenging the supposed aestheticism of the older professorial critic, it give this professional class a new professional mode, with the likely outcome that the proliferation of critical close readings will be replaced by the proliferation of literary typologies, all ingeniously elaborated. In other words, this type of formalism lends itself to the grand professorial synthesis. As a method of criticism it crosses decisively from the amateur and extra-institutional dimension of the professorial New Critic into the wholly professional realm of the professor as systemic synthesizer.

Despite these and other defects, Frye gave University literary studies an impetus in terms of changing habits of thought and, as can be seen clearly from our historical perspective, in terms of opening literary studies to a new future. Frye's method made it possible to talk again about genre, expanded the analysis of symbols to embrace the 'polysemous' nature of texts, and stimulated a new interest in recurrent narrative structures or myths. Frye also anticipates many aspects of the French structuralism, with its roots in linguistics and its example in anthropology, which began to have a substantial influence in America that can be dated from the Baltimore Structuralism Conference of 1966.[45] Frye talks about discovering 'a few of the grammatical rudiments of literary expression',[46] implying a model similar to that of structuralism, which treats an individual work as the product of the implicit generic rules which allow the very possibility of its creation. This model is politically favoured by both Frye and the structuralists, since it reverses the premium set on genius by Kant and the Romantics. Kant, with his acceptance that events in nature are rule-based, also accepted the idea that artworks must be built upon rules. Kant, however, refused to accept those eighteenth-century models which claimed that the rules of art were a set of discernible prescriptions that demanded conformity and left no room for genius. So the 'genius' in Kant's account is the artist who has the ability to set new implied rules by creating an original artwork. The genius is a force like nature, giving rules, but the artwork remains regulated by new rules and is not a merely eruptive, unaccountable singularity or event. Frye's approach takes little account of novelty and change and certainly does not allow for the equation of the creativity of genius with that of nature itself that Kant outlines. These theoretical matters depend on many others, and much of what can be said about Frye's example can be said, both for and against, about the vogue for French structuralism which was to succeed him. This will be picked up in a later chapter.

*

I will close this chapter with an extraneous discussion. Frye's work is a marker in the process of professionalization of literary studies. He emphasizes that the scientific study of literature is entirely different from the activity practised by the 'man of taste' or aesthetic critic, and relentlessly excludes poets (i.e. literary artists) from the realm of criticism: 'The poet speaking as critic produces, not criticism, but documents to be examined by critics.' Moreover, he denies the right of any socially interested system, 'Christian, democratic or Marxist',[47] to influence criticism, and concurs with the New Critics that poets cannot speak directly to readerships in any interested way. In terms of Frye's desire to develop a formal science of criticism this is all conceivably necessary but, analysed as a performative act, seems concerned with the policing of boundaries: the division of labour, the separation of intellectual disciplines, the affirmation of a category of literary utterance distinct from any other kind of utterance, and the social separation of the university critic *qua* critic from extra-institutional groups of all kinds. For African Americans, the theory of literature at mid-century was a quite different matter, and had to be constructed in a different place, as part of a strategy of literary production in the manner of earlier literary movements. The work that was done through the middle of the century became the foundation of an African American literary and cultural theory which over several decades was forced into universities and gradually became the basis for the construction of programs of study and the creation of faculties.

While the American university critics could draw on 'the' tradition of English and indeed world literature, African Americans had been disproportionately denied literacy during and after slavery, had been in many regards broken from their traditional culture which survived as a complex residue but not an intact entity, were in large part divorced from African languages if not perhaps from certain speech habits or inflections, and had reference mainly to oral and musical tradition rather than the products of bourgeois art on which European-derived cultural theory depended. The one substantial African American literary tradition of the nineteenth century was the slave narrative, an autobiographical genre which did not meet the criterion of artistic autonomy preferred by the literary academics. From early in the 1920s, however, it became apparent to the whole of America and beyond that African American culture had produced a major modern music – jazz – and debate among white commentators began about whether this could properly be regarded as an art form. Educated African Americans, termed the 'talented tenth' by W. E. B. Du Bois in *The Souls of Black Folk* (1903), began to aspire to European-style cultural accomplishments, and in the literary field this led to the artistic movement known as the Harlem Renaissance, a group which produced mainly poetry and fiction, and looked to other American and European avant-garde art movements as its model. This group also produced important writing on the theory of Negro identity and culture, which of necessity would have to blend tradition, memory, adaptation, compromise and sheer invention. The cultural theory about Negro identity, art and culture was speculative and prescriptive, a set of proposals for the theoretical basis of action rather than a reflective survey of the totality of human accomplishments to date. Sometimes the literary efforts of the Harlem Renaissance group seemed more geared to the expectations of a fashionable white audience than to any substantial project of Negro ethnic self-definition, but essays and articles written at this time can now clearly be seen as essential theoretical formulations of the future, and the topics they tackle remain the stock of African American cultural theory to this day. These include Alain Locke's contribution as editor of *The New Negro* anthology (1925), Langston Hughes' 'The Negro Artist and the Racial Mountain' (1926), and, in a highly critical response to the limitations of this group, Richard Wright's 'Blueprint for Negro Writing' (1937).

A key figure in the formation of African American literary theory is Ralph Ellison, whose novel *Invisible Man* was published in 1952 and was swiftly adopted on school curricula. Ellison was able to benefit from the example of Richard Wright, who had been the first internationally successful African American novelist, but was perhaps a more palatable figure in 1950s American than the communist Wright. Rather than produce a series of novels, Ellison used the platform of his success to write and speak widely on issues of African American culture. The early essays were assembled in *Shadow and Act* (1964), which is a key document in African American cultural theory. Of equal importance as an intervention in critical theory is *Invisible Man* itself. James Joyce's *Ulysses* is an important precedent for Ellison if not a direct model, in the sense that neither *Ulysses* nor *Invisible Man* is simply a production-line novel that came out rather well and happened to be successful. Rather, the centrality of each novel was planned by its author. Critical theory has still not caught up with *Ulysses*, which continues to astound by constantly appearing to go beyond the critical theory that is brought to bear on it. Ellison had not perhaps planned a work of such scope, but the goals of *Invisible Man* are more immediate. A key theme of the novel is the construction of identity from available discourses – literary, political, folkloric and vernacular. The protagonist is a skilled orator who in defeat turns to writing his auto-biography. The structure of the whole work is predicated on testing the mysterious relationship between language, symbol, narrative, on the one hand, and selfhood or social destiny on the other. This is not an abstract, existential question, although the novel certainly draws on existentialism as one of the available discourses from which it is assembled. The question acquires concreteness in the context of the aftermath of slavery, and the distant model is *Ulysses* and its modelling of colonial identity as a problem compounded by the obvious limitations of the concept of identity. This will be a theme of later postcolonial literature and theory; indeed, the connections between African American writers and the developing *négritude* movement at this time should not be overlooked. African American cultural theory has supplied an important model and example for the postcolonial situation of which it is obviously part.

One motif of African American cultural theory to which Ellison gave substance (even if he was not the first to touch on it) is the extent to which jazz music can serve as a metaphor for African American existence and a model for literature. The frequent recourse of African American literary theory to the paradigm of jazz and blues could be seen as a weakness. Why attempt to furnish an explanation of one art in terms of another which presumably requires further and equally copious theorization? But the recourse to jazz and blues is more than metaphorical. It throws down challenges about the nature of literary expression: about extra-linguistic meaning, about the role of the body, about the vernacular tradition, about the coding of repressed meanings, about the role of the individual in the group, and about the status of the expressive voice. Ellison does not work all of these ideas through – indeed, it is not clear that they can be worked through – but his writings set down a palette which academic professionals have subsequently developed. For Ellison, a trained musician, jazz is the music of the big bands, in which the soloist is set against a highly ordered background. Ellison disliked modern jazz and, like Adorno, found in the virtuosic and drug-troubled Charlie Parker and his music only the example of the pathos of Negro sacrifice, not the triumph of the Negro and American preservation of identity in the moment of integration of the individual with the collective: 'the individual's willingness to discover his true self, upon his defining himself – for the time being at least – against his background.'[48] Ellison is also responsible for consolidating the theme of the masked and double identities of subject people, although his is not the first literary embodiment of this theme. While academic literary theory polices the boundaries of what might or might not be properly said, or what might or might not constitute the proper object of a critical inquiry, the kind of formula used by Ellison and elsewhere in early African American theory is aimed to open troubling inquiries: 'Perhaps the most insidious and least understood form of segregation is that of the word [. . .]. For if the word has the potency to revive and make us free, it has also the power to blind, imprison and destroy.'[49] This is not a theory, but a massive theoretical stimulus, one which insists on society as its real object, and refuses the demarcation of academic discipline. Ellison is as familiar with symbolism as any New Critic; he was inspired to pursue his literary career by his encounter with *The Waste Land*, and his novel reflects symbolist tradition quite as much as existentialism or the American vernacular. Ellison as theorist takes a qualified distance from New Critical norms and presuppositions, although his work is quite as aware of the ironic space between words and the mute 'identity' of the inner 'Invisible Man' who can only listen as any Eliot, Ransom or indeed Beckett.

Ellison's refusal to insist on *Negro* identity, his rounded attacks on the politics of Richard Wright's protest novels, and his endorsement of a notion of free American identity have led many to question his loyalty to the African American cause. These criticisms certainly have grounds. Yet even though African American writers and theorists who came after Ellison tended to have a more radical agenda, Ellison set the model, and while Frye elaborated his discovery that all literature was part of one great system, Ellison set a different agenda – an agenda concerning textuality, force and identity; canon and race or ethnicity; and the institutional organization of culture. These questions would gradually become more widely addressed.

Chapter 3

Reconfiguring English Studies

The moment of theory is closely identified with the intellectual impetus given to Marxist cultural theory by the introduction of the thought of French Marxist Louis Althusser into Britain. The ground for the eager reception of Althusser had already been well prepared during the 1940s and 1950s by the general British experience of socialism as well as Marxism, and in particular by the work of Richard Hoggart and Raymond Williams. The transition from the dominance of Leavisism to the dominance of something called 'theory' is not easily described in terms of a linear narrative of development, not least because Leavisism, despite its anti-Marxist roots, is so clearly involved in the development of theory in the British context. Theory in its heyday was somewhat triumphalistic, and presented itself as a sort of enlightenment, a scientific dispersal of the darkness of a mode of study previously mired in ideology. Yet 'theory' in a moment of reaction against Marxism (Foucault) also produced the notion that narratives of scientific progress should be regarded as themselves mythological, and that shifts from one discursive paradigm to another might be thought of as ruptures, certainly, but not as the product of an incessant ascent towards the light. Whatever the novelty of theory, the notion that it replaced a pre-theoretical past was certainly incorrect, even if such figures as Richards and Ransom had developed theory towards a different end, nor was theory original in its guise as a form of political praxis, as Leavis's transposition of Leninist activism to the classroom had already adopted this model.

A further complication of the view of theory as a moment of progress arises simply from the lateral aspect of its development – the fact that various strands of Marxist theoretical thought existed outside Britain but were not well known or easily accessible, and therefore were not available even to people, such as Williams, who were working in the same areas. The specific problem which the importance of Marx creates not only for the mapping of literary theory but also for its practice in the English-language context is that Marx belongs to the tradition of classical German philosophy. This modern German tradition has influenced English literature, culture and criticism only at certain times and in certain respects. Emphatically, the period of 'theory' in English literary studies in Britain was characterized by the deliberate importation of German Marxism alongside texts of French and Italian Marxism, largely at the advocacy of the journal *New Left Review* under the editorship of Perry Anderson. The exercise of importing European Marxism and presenting its texts collectively under the heading 'Western Marxism' was a deliberate act intended both to accuse British socialist intellectuals of lacking a coherent theory of society and to rectify that lack. This relatively sudden importation began a grafting process in which a variety of Marxist texts (which did not among themselves amount to a single, coherent tradition) as well as other theoretical ventures (especially French versions of psychoanalysis, linguistics and structuralism) were suddenly introduced into a climate which was not intellectually well prepared to receive them. The effect of this on the small number of established communist and socialist academics was initially challenging, since it obliged them to come to terms with what appeared to be a massive intellectual backlog. As the uptake of theory spread, left-leaning academics sought to acquaint themselves rapidly with a range of theoretical texts, adapt these texts to the study of literature and culture, and confront traditionalist colleagues with a series of attacks on curriculum and methodology which sometimes resulted in bitter disputes in Departments of English heavily polarized around the acceptance or rejection of 'theory'. The theory adopters faced certain difficulties which were both intellectual and practical. These were of two kinds. One was the assimilation of a variety of theories by individuals who in many cases lacked good knowledge of the background on which theory was based, especially the background of classical German philosophy, and who in some cases lacked the necessary linguistic skills to master the new materials and relied therefore on the arrival of translations. The intellectual struggle to assimilate theory resulted in a characteristic unevenness and eclecticism, arguably compensated in part by a refreshing sense of commitment and urgency. The second and greater difficulty was the task of complete revision of the subject of English which the theorists set themselves, a process which took the form both of revisiting every aspect of English literary study, and of a potentially almost indefinite expansion of the discipline into cultural studies in general. The creation of cultural studies in Britain was not merely a consequence of the expansion of English studies, but served as a stimulus to English literary studies even where it became institutionally separate from it. Indeed some English Departments converted into Departments of Cultural Studies. The expansion of the theoretical basis of English as well as the open-ended increase of its potential objects to include all the artefacts of mass culture was not, however, matched by increased interest in European languages, literature and culture. For better or worse, the creation of a canon of European theory was not accompanied by any corresponding growth of interest in European literature and culture, and the cosmopolitan basis of 'theory' appears mostly not to have dislodged the Anglophone bias of 'English'.

The impact of Marxism on theory is lateral, then as well as linear, and is social (in terms of the historical actuality of communist politics) as well as intellectual. The political and intellectual influence of Marxism from the latter half of the nineteenth century onward is evidently colossal, yet the development of a Marxist theory of culture lagged some decades behind, and took place overwhelmingly in national situations in which either it was administratively imperative to have a prescriptive theory of culture – as in the Soviet Union, where all aspects of civic life had to be theoretically led – or it was found desirable by relatively small numbers of intellectuals to develop a theory of existing bourgeois culture as an ideological mechanism in nations where revolution had not yet been accomplished. In the latter case, the theory of culture might serve as an extension of political struggle, or as a qualification of Marxist certainties. The substantial Marxist developments which contributed to the origin of theory supplied key arguments which Marxism originally lacked, and in doing so went beyond Marxism.

Did Marxism lack a theory of culture, and was it essential to insist on the notion of culture and to theorize that notion? Marx certainly did not lack a theory of human culture in the broadest sense of that term. The Marx who was known at the beginning of the twentieth century was a theorist of capital and of class struggle. It was well understood that his theory of the revolutionary overthrow of capitalism predicted a complete transformation of human culture, although it did not predict what forms the new society would take. Marxists valued Marx for his analysis of the workings of class society and for his detailed account of the workings of capital which purported to show that the irrationality of market economies led to increasingly severe crises and the complete impoverishment of the industrial working class – a description which certainly matched many aspects of the nineteenth-century economy of England, which was Marx's principal object of study. Marx's entire emphasis was on what he thought of as being material reality, as opposed to the world of ideas, and his analytical emphasis on economic life was geared to looking at the processes of society's self-production, rather than trading in idealistic notions of what humanity was or might become.

For Marx, economic processes were absolutely dominant: the available means of production (industrial technology) determined the shape of the social relations of production (class society), while the state had the function not of preserving justice for all, but of ensuring the continuation of capitalist property relations, in particular through its control of the police and army, which could suppress any threat to the existing order. Marx was resistant to the notion that society could be changed by changing people's ideas, and his well-known theory of ideology suggests that it is the actual shape of society that gives shape to ideas, rather than vice versa.

> In the social production of their life, men enter into definite relations that are indispensable and independent of their will, relations of production which correspond to a definite stage of development of their material productive forces. The sum total of these relations of production constitutes the economic structure of society, the real foundation, on which rises a legal and political superstructure and to which correspond definite forms of social consciousness. The mode of production of material life conditions the social, political and intellectual life process in general. It is not the consciousness of men that determines their being, but, on the contrary, their social being that determines their consciousness.[1]

This is Marx's summary formulation of 1859, with its often-quoted final sentence. It is a terse modification of the extended treatment offered by Marx and Engels' extended polemical study of 1845, *The German Ideology*. In 1859, Marx had turned his attention entirely to the theory of money in general and capital in particular. In 1845, the early and formative period of Marx's thought, it had been more important to denounce at length the notion that society could be modified by a critique of its ideas. Marx's emphasis on the social relations of production, once it eventually became applied to the production of literature and culture, would prove massively enabling, not least to those who sought some leverage against the dominance of a New Criticism which seemed to abstract literary texts from their social situation. Yet, even as we note the critical leverage these ideas grant, we should also set a question mark against the guiding opposition between the terms 'material' and 'ideal' on which Marx and Engels' analysis of ideology rests:

The ruling ideas are nothing more than the ideal expression of the dominant material relationships, the dominant material relationships grasped as
ideas. [. . .]

Consciousness can never be anything else than conscious existence, and
the existence of men is their actual life-process. If in all ideology men and
their circumstances appear upside down as in a *camera obscura*, this phenomenon arises just as much from their historical life-process as the inversion
of objects on the retina does from their physical life-process. [. . .]

We do not set out from what men say, imagine, conceive, nor from men
as narrated, thought of, imagined, conceived, in order to arrive at men in
the flesh. We set out from real, active men, and on the basis of their real-
life process we demonstrate the development of the ideological reflexes
and echoes of this life-process. The phantoms formed in the human
brain are also, necessarily, sublimates of their material life-process, which is
empirically verifiable and bound to material premises. Morality, religion,
metaphysics, all the rest of ideology and their corresponding forms of consciousness, thus no longer retain the semblance of independence.[2]

These passages blend highly enabling insights with a figurative language
which seems suspiciously elementary. That ideas are the 'expression' of
material relationships valuably establishes that ideas must be considered
in their social situation, but problematically implies that the whole domain
of symbolic exchange is 'ideal' (i.e. exists as ideas) while other forms of
exchange are 'material' (even though purportedly 'material' relationships
are mediated by the symbolic in the form of money). Marx and Engels
are using philosophical terms, but in a polemical manner. They do so
to great effect, but leave a curious rhetorical residue from which their
intended meanings cannot easily be freed. A similar blend of effective
intellectual polemic and potential terminological chaos is found in the
second paragraph, which suggest that ideas 'invert' reality, by which
Marx and Engels mean to suggest that the idea of the authority of God,
for example, is a disguised reflection of the real authority of class society.
Simple as it is, this notion of inversion is vital to the emphasis of later
Marxist interpretations of cultural texts as ideological vessels. At the same
time, it depends on a stark opposition between false consciousness and
the apprehension of reality which is likely to prove unsustainable in the
analysis of complex (and indeed simple) cultural objects. The reference
to ideas as 'phantoms' is one of several uses by Marx of the metaphor of
ghosts – famously in the description of communism as a 'spectre' haunting
Europe. While the metaphor is polemically effective, the notion of ideas
as phantoms – semblances of the real lacking material substance – really
works against the alternative which we might expect from Marx – the

proposition that ideas are themselves productive forces – and the airy claim that philosophy, religion and other intellectual discourses are now shifted from apparent independence from the real to tainted immersion in it clearly suggests something that cannot easily be demonstrated.

Further paragraphs in *The German Ideology* argue that the false notion that consciousness determines reality is a product of the division of labour in society. The division of labour, in which socially necessary tasks are carried out by different groups of workers in order to increase the efficiency of production, is here applied to intellectual workers as a fraction of the ruling class whose thinking they carry out:

> Division of labour only becomes truly such from the moment when a division of material and mental labour appears. From this moment onwards consciousness *can* really flatter itself that it is something other than consciousness of existing practice, that it *really* represents something without representing something real; from now on consciousness is in a position to emancipate itself from the world and to proceed to the formation of 'pure' theory, theology, philosophy, morality etc. [. . .]
>
> The division of labour [. . .] manifests itself in the ruling class as the division of mental and material labour, so that inside this class one part appears as the thinkers of the class (its active, conceptive ideologists, who make the perfecting of the illusion of the class about itself their chief source of livelihood) while the others' attitude to these ideas and illusions is more passive and receptive, because they are in reality the active members of this class and have less time to make up illusions and ideas about themselves.[3]

Marx argues that the division of labour is in its primary form nothing more than the 'division of labour in the sexual act', a thought developed by Engels in *The Origin of the Family, Private Property and the State* (1884), and which feminist theory from the 1970s would turn into a substantial materialist and ontological inquiry. Marx claims that the division of labour only becomes truly such when the division of 'material and mental labour' establishes itself. On the one hand, this is a complex claim which has many applications to later cultural theory, since the claim is not only that intellectual or cultural products are class-partisan in character, but implies that the very form which these activities adopt is itself a product of the alienation of human labour created by the division of labour. This means that discourses such as ethics and philosophy do not embody the transcendence of the human condition or embody its highest moment or furthest development, but are instead constitutively untrue, part of the limitation of human 'species being' (in Marx's term). On the other hand, Marx and Engels simply refer in a mocking polemical manner to the products of intellectual labourers as being to create 'illusions and ideas' about the ruling class of which they form a fraction. While this mocking attitude to the abstract irrelevance of 'ideas' dramatically performs the task of steering the reader to concentrate on the task of analysing society and anticipating the meaning and purpose of future change, the radical dismissal of the state of existing culture is so one-sided as to require substantial further investigation if it is to be maintained in any form.

Marx and Engels created the grounds for a possible analysis of culture (in the restricted, superstructural sense), but made no attempt to pursue it. The absence of a Marxist theory of culture played an important role after the Russian Revolution, when a debate started concerning the merit of bourgeois culture and the desirability of creating a new, modernist, proletarian culture (*Proletkult*). Lenin and Trotsky both wrote on the merits of the bourgeois novel in terms of its ability to give insight into the totality of society, in effect testifying to its ability to challenge ideology and serve revolutionary consciousness, even when its creators were allied to the bourgeoisie. The chief literary-theoretical defender of the bourgeois novel from a Marxist perspective was the Hungarian Georg Lukács, whose work I examine in Chapter 6. The advocates of new proletarian art were perhaps more true to the spirit of Marx's claim that communism would bring about a new state of human being which was unpredictable from the perspective of capitalist society, but which would overcome the loss of authentic being attendant on the division of labour.

The Soviet experience did have a direct effect on other European countries during the 1930s and even before, not least through the direct intervention of the Communist International in the strategy of the various national Communist Parties, although the context of discussion was not the same in those countries, in which communists and other socialists were preparing for revolutionary struggle, as in the Soviet Union, where socialism of a sort had already been accomplished. In one respect, Marx had not neglected to supply a theory of culture, since the very substance of his thought concerned the transformation of human society in its entirety. It is rightly argued that Marx's philosophy is in essence ontological, not simply political or economic, a view that was not always clear in the early decades of Marxism when Marx's early writings, which revealed the philosophical basis of his thought, were simply not known. *Critique of Hegel's Doctrine of the State* (1843–4, first published 1927) and *Economical and Philosophical Manuscripts* (1844, first published 1932) were among the most important of Marx's works to have little impact in

Europe until after the Second World War, though they are crucial for the development of a Marxist theory of culture. One effect of the absence of a Marxist theory of culture in Britain and America before the Second World War was the reduction of the politics of culture to a demand for 'commitment' on the part of the literary author – a demand which did not do justice to the more complicated questions either of the political function of the text or of the autonomy of the literary object, making it easy for figures such as Leavis and Ransom to define their practice against the politics of commitment. It is also easy to see why Raymond Williams was so unsatisfied with the Marxist approach to literature. Williams felt that culture could not simply be regarded as an ideological veil disguising the true nature of social reality, but also that the object of culture had not been properly defined. Far from being an ideological veil, culture might be part of a complex system of social being that could not simply be expressed in terms of capital and the alienation of the commodity form, and the culture of certain tightly knit working-class groups might be part of a value system already antithetical to capitalism.

The need for a development of Marxist cultural theory in Britain arose both from the fact that it remained underdeveloped in Marx's own work, and from the fact that the full philosophical tradition of Marxism had still not been fully developed anywhere, in part because the relative obscurity of Marx's early writings meant that certain perspectives on Marx simply were not available, and in part because the struggle to create revolution and fight Nazism had resulted in the need for a direct politics of commitment, not the indirect politics of cultural critique.

Before passing on to a discussion of the work of Richard Hoggart and Raymond Williams, the two figures most closely associated with the transformation of literary into cultural studies which prepared the ground for the transformation of literary theory, it is worth paying attention to the question of Marx's materialism. Following the introduction of Marxism into literary theory, the terms material and materialism, with their evident allusion to the assumed concrete actuality of matter, are found deployed in many literary-theoretical contexts. When faced with the theological niceties of matter it is tempting to resort to ironic play, a temptation which Marx and Engels did not resist when they penned their polemic against Feuerbach, Bauer and Stirner in *The German Ideology* (1845) and against Proudhon in *The Poverty of Philosophy* (1847). The tone of gleeful irony is one that assails Marx whenever he seeks to deal with metaphysics, and returns most notably, and not accidentally, in the passage dealing with the fetishism of the commodity in *Capital*. The famous essay on Feuerbach in *The German Ideology* which we have already discussed offers another opportunity to observe the term materialism in a context of rhetorical and analytical slippage.

We find in Marx a frequent rhetorical hostility towards 'abstraction' that is, as Marx sees it, towards the form of Hegelianism adopted by the young Hegelians, most notably by Feuerbach, which Marx characterizes as 'idealism' in opposition to 'materialism'. Marx's resistance to 'idealism' takes the form of a constant recourse to the concept of the material, which Marx, following Hegel, will refer to as 'particularity'. The account of the commodity in *Capital* is organized around this opposition of the material particularity of the commodity (its use value) as opposed to its exchange value which has 'absolutely no connection with the physical nature of the commodity and the material (*dinglich*) relations arising out of this'. This is not the space for a detailed critique or commentary on the text of Marx, yet *The German Ideology* especially remains one of the most influential texts of modern thought even among those who are unfamiliar with it, and it impinges on all of us inasmuch as we retain the use of the term 'materialism' in the context of cultural analysis, with all the connotations that term embodies of opposition to a certain reading of Hegelian idealism.

It does not need to be said perhaps that Marx's attempt to refute Hegel results in an undialectical, one-sided view of consciousness as either cut off from 'material reality' or (in *The German Ideology*) as a 'sublimate' of it like a rising gas. Yet Marx's anti-Hegelianism owes so much to Hegel that it comes back to universality not in the form of Hegel's absolute idea, but in the form of communism. For we learn from *The German Ideology* that communism 'turns existing conditions into conditions of unity'. Communism as it were comes out of the other side of the alienation of nature, which, as Hegel's *Phenomenology* (1807) claims, begins with the displacement of sense certainty, and restores material reality by identifying it entirely with thought. 'The reality which communism creates is precisely the true basis for rendering it impossible that anything should exist independently of individuals, insofar as reality is only a product of the preceding intercourse of individuals.'[4] Communism will not allow the movement of money and commodities which denies the individual access to the real. A direct relationship to materiality will be restored. Under communism, the return to a new materiality, once property relations have been abolished, will result in the emergence of a new 'universality', not a universality of money and the infinite fungibility of constant exchange in which every material reality melts away, but a new state of being, an *ontological* universality. While the argument for communism or socialism might be generally cast in the form of a struggle for a rational and just society, it is striking that Marx's argument for communism should adopt not just the rhetoric but even the form of a program for the restoration of a nature which is considered lost. Marx's optimism is far from the pessimism of Ransom, which finds only brief glimpses of the particular actuality of nature in the nuanced reading of the privileged literary artefact, bracketed from history; for Marx, it is the transformation of society itself which will restore reality, and only the most profound historicism which will make the necessity and course of this transformation visible to the predictive scientific consciousness.

*

The intellectual link between the vision of the Leavises and the transformation of the methodology and object of English is found in the work of Richard Hoggart, who co-founded the Birmingham Centre for Contemporary Cultural Studies in 1963[5] and is best known for *The Uses of Literacy: Aspects of Working-Class Life, with Special References to Publications and Entertainments* (1957). Hoggart was of upper-working-class origins, grammar-school educated on a scholarship, and a graduate of Leeds University.[6] This trajectory from working-class origins to provincial university accounted for Hoggart's passionate interest in working-class culture and his commitment to workers' education programs run as extra-mural ventures by the universities where he worked. However, his language and approach have many features in common with the combative pessimism of the Leavises, whose work he cites at key junctures. In *The Uses of Literacy*, Hoggart criticizes 'a middle-class Marxist's view of the working-classes' for 'part-pitying and part-patronising working-class people beyond any semblance of reality', and claims that 'it is some novels, after all, that may bring us really close to the quality of working-class life – such a novel as Lawrence's *Sons and Lovers*, at least, rather more than popular or more consciously proletarian fiction'.[7] Hoggart's dismissal of 'middle-class' Marxism does not even begin to engage the possibilities of Marxist cultural analysis. However, his gesture towards Lawrence is supplemented by praise for 'the detailed surveys of working-class life which sociologists have made during the last twenty years', work which succeeds in conveying the 'claustrophobic impression' of working class life in all its 'concreteness'.[8] The notion of 'concreteness' would have been vividly found in the Mass-Observation studies of the working class which Hoggart cites in his bibliography: *The Pub and the People* (1943) and *Puzzled People* (1947).[9] Hoggart's study emulates Mass-Observation work in that it assembles and sorts vernacular materials in an impressionistic and documentary fashion. Yet while Mass-Observation in its earlier manifestations had insisted for political reasons on the absence of a metacommentary, Hoggart weaves himself into his material as an almost belletristic critic intent on mediating the raw materials through his own sensibility for the benefit of a like-minded elite audience: 'The strongest impression, after one has read a lot of these stories, is of their extraordinary fidelity to the detail of the readers' lives.'[10]

Hoggart's lack of theory may seem to some contemporary readers merely quaint. The deliberate vagueness of the subtitle of his book may be taken to suggest a lack of rigorous focus. However, it is important for us to understand that Hoggart is searching for a mode of grasping the reality of the life of the majority which will, certainly, reflect the Leavisite 'sensibility' of which he clearly considers himself a bearer, but which will not make the working class a mere object of a scientific or political metalanguage. This leaves Hoggart with a practice – workers' education in extra-mural classes – but a defective theory. Hoggart does little more than paraphrase Q. D. Leavis's *Fiction and the Reading Public* (1932) when he laments a lack of 'serious reading' in the working class: 'There are many movements towards increasing and improving the minority; there are much larger and on the whole more successful movements toward strengthening the hold of a few dominant popular publications on the great majority of people.'[11] Yet in 'Schools of English and Contemporary Society' (1963), only a few years after *The Uses of Literacy*, Hoggart set out a blueprint for the academic practice of 'Literature and Contemporary Cultural Studies' which anticipated the future direction of cultural studies. This field would partly draw on existing approaches, especially F. R. Leavis and Denys Thompson's *Culture and Environment* (1933) and Q. D. Leavis's *Fiction and the Reading Public*.[12] The residue of Leavisism is seen, first, in the commitment to the study of the contemporary; second, in the desire to grasp the life-world of the majority concretely and not theoretically; finally, in the continued privileging of literary-critical sensibility as the standpoint from which all cultural objects were to be viewed. It is worth stressing the connection to Leavis of early cultural studies not merely because it clarifies the social situation of its origins, but also because it contradicts the emphatic anti-Leavisism which has accompanied the introduction of theory in Britain, and, further, because it helps to explain the eclecticism of theory in the British context. This eclecticism occurs because the movement to cultural studies – the main impulse towards 'theory' – was not led by European-style intellectuals but produced by the social flexibility of the education system itself which created the Janus-like figure of the grammar-school educated man, recently emerged from the concreteness of working-class life but not identified with any ready-made method of placing the working class he had recently left as his 'object'. This eclecticism is the product not of confusion but of dissent. Hoggart defines the field of cultural studies in terms of three parts: 'historical and philosophical', 'sociological', 'literary critical', with the latter said to be the 'most important'.[13] The 'historical and philosophical' aspect refers to what Hoggart calls the 'cultural debate' exemplified in Raymond Williams' *Culture and Society 1780–1950* (1958), a text designed to historicize the term culture and restore the full breadth of its meanings in order, it can be argued, to make everything pertaining to culture in all of its aspects available to consciousness and therefore open to change. That is to say, shifting the term 'culture' away from the narrow notion of 'high culture' achieves a dual political purpose: it reveals the ideological dimension of high culture as the culture of the bourgeoisie and demonstrates that the lower classes are not merely culture-less. The effect of historicizing the term is radically to bring to light the immanence of culture in a way that is materialist and political but not objectivizing and scientific. Indeed, Hoggart's second grouping – the 'sociological' inquiry – picks up directly from Williams in finding both sociological and popular terms for cultural groupings and phenomena in use at that time (the highbrow, the Angry Young Man) too thin and under-researched.[14] Hoggart proposes research into all aspects of cultural production and consumption as a 'sociology of literature or of culture' which should look at (a) writers and artists, (b) audiences, (c) opinion formers and their channels of influence, (d) the 'organization for the production and distribution of the written and spoken word' and (e) 'all sorts of interrelations' both functional and imaginative.[15] While the scholarship of our own time will now routinely make these different strata the object of investigation in terms of cultural *history*, it is notable that Hoggart seeks to grasp the *contemporary* culture by these means. The third part of Hoggart's field is the literary critical. Just as Leavis advocated the application of literary sensibility to advertising, Hoggart urges its use in the reading of all manner of contemporary cultural objects: 'film criticism; television and radio criticism; television drama [. . .]; popular fiction of many kinds [. . .] the press and journals [. . .]; strip cartoons; the language of advertising and public relations; popular songs and popular music [. . .].' Though 'increasingly machine tooled', such arts may contain 'brittle voices' which authentically open out on to human experience, and we should recognize the 'meaningfulness of much popular art' by imaginatively entering into it.[16]

*

Hoggart was a true innovator and set a key example for English studies and its offshoot, cultural studies, but the transition from Cambridge English to the period of theory is more completely realized in the work and career of Raymond Williams. Williams' work is of particular interest because it represents a genuine transition from Leavisism to theory, and his career and example are of pronounced importance for the reshaping of English studies itself, and for the divergence of English studies into the various fields of cultural studies. Williams was born in Wales to a working-class family, and it is this background which shapes his intellectual commitments. Following study at Cambridge and service in the Second World War, he became an adult education tutor for the Oxford University Delegacy for Extra-Mural Studies, until 1961 when he became a Fellow of Jesus College, Cambridge. Williams was from an English-speaking part of Wales and not notably nationalist in outlook, but ethnic difference subtly conditioned Williams' attitude to the notion of a national literary tradition which he encountered at Cambridge. However, Williams did not reject the notion of a common culture. The sense of community which he found in Welsh working-class areas shaped his commitment to socialism and led him in his early work to validate the term 'community' as an alternative to national tradition. More than this, Williams' class background led him to question the object of literary studies. While English studies focused on a great tradition which supposedly shaped national culture and consciousness, Williams was aware of all the aspects of the everyday life of the groups who did not participate in shaping national literary consciousness, and asked how this texture of 'culture' might be brought into knowledge and theorized. The shift from 'literature' to 'culture', then, has its roots in class and ethnic difference, but this did not mean that the shift was the automatic product of such difference; it needed to be thought.

In Williams' work part of the means for thinking the shift was supplied by the theoretical climate and practical activity of English studies itself. Williams was influenced in his overall orientation by Leavis and Richards, and his project became differentiated from theirs progressively and not by way of a sudden rupture or enlightenment. Like Hoggart, Williams was particularly influenced by the Leavises, whose project could be construed as 'radical middle class'. Its emphasis on 'tradition' was anti-Whig, in that it vigorously opposed the socially disintegrative effects of the Industrial Revolution, but was not truly Tory, in that it made strategic use of a Tory idea of organic community as supposed to have been evidenced in the Elizabethan period only in the knowledge that the social relations of Elizabethan England could never be restored. The Leavisite position avoids Whig, Tory, Conservative and Labour or socialist positions. In other words, its apparent conservatism is a kind of strategic bulwark against both capitalism and socialism. 'Culture' becomes a third position, beyond the class interest of the propertied and the propertyless. The notion that culture might ameliorate or correct the effects of the Industrial Revolution can be adapted by socialists, and Williams set about this in his early and important work, *Culture and Society 1780–1950* (1958). *Mass Civilisation and Minority Culture* was only one text in what Williams identified as a tradition of works that distinguished culture from society. The Leavises' work offered other suggestions for Williams' evolving project. *Fiction and the Reading Public* suggested that literature should not be seen simply from the idealized position of the present-day, culturally equipped reader standing at the apex of tradition, but grasped in the context of a history of publication in which class, textual ideology, modes of production, and the constitution of readerships all played a part. Q. D. Leavis did not herself use these terms, which reflect more the historical methodology of recent scholarship, and indeed her work is geared to a defence of minority culture rather than its critique, but her work suggests the move from reading literature to historically grasping culture in all its mediations on which Williams and the tradition of cultural studies would build. The third of these works, *Culture and Environment*, suggested that literary studies could be broadened to include other textual objects. Leavis and Thompson were interested in creating a kind of 'sensibility', in their term, which would be differentiated from its cultural environment. They thought that the reading skills learned in English studies ought to be applied to objects such as advertisements, newspaper articles, and other textual artefacts thought of as being manipulative rather than truthful, in order to identify the rhetorical devices of such texts and thereby counter the manipulative intentions of their producers. Leavis was opposed to Marxism, but his work nevertheless showed that English studies lent itself to a practice of ideology critique in which subtle modes of textual interpretation could be brought to bear on an expanded range of cultural objects.

Another aspect of Leavisism which lent itself to the socialist project was the emphasis on creating an 'armed minority' of skilled literary interpreters whose goal would be to act in schools as educators spreading the 'sensibility' which the texts produced in modern capitalist society were intended to negate. This idea converged with the different tradition of Adult or Workers' Education, in which Williams was involved from 1945 to 1961. In the later nineteenth century, many opportunities for workers' self-education had been brought into existence, in the Mechanics Institutes, co-operatives and trades unions. This working-class self-organization was complemented by the development of University Extensions, departments of extra-mural education under the umbrella of established universities which sent extension lecturers out into working-class communities to give lectures and establish regular classes. Alongside the demand for subjects useful to socialist politics, such as history and political economy, English, and the notion of a national culture which accompanied it, came to take on a key role. The popularity of English seems to have reflected on the one hand the desire of working-class people to participate in a national culture, and on the other the desire of the more privileged to follow the agenda set by Matthew Arnold in *Culture and Anarchy* – the amelioration of the demand for socialism through the dissemination of culture.[17] The tension in the very constitution of adult education in the nineteenth century was of importance in one form or another throughout the twentieth century, since it involves a complex negotiation between those classes or other entities which purport to be the bearers of culture, and those which aspire to possession of or entry into culture – a negotiation or struggle in which the very notion of culture becomes contested and strategically transformed. A basic element in this negotiation is the competition within adult education between the view that workers' education should facilitate the development of a class identity or culture, and the notion that it should seek to induct workers into a national identity or culture, transcending class. In the period before the Second World War, the Workers' Educational Association (WEA) had continued to air debates between those who wanted to maintain the working-class basis of adult education, thereby conserving the regional and class identities coded within it, and those who wanted to take adult education to a broader audience, who tended to be more committed to the idea of high culture.[18] The content of adult education was affected not only by politics, but also by the model of teacher–student interaction, in which the views and needs of the students assumed particular importance. Adult education in the area of culture was frequently interdisciplinary, shaped to address a broad area of inquiry, and was later credited by Williams as the forerunner of modern cultural studies, especially in its emphasis on the forms of contemporary culture:

When I moved into internal university teaching, when at about the same time Richard Hoggart did the same, we started teaching in ways that had been absolutely familiar in Extra Mural and WEA classes, relating history to art and literature, including contemporary culture, and suddenly so strange was this to the Universities they said 'My God, here is a new subject called Cultural Studies.' But we are beginning I am afraid, to see encyclopaedia articles dating the birth of Cultural Studies from this or that book in the late 'fifties. Don't believe a word of it. That shift of perspective about the teaching of arts and literature and their relation to history and to contemporary society began in Adult Education, it didn't happen anywhere else.[19]

Williams might have added that the very notion of English studies, let alone that of cultural studies, had been developed first in the context of adult education, before being taken up within English universities at the end of the nineteenth century. This is worth remembering, because it modifies the commonly received perception that English was once an originary and pure discipline from which the hybrid and polyvalent cultural studies was a promiscuous development that it was necessary to hive off into a separate university department.

Williams' *Culture and Society* is a particularly interesting and influential document of the moment in which the socialist inflection of adult education began to manifest itself at the level of disciplinary debate within the University 'proper' at a high level of theoretical articulation. This work has limitations which make it appear now as the record of an incomplete intellectual struggle, but the political forces which shape it, and the reshaping of academic fields which it anticipates, are still very much in evidence. Although I have used the short-hand term 'limitations', it is more accurate to suggest that the text bears the mark of a specific historical impasse – the apparent inability of Marxism to supply a theory of culture which might properly incorporate the tradition of refinement characteristic of criticism and scholarship in the arts and literature, and the inability of the modes of criticism and scholarship which existed at that time properly to construct their object and reflect the totality of its contexts. Williams shows no awareness of other national traditions which were giving theoretical shape to cultural issues in other enclaves – such as the German-language aesthetic debates of the Frankfurt School – despite the presence in England of the émigré social theorist Karl Mannheim, who shared the influence of Marx and Weber common to the Frankfurt School group, and whose activity in the context of adult education in the 1930s pointed the way to a more sociological approach to culture.[20] Raymond Williams had left the Communist Party before the

Second World War, disillusioned with Stalin and 'democratic centralism', and the model of socialism implied in his early work has points of contact with the common strand of British Labourism or 'workerism' (an identification with the working class in its current state of existence) and with Fabianism (an explicit renunciation of revolutionary means). His rejection of Marxism in the field of culture is a response to early British attempts to formulate a Marxist literary theory: in Christopher Caudwell's *Illusion and Reality* (1937) and Alick West's *Crisis and Criticism* (1937). Williams' basic objection to Marxism at the time of *Culture and Society* is that the model of (economic) base and (cultural and institutional) superstructure tends to suggest that literature and the arts are purely of secondary importance. The effect of this is to oblige Marxist commentary on literature to spend time justifying the importance of literature (an importance which in most other contexts might otherwise be taken for granted) and to assume the task of categorizing literary works according to their compatibility with socialism.[21] Williams declares himself 'not a Marxist'[22] and therefore not interested in resolving the problems of Marxist cultural commentary. Even though he at this time rejects Marxism, Williams' own project is shaped by it, and specifically by the problems suggested to him by the base–superstructure model:

> [...] there seems to be a general inadequacy, among Marxists, in the use of 'culture' as a term. It normally indicates, in their writings, the intellectual and imaginative products of a society; this corresponds with the weak use of 'superstructure'. But it would seem that from their emphasis on the interdependence of all elements of social reality, and from their analytic emphasis on movement and change, Marxists should logically use 'culture' in the sense of a whole way of life, a general social process. [...] The difficulty lies [...] in the terms of Marx's original formulation: if one accepts 'structure' and 'superstructure', not as the terms of a suggestive analogy, but as descriptions of reality, the errors naturally follow. Even if the terms are seen as those of an analogy, they need [...] amendment.[23]

Williams dislikes the manner in which Marx's analogy of base and superstructure – which refers to the foundations and superstructure of a building – has been treated literally, leading Marxist commentators to treat cultural products as secondary products of a determining economic base, which are then likely to be given reductively ideological readings. The key here is that for Williams it is not simply that cultural objects such as high literary texts have been badly analysed, but that the base–superstructure model has tended to prevent a broadening of the notion of culture to include 'a whole way of life, a general social process' – the innumerable aspects of what Williams will in much of his work call 'communication'.

The notion of 'communication' is itself problematic, since it implies a simple division between transmissible contents and modes of transmission which is idealist and likely to create numerous false problems if introduced as an alternative to 'ideology'; but the key here is Williams' desire to resist the model of culture as ideology, in this case by establishing 'communication' as a more neutral term which, unlike the notion of a top-down, ruling-class ideology shaping consciousness, leaves space for the possibility that any individual or group within society may be able to originate and transmit contents, as well as receive and absorb them. The notion of communication is part of the broad shift involved in Williams' reshaping of 'culture' as an object of study. On the face of it, Williams' desire to account for culture as an ensemble of relations (he does not even qualify these as 'symbolic' relations) might be expected to have an anthropological impetus. Yet the whole of *Culture and Society* is dedicated to what we might now call an archaeology or genealogy of the term 'culture' in English literature which demonstrates the unfolding centrality of this term in the use to which Williams puts it. This is done, I think, not simply to claim the authority of tradition for Williams' own evolving position, but to demonstrate that 'culture' is indeed the term under which modern society (since the later eighteenth century) has acquired a knowledge of itself and its own identity. If this summary is correct, it reveals important characteristics of Williams' approach to culture. This is not an anthropological approach which will scientifically categorize a culture from the outside, nor is it a politically revolutionary approach which suppresses the complexities of culture in the interest of revolutionary clarity. For Williams, the investigation of culture is dependent on the intimate, direct knowledge of cultural contents on the part of the commentator. His position, perhaps accidentally, reflects then current anthropological debate about the position of the anthropological observer, but his stance reflects other considerations: the demand of literary close reading method for the nuanced involvement of a native speaker, and his insight that many hitherto excluded cultural objects were themselves transient or not really recognizable from a high cultural perspective. The overall effect of this is seamlessly continuous with his literary training, in that it grants supremacy to the idea of national tradition.

Culture and Society traces the use of the term 'culture' in a variety of British essayists who are mostly conservative in outlook. Indeed, Williams' stance in making substantial use of figures such as Burke and

Coleridge seems remarkably un-socialist at first glance, although the inclusion of Ruskin and Morris conforms to the palette of the British labour movement.

> I wish to show the emergence of *culture* as an abstraction and an absolute: an emergence which, in a very complex way, merges two general responses – first, the recognition of the practical separation of certain moral and intellectual activities from the driven impetus of a new kind of society; second, the emphasis of these activities, as a court of human appeal, to be set over the processes of practical social judgment and yet to offer itself as a mitigating and rallying alternative. [...] The idea of *culture* would be simpler if it had been a response to industrialism alone, but it was also, quite evidently, a response to the new political and social developments, to *Democracy*.[24]

In some ways, Williams' project reflects a desire to redeem conservative thinkers from socialist mistrust, for example by asserting the importance of the social commitment of the English Romantic poets against received views of their absorption in personal emotions.

> What were seen at the end of the nineteenth century as disparate interests, between which a man must choose and in the act of choice declare himself a poet or a sociologist, were, normally, at the beginning of the century, seen as interlocking interests: a conclusion about personal feeling became a conclusion about society, and an observation of natural beauty carried a necessary moral reference to the whole and unified life of man.[25]

As well as mapping the term culture, Williams is hinting here at his own version of the theory of 'dissociation of sensibility' propounded by Eliot. However, Williams connects the ideas of 'culture' and 'experience' in ways that seem not to reflect a fundamental disturbance of consciousness (such as that implied by Eliot or, in an entirely contrasting fashion, by Marx), but to affirm and even celebrate the validity of the personal and social against the economic. It seems at first odd that he discovers that process in the work of Thomas Carlyle, a figure held to be mainly reactionary by the left, but in Carlyle's *On Heroes and Hero Worship and the Heroic in History* (1841) Williams finds the full realization of the notion of culture first propounded by Burke and Coleridge: 'It is here [in Carlyle's 'Man-of-Letters Hero'] that the idea of culture as the body of arts and learning and the idea of culture as a body of values superior to the ordinary progress of society, meet and combine.'[26] At this stage in his thinking Williams (1) assumes that the coming into being of a notion of culture reflects the reality that culture exists as a domain which is at very least non-identical with the economic; and (2) seeks to defend a notion of culture which embraces all aspects of social life against any privatized notion of the aesthetic, such as that made explicit in the aesthetic movement. His discussion of the psychologist turned literary theorist I. A. Richards makes clear this emphasis on the collective against the individual:

> [. . .] nearly all theoretical discussions of art since the Industrial Revolution have been crippled by the assumed opposition between art and the actual organisation of society.
>
> All that Richards has taught us about language and communication, and for which we acknowledge our debt, has to be reviewed, finally, when we have rid ourselves of those vestiges of Aesthetic Man – alone in a hostile environment, receiving and organizing his experience – which Richards, even as a brilliant opponent, in fact inherited.[27]

Williams' work in *Culture and Society* represents very much a turning point, not only for him but for English studies as a whole. The idea of culture, backed by an uncertain validation of 'experience', soon became dissatisfying to Williams himself. The retrospective judgements and clarifications he made in a later series of interviews published as *Politics and Letters* give a kind of career overview and are fair in both their defence and their rejection of his own positions in the late 1950s, especially as regards his uncritical endorsement of the idea of a 'national culture':

> *Culture and Society* is not a book I am greatly attached to now. But ironically it is the very success of the book which has created the conditions for its critique.
>
> The whole notion of the rise of a national literature, the definition of a nation through its literature, the idea of literature as the moral essence or spirit of the nation – these are supports of a specific political and social ideology. All I can say is that I did not see that when I was writing *Culture and Society*. [. . .]
>
> I would myself no longer use the word 'community' in the way I did in *Culture and Society*.[28]

These reservations are well made. We should note, first, that Williams is correct in his assessment of the ground-clearing effect of *Culture and Society*, but we might also add that the hybrid of labourism and Leavisism which Williams offers in the absence of a distinct Marxist analysis has a logic of its own and has not simply been swept aside by a higher scientific truth. *The Long Revolution* (1961) was planned to extend the work of *Culture and Society* in areas of 'questions in the theory of culture, historical analysis of certain cultural institutions and forms, and problems of meaning and action in our contemporary cultural situation'. Williams explains his title as follows: 'It seems to me that we are living through a long revolution, which our best descriptions only in part interpret. It is a genuine revolution, transforming men and institutions; continually deepened and extended by the actions of millions, continuously and variously opposed by explicit reaction and by the pressure of habitual forms and ideas.' This revolution is said to be hard to define due to its complexity. Williams' title rejects the Bolshevik emphasis on rapid, revolutionary social change. Cultural change is democratic because it is the mode in which the masses ('millions') can communicate their desire for social justice which it seems that Williams presumes to be spontaneous, although 'if we take the criterion that people should govern themselves [. . .] it is evident that the democratic revolution is still at a very early stage'. Williams does not, in 1961, begin to think of culture as a material process, although his desire to investigate 'institutions' points towards this. Unlike economistic Marxists, Williams insists on the centrality of the relation between culture and social change: 'The complex interaction between the democratic and social revolutions is at the centre of our most difficult social thinking.'[29]

The Long Revolution argues that attention must be shifted away from the aesthetic function of art to its communicative function, which Williams claims has generally been ignored by aesthetic theory. The advantage of this is that it seeks to displace emphasis on the private consciousness, an emphasis which Marxist thought has always considered ideological and bourgeois in character, as it over-privileges the individual and directs understanding away from the collective basis of social existence. Williams also seeks to disrupt the formalist element of emphasis on the work to an attention to the social dimension of the work. Once again, Williams certainly predicts numerous threads in recent literary theory. However, in having recourse to the term 'experience' he established a model which invites objection:

> It seems better to speak of art in terms of the organization of experience, especially in its effect on a spectator or an audience. [. . .]
>
> Communication is the process of making unique experience into common experience, and it is, above all, the claim to love [. . .]. It is of the utmost importance to realize this sense of communication as a whole social process.[30]

There must be an objection to the emphasis on experience, which privileges what subjects feel or know about the society they belong to *above* any fact, analysis or speculative claim which might be produced by the process of investigating or reflecting that society. The term 'communication' is promising inasmuch as it proposes to broaden the object and approach of literary studies, yet in projecting an unanalysed notion of communicating subjects it falls back really from the Marxist position which treats consciousness itself as a *product*, more than a *producing* entity.

In describing 'culture', Williams does not seek to collapse all artefacts and practices into a single category, but suggests a ternary system which in effect reproduces then current judgements about high and low culture, with a third category for objects not previously considered cultural at all. 'There are three general categories in the definition of culture': the 'ideal', the 'documentary' and the 'social' – the last one including 'meanings and values not only in art and learning but also in institutions and ordinary behaviour', 'meanings and values implicit in a particular way of life, a particular culture'.[31] Williams considers these categories to be objectively in conflict – Marxists would say 'contradictory' – yet to us high ('ideal') and low ('documentary') culture appear less as separate categories than the third of these – the 'social' – and it is the latter which seems most problematic in Williams' system.

In his aim to 'define the theory of culture as the study of relationships between elements in a whole way of life' and document the 'particular sense of life' at the level of 'small differences in style, speech and behaviour', Williams coins the term 'structure of feeling'.

> In one sense, this structure of feeling is the culture of a period: it is the particular living result of all the elements in the general organization. [. . . I]t is a very deep and very wide possession, in all actual communities, precisely because it is on it that communication depends. [. . .]
>
> Once the carriers of such a structure die, the nearest we can get to this vital element is in the documentary culture, from poems to buildings and dress-fashions, and it is this relation that gives significance to the definition of culture in documentary terms. [. . .] The significance of documentary culture is that, more clearly than anything else, it expresses that life to us in direct terms, when the living witnesses are silent.

In an attempt to map this set of terms on to the England of the 1840s, Williams struggles to define a 'dominant social character' of the period, since he finds also 'alternative social characters' which 'affected, in important ways, the whole life of the time. [. . .] In some respects, the structure of feeling corresponds to the dominant social character, but [. . .] the structure of feeling is not uniform throughout society.'[32]

High cultural literature keeps its centrality in this model, but second-rate literature has a valuable documentary function of its own. The

> connection between the popular structure of feeling and that used in the literature of the time is of major importance in the analysis of culture. It is here, at a level even more important than that of the institutions, that the real relations within the whole culture are made clear: relations that can easily be neglected when only the best writing survives, or when this is studied outside its social context.[33]

Beyond cultural artefacts of any kind lie the elusive social relations of changing social and political institutions which themselves embody an expression of what we might now call the collective imaginary – akin to what Walter Benjamin in his discussion of the Parisian arcades called 'wish images', 'images in the collective unconscious in which the new is permeated with the old'.[34] However, while Benjamin located these utopian images in architectural features, Williams prefers to prioritize the less imagistic domain of actual social organization as the arenas of collective utopian wish:

> In a quite different way, in new institutions, the slow creation of different images of community, different forms of relationship, by the newly-organizing workers and by middle class reformers, marks a reaching out of the mind of comparable importance. We cannot understand even the creative part of a culture without reference to activities of this kind, in industry and institutions, which are as strong and as valuable an expression of human feeling as the major art and thought.[35]

Williams later admitted that his emphasis on a general cultural process had been mistaken, but defended it as an understandable response to what he took to be the prevalent economism of that time: 'I [. . .] abstracted my area of emphasis from the whole historical process. In the effort of establishing that cultural production was a primary activity, I think that at times I gave the impression – especially with my emphasis on "experience" – that I was denying determinations altogether [. . .]. It took me a long time to find the key move to the notion of cultural production as itself material.'[36] Williams explains that he still returns to the much-criticized idea of the 'structure of feeling' 'from the actual experience of literary analysis rather than from any theoretical satisfaction with the concept itself', noting that there is a kind of residue in the reading of a work which remains even once it has been accounted for in terms of the social totality which shapes it.[37] Responding to later theory's critique of the notion of presence as ideological (Althusser) or as simple impassive deviation (Derrida), Williams qualifies, rather than retracting, his basic idea:

> I think that I quite simply confused the quality of *presence*, which distinguishes a structure of feeling from an explicit or codified doctrine, with the historical present – which is another matter altogether. What I would now wish to say is that while a structure of feeling always exists in the present tense, so to speak grammatically, I do not now think it more recoverable or less accessible in the temporal present than in the past.[38]

Yet the unnamed interviewer in this exchange rebuts this effectively: 'that one should attempt to interpret a whole social structure by the canon of actually living within it, if taken seriously, is centrally disabling [...]. There is a deep disjuncture between the literary text from which an experience can be reconstructed and the total historical process at the time. There is not a continuity at all.'[39] Indeed, Williams' attempt to defend the inarticulated notion of 'experience' gives ammunition to those of his unsympathetic critics who have mocked his discovery of conflict and trauma at every turn:[40]

> [...] the peculiar location of a structure of feeling is the endless comparison that must occur in the process of consciousness between the articulated and the lived. The lived is only another word, if you like, for experience: but we have to find another word for that level. For all that is not fully articulated, all that comes through as disturbance, tension, blockage, emotional trouble seems to me precisely a source of major changes in the relation between the signifier and the signified, whether in literary language or conventions.[41]

So even in later decades Williams maintains his opposition to the Althusserian view 'that all experience is ideology, that the subject is wholly an ideological illusion'.[42]

The Long Revolution features chapters on education, the reading public, the popular press, 'standard English', social history of English writers, social history of dramatic forms, realism and the contemporary novel, followed by a final and widely noted section on 'Britain in the 1960s'. It is certainly a key text in the formation of cultural studies and also in the expansion of English studies, as it questions the boundaries of the literary, investigates other modes of textuality, assesses the creation of literacy and construction of readerships, and attempts a social history of literary forms – modes of inquiry now taken as standard and still pursued today. Here, however, I have wished to emphasize not the trajectory of cultural studies as a hybrid discipline itself, but the exact shape of the moment in which theory is received in Britain, not from the perspective of the Leavisism against which theorists usually believed themselves to be at war, but in terms of labourism, left Leavisism, and, in the background but nevertheless essential, the adult education agenda. Williams' work shows that the moment of the arrival of theory is certainly prepared within English studies, but also that resistances to theory rooted in socialist and labour thought – in the particular experiences of the British working class and the British left – were already in place, and begin to account for elements in the process of the adaptation of theory. Although Williams can hardly be termed a feminist, it is the tradition of socialist feminism in particular which would resist the scientific and transcendent posture of Althusserian theory, and continue to insist on the politically progressive value of experience and its consolidation and communication.

Chapter 4

The Politics of Theory

The British background of the postwar transformation of English studies and the eruption of 'theory' which reached its climax in the 1970s was the political situation of the non-Labour left in the 1950s. In essence, communists and Marxists were a small and isolated body of intellectuals, and the working-class labour movement had lost its political impetus. What changed the situation of these intellectuals was the formation of a small New Left in 1956, in response to the suppression of the Hungarian uprising by the Soviet Union, and to Khrushchev's denunciation of Stalin. This was a key moment for the British left, which made possible a break with Stalinism and hence a broad reconsideration of the basis of radical socialist politics. As well as the formation of a New Left group around the journal *New Left Review*, there was the larger-scale example of CND, the Campaign for Nuclear Disarmament, as a response to the Cold War and the proliferation of nuclear weapons. The first major success of CND was the Aldermaston march of 1958. The New Left grasped several important lessons which transformed the shape and flavour of the British left. Hungary showed that it was no longer necessary or desirable to align the hope for socialism with the Soviet Union. CND showed that a form of radical politics was possible which could unite intellectuals, students and other independents, and need no longer be rooted in the assumption that the working class and its organizations were the only possible agency of social change. In this climate, and against a background of rising prosperity deemed likely to blunt the revolutionary desire of the working class, culture itself increasingly became the focus for politicized theory.

The social base of the left remained narrow in the 1960s in Britain, but the change in intellectual climate which it engendered was important.

Under the editorship of Perry Anderson from 1961, *New Left Review* set its face both against the ideas of the old Labour movement and against the ideas of Hoggart and Williams, which were deemed to be rooted in an unexamined valorization of the category of 'experience' and in the textualist mode of English studies propagated by Leavis. *New Left Review* saw its task as equipping the British left with a theory which it had hitherto lacked. It is this emphasis on theory which conditioned the intellectual climate on the left for the next two decades, and the political emphasis on theory strongly influenced the battle of literary theory against an unenlightened pre-theory which in fact shared the same ethical fervour and many of the same ideas. *New Left Review* was mainly concerned with Marxist philosophy, and therefore in part with the Marxist theory of culture. It proceeded by importing essays on Marxist political theory from other European countries, especially Germany, France and Italy, and by commissioning translations of important books under the NLR imprint. *New Left Review* was a journal of intellectuals and had no mass political constituency nor any aim to create one. Its immediate and lasting influence was to create a new construction, 'Western Marxism', which brought together the work of theorists in different national traditions who had worked independently of each other, and wove them into a body of documents and a way of thinking which went beyond the sum of its parts.

The work of Louis Althusser was of particular importance for these British left intellectuals as it appeared in a series of translations by Ben Brewster, beginning with *For Marx* (1965; translated 1969) and followed by *Reading* Capital (1965; translated 1970) and *Lenin and Philosophy* (1969; translated 1971).[1] The speed at which Althusser was translated, adopted and imitated suggests that the theoretical vacuum on the British left which Perry Anderson so often denounced was indeed a reality. Indeed, Althusser's own work had been framed to fill a comparable gap on the French left. *For Marx* collected essays which Althusser had published in Communist Party journals between 1960 and 1965. New Left commentators would frequently emphasize the difference in situation of the British and French Communist Parties. The British left was dominated by the Labour Party, whose reformist, basically Fabian approach had led to electoral successes which seemed to have pre-empted the development of a Communist Party with revolutionary goals. As a consequence, British communists were few in number, had a very limited electoral presence, and in the period following the Second World War the Party's members could regard their French counterparts with envy. The French Communist Party (PCF) experienced considerable electoral success, in part due to its role in the resistance to German occupation, polling 20–25 per cent of the national electorate in the two decades following the war and periodically earning representation at ministerial level. The PCF would later be politically compromised in the eyes of some French leftists by its adherence to the Moscow line, its ambivalence about French imperialism in Algeria and Vietnam, its opposition to the student radicals participating in the May 1968 protests, and its support of the Soviet suppression of Czechoslovakia in 1968. Along with the bureaucratic centralism with which they were bound up, these factors combined by the later 1960s to make the PCF into an object of antipathy to many left intellectuals in France. It might be thought that the comparative success of the PCF in the 1940s and 1950s could have led to a florescence of Marxist theory. However, as Althusser himself explained,[2] the emphasis on practical activity, the dependence on the doctrines codified by the Communist Party of the Soviet Union, and the lack of an adequate reading of Marx in virtually all quarters had meant that France suffered a lack of theoretical tradition on key aspects of Marxism quite as significant as that in Britain, despite and indeed because of the size and success of the PCF.

In his 1968 essay 'Components of the National Culture', Anderson predicted the development of a political student movement in Britain in the mould of movements already highly visible in other countries, such as France and the United States. The immediate objective of this movement would be 'the fight against the authoritarianism of universities and colleges' as well as 'alliance with the working class and struggle against imperialism.' Like many radical socialists and Marxists, Anderson saw the student movement as supplying an example to, and even substitution for, the relatively moribund labour movement. Anderson argues that students must struggle not only against the authoritarianism of universities but against their educational programs, demanding 'a direct attack on the reactionary and mystifying culture inculcated in universities and colleges, [. . .] which it is one of the most fundamental purposes of British higher education to instil in students,' quoting Louis Althusser's claim that 'the number one strategic point of the action of the dominant class' is 'the very *knowledge* students receive from their teachers', which is 'the true fortress of class influence in the university'.[3] According to Anderson, student revolt has not taken place in England because of the lack of a left intellectual tradition comparable to that found internationally, the key absence of which is any national tradition either of classical sociology or of Marxism. The reasons for this are said to include the lack of a radical bourgeois intellectual tradition in the nineteenth century, and the domination of most areas of British intellectual life by a 'White emigration' of European émigré counter-revolutionary thinkers in the interwar period. Anderson surveys a number of intellectual fields – philosophy, economics, political theory and others – in which British intellectual life has either developed in an anti-theoretical fashion or (as in the case of Keynesian economics) arrived at an impasse. Two strands which he discusses are of especial importance for us here.

This narrative has so far made little mention of psychoanalysis because its influence in literary theory and indeed in British thought in general was very limited until the period of high theory. This is paradoxical not least because Freud's own work made substantial reference to literature – the Oedipus complex takes its form and name from a literary character, and several of his essays have a literary topic, notably 'The Uncanny' (1919), which discusses mainly literary effects. As Anderson notes, the effect of psychoanalysis on British culture is 'virtually nil', despite the existence of an important British school of psychoanalysis with the work of Melanie Klein as its most outstanding achievement, and also despite the existence of the outstanding Hogarth Press edition of Freud which had set a standard worldwide. Although outstanding, this edition was expensive, and the desire of British Freudians to avoid the vulgarization of psychoanalysis had combined with the generally unreceptive intellectual conditions to confine Freud's work to a professional enclave. Freud's work has massive implications for sociology, anthropology, philosophy and aesthetics which insular British thought has been denied. Anderson cites Althusser, once again, on the near-Copernican significance of Freud's discovery of the unconscious:

> It was not in vain that Freud sometimes compared the critical impact of his discoveries with the upheaval of the Copernican revolution. Since Copernicus, we know that the earth is not the centre of the universe. Since Marx, we know that the human subject, the economic, political or philosophical ego is not the centre of history – we even know, against the Enlightenment and against Hegel, that history has no centre, but possesses a structure without a centre . . . Freud has shown us in his turn that the real subject, the individual in his singular essence, does not have the form of an I centred on the 'ego', 'consciousness' or 'existence' – that the human subject is decentred, constituted by a subject which itself has no centre.[4]

Althusser's version of Freud is mediated by Lacan and represents what for a time became a central enabling claim of theory. What was important in Freud was not his development of therapeutic modes to bring about the adaptation (i.e. social normalization) of individual subjects, but his 'discovery' or construction of the notion of the unconscious. Freud's thought is here mediated by the linguistic structuralism of Ferdinand de Saussure, which saw language in terms of a system of differences rather than in terms of individual utterances. The convergence of linguistics and psychoanalysis had received extensive speculative treatment in the work of Jacques Lacan. The interest of 'theory', and equally of literary theory, did not stem from a desire either to perfect the treatment of any variety of mental illness or to refine the discipline of linguistics. The Freudian idea of the unconscious and the Lacanian suggestion that the unconscious was like a language – that is, a structure of signs without an articulating intention or ego at its centre – allowed for a number of developments. In general, it appeared to give a psychological basis to the notion of ideology. It did this by linking desire to the formation of ideology, and allowing for the speculative examination of the investment of desire in ideological formations. Perhaps the main shift in Althusserian Marxism was from the Marxist emphasis on ideology as the *conscious* framework of ideas to an emphasis on the *unconscious* ideological structures of society which 'interpellated' the subject.[5] In relation to literary theory, it suggested that texts could be read in terms other than those suggested by their authors, other than those suggested by a reconstruction of authorial intention, and other even than any mapping of the conscious knowledge of the work's own period. Literary analysis could be shifted away not only from author-centred interpretation, but away from what the text actually appeared to say or imply to what it did *not* say.[6] The unconscious could be plotted not in terms of the author or any fictional character, nor even as the collective unconscious of a society or a race, but as a complex and always (by definition) speculatively reconstructed (because unknown) nexus of drives grasped as the absent motivations of the structures in which they could be detected, but having no particular locus in any individual or collective outside the text.

One political advantage of this shift was that it facilitated the assault on Marxism's ideological *bête noire*, the bourgeois self. Bourgeois society was held to legitimate itself by a fetishistic celebration of the power of individual action. In this way, entrepreneurs or other powerful individuals could be celebrated as the agents making history. On the one hand, this served to mask the real narrative of history, which Marxism holds to be the product of shifts in class power, and deny the truth that the proletariat would be the collective agent or 'subject' of coming historical change, not any individual agent. On the other hand, 'bourgeois individualism' made a myth of the wealth-creating power of the individual capitalist as a way of justifying disparities of wealth and denying the process of extraction of 'surplus value' (or profit) on which capital accumulation was based. Therefore any undermining of the ideology of the individual was seen as demystifying key legitimating bourgeois myths concerning the role of the individual in the creation of history and in the creation of wealth. In terms of cultural analysis, cultural artefacts of all kinds could be construed as texts and read in terms of the unconscious motivations of their structures. The idea of the unconscious in these contexts would be highly generalized. In Freud's clinical theory it is always a matter of the suppression of traumatic experiences which shape individual development. In some of his later works, especially *Civilization and its Discontents* (1930) and *Moses and Monotheism* (1934–8), Freud suggested models for transition from the individual case of the analysand to the role of the psyche in broad social and historical processes. In fact, literary theory made free use of Freud's notion of the unconscious in its habit of reading against the grain, which often involved the identification of something *not* included in a text which could be described as in some way strategically *repressed* by the text.[7] In its broadest form, in the convergence of Marxism and psychoanalysis, the fact that any cultural text embodies only a partial and particular presentation of the social totality – the totality which Marxist science makes it its job to present and which bourgeois ideology is held to suppress – makes it possible to construe a text in terms of the repressed unconscious of that which it chooses not to mention, but which always erupts into it.

Anderson's article claims that the revolution promised by Freudian theory has been denied to British thought; as the link to Althusser makes clear, it is the potential of psychoanalysis to contribute to a thinking of social totality which is unfulfilled in British thought that in nearly every branch considers its object empirically, locally and sceptically. The principal exception to this refusal of totality has been, according to Anderson, literary studies. Of course, literature and literary studies were in any case at that time accorded a high role in culture. Volume 3 of Cox and Dyson's *The Twentieth Century Mind: History, Ideas and Literature in Britain, 1945–1965* (1972) is admittedly the product of the editors of a literary journal, but is remarkable for granting more pages to 'The Novel' than to the entirety of political, diplomatic, economic and social history, and as many pages to literary criticism as to physics. The story of literary criticism told in this volume (by its editors) carries virtually no reference whatsoever to the currents named by Anderson. Literary criticism is the product of a smooth succession, according to these conservative authors, who give a quite different account of the period we are now examining.

Mention is made of Marxist literary theorists, Georg Lukács and Lucien Goldmann, and due space is made for Hoggart and Williams, but to Cox and Dyson the mainstream of criticism is borne by their own journal (*Critical Quarterly*), Frank Kermode, W. H. Auden, Lionel Trilling and the 'irritating' Northrop Frye.[8] Anderson has quite as much respect for the trajectory of English studies as Cox and Dyson, but senses in literary criticism a potential for intellectual responsibility to the future of society that Cox and Dyson do not even hint at in their account. In Anderson's words: 'Suppressed and denied in every other sector of thought, the second, displaced home of the totality became literary criticism.' With Leavis,

> English literary criticism conceived the ambition to become the vaulting centre of 'humane studies and of the university'. English was 'the chief of the humanities'. This claim was unique to England: no other country has ever produced a critical discipline with these pretentions. They should be seen, not as an expression of megalomania on the part of Leavis, but as a symptom of the objective vacuum at the centre of the culture. Driven out of its expected habitat, the notion of the totality found refuge in the least expected of studies.[9]

Despite his radicalism and importance, Leavis was unable to theorize his discipline, but Anderson concludes that it was 'no surprise' that the work of Raymond Williams should have emerged from the context of English studies.

The combination of the ethical concerns of Leavisism and its corresponding but untheorized orientation towards the total social process made the left strand of English studies into a very receptive and constructive element of the *New Left Review* project, although unpleasant arguments over theory were a common feature of many Departments of English during the 1970s, with divisions based mainly on politics and also on age. The tone of Anderson's rejection of British empiricism was widely echoed. The lack of a developed theory in Leavis's own work made it easy for theorists to denounce the defenders of something which suddenly seemed like tradition. The influx of theoretical models from other disciplines (linguistics, anthropology, psychoanalysis, philosophy) proved a heady addition to a subject which already had grand ideas of its own scope. However, I have chosen to shape this narrative from the perspective of the *New Left Review* in order to emphasize the *political* dimension of the new theory and stress the role of left intellectuals (within and without English) and the over-riding concern of the left at this time to find a basis for political praxis.

Theory did not provide such a basis. In his review of the trajectory of European Marxism in *Considerations on Western Marxism* (1976), Perry Anderson noted that theory had changed the essence of Marxist thought, creating 'a basic shift in the whole centre of gravity of European Marxism toward *philosophy*' in a discourse dominated by professional philosophers with University positions.[10] Anderson notes that this movement into philosophy was shaped by external political events (the rise of Nazism) but enabled by the belated discovery (in the 1930s and after) of Marx's early philosophical writings. It was a paradox of history that the movement into philosophy reversed Marx's own movement out of philosophy and into politics. A key effect of this professionalization had been a tendency to produce works *on* rather than *in* Marxism, often in a specialized vocabulary that in no way addressed a working-class audience. Marxist discussion was increasingly referred both to bourgeois thought of one kind or another, or to the pre-Marxist philosophy which was held to explain or supply the philosophy which Marx himself never mapped out. Moreover, Western Marxism had retreated from the internationalism of political Marxism into isolated national fractions. By contrast, Anderson praised the economic and political writings of Trotsky, and concluded that in the wake of the events of 1968 in France and elsewhere, Western Marxism was unlikely to supply a viable fusion of theory and practice: 'After the prolonged, winding detour of Western Marxism, the questions left unanswered by Lenin's generation, and made impossible to answer by the rupture of theory and practice in Stalin's epoch, continue to await replies. They do not lie within the jurisdiction of philosophy.'[11] It should be added that in the 1960s and 1970s *New Left Review* represented a relatively isolated sect of the radical left, the majority of whom in these decades turned to Trotsky as an alternative to Stalin, blamed Stalin's policy of 'socialism in one country' for betraying the project of global revolution, and preferred the praxis of reviving Leninist revolutionary cadres to academic practice.[12]

Another key influence on literary theory was the Centre for Contemporary Cultural Studies inaugurated in 1963 at the University of Birmingham under the directorship of Richard Hoggart. Partly originating in the English Department, the creation of the CCCS represented the moment in which literary studies attempted to step out of its self-imposed boundaries and place its hitherto privileged texts among a range of other cultural objects. Literary theory always borders on cultural theory, and the eclectic method of both literary and cultural theory tends to force a questioning not only about the privileging of certain literary texts among others, but about the privileging of literary texts of any kind among all other cultural objects, creating an intellectual and political pressure on literary studies to abolish itself. Cultural studies was a mixed discipline, a kind of sociology with a strong streak of Leavisite literary criticism. In its early period, the Centre focused on the culture of the working class along lines established by Hoggart and Williams. Later, and under the leadership of Stuart Hall, the focus shifted to the ideological function of the media. A key challenge of cultural studies to the discipline of English was its refusal to accept a generalized model of mass culture and mass audience from which the consumption of privileged texts was set apart. The example which cultural studies offered to English was the theoretical range of its method, which by the 1970s had embraced the semiology of Roland Barthes and Umberto Eco, the Marxism of Louis Althusser and Antonio Gramsci, the linguistically influenced psychoanalysis of Jacques Lacan, and the theories of discourse and power found in the work of Michel Foucault.

*

At the time of Anderson's 'Components' essay, feminism had only just begun to come into view as a renewed cultural force, in what is sometimes referred to as the 'second wave' of feminism. While Marxist theory had a development in Britain simply unmatched in the United States, feminism in Britain was muted by its origin in socialism, while American feminism was emboldened and enabled by its origin in the civil rights movement. The first wave of American feminism came in the nineteenth and early twentieth centuries. The early 'woman's movement' had debated the 'woman issue' and its leaders became very well-known figures. One of its more radical accomplishments had been the publication of *The Woman's Bible* (1895), edited by a committee of women including Elizabeth Cady Stanton, three of whom were ordained ministers. *The Woman's Bible* was published in response to opponents of the woman's movement who cited the Bible as an authority for women's subordination. In reply, *The Woman's Bible* presented a systematic analysis and critique of the treatment of women's role in the Bible. It was received with outrage even by most members of the Suffrage Association at that time, who thought it sacrilegious, but from our point of view it looks like an early example of feminist criticism, and its combination of scholarship and activism is an early example for later feminist programs.

The major gap in feminist history comes between 1920 and 1960. In the United States, public interest in women's rights effectively disappeared in this period.[13] The same is true in Britain, where women's aspirations, to the extent they were articulated at all, tended to be subsumed under socialism. The reasons for this decline in interest are not clear, but certainly include the war and recession. In the United States, women's rights began to surface again in the 1960s with the creation of President Kennedy's Commission on the Status of Women (1961), which submitted its report *American Women* in 1963. The Equal Pay Act (1963) and the Equal Rights Act (1964) were landmarks for the rights of women (among others). The background of the women's liberation movement was the civil rights movement. Nineteen-sixty had seen the formation of the Student Non-Violent Coordinating Committee (SNCC) by black students in Southern colleges. The SNCC was the backbone of a multiracial movement until it banned white members in 1966. Some of the white women in the SNCC who had already begun to discuss women's politics migrated to the National Conference for a New Politics called in 1967. It was there that Jo Freeman and Shulamith Firestone attempted to present a resolution calling for civil rights for women. The conference refused to hear them, but agreed to hear a resolution on Native American rights. That refusal was in effect a landmark in the formation of women's liberation: angered that women were not recognized as an oppressed group while Native Americans were, Freeman and Firestone went on to found the first women's groups in Chicago and New York.[14] These organizations soon recruited a sizeable cadre, made up in particular from women who had been involved in civil rights, and also from those in the peace movement and left political organizations. These groups organized initially around the issue of 'women's oppression', somewhat vaguely conceived, and achieved a notable emergence into the public sphere when they disrupted the Miss America contest in 1968 with a demonstration.

The British background did not include a civil rights movement, but did include a background of socialism. British women's liberation emerged from socialism and continued to have a large socialist-feminist and Marxist-feminist component. Juliet Mitchell's 'Women: The Longest Revolution' was published in *New Left Review* in 1966 and represented a turning point in the discussion of women's issues.[15] Mitchell argues that the goal of women's emancipation was inadequate, and offered an examination of women's oppression in the context of socialist history. Just as Perry Anderson had criticized the lack of 'theory' in British socialism, Mitchell argues that economistic socialist theory does not give a full account of women's oppression. Attention must be broadened to include all of the formations which conditioned women: productive, reproductive, sexual and social. Only the transformation of all of these, and not just the fight for women's rights, would bring about anything like a liberation of women. Mitchell's *Woman's Estate* (1971) continued to denounce the inadequacy of the socialist containment of feminist politics, although it did not renounce this frame:

> Feminism, then, is the terrain on which a socialist analysis works. It is by definition available to all women, whatever their class [. . .]: *it is about being a woman.* [. . .] The trouble is that 'socialists' try to prevent feminists from having their 'feminist consciousness' by asking them to subscribe to a working class 'ideology' – which can no more exist than feminist ideology. [. . .] The oppressed consciousness of all groups contributes to the nature of this socialist ideology – if any oppressed awareness is missing from its formation that is its loss.[16]

British feminism is linked to socialism, and its theoretical concerns are broadened in line with the expansion of Marxist theory in the pages of *New Left Review*. The tension between socialism and feminism which Mitchell signposts here, although usually in Britain internal to both, could not very easily be dissolved.

As well as this theoretical impetus, early feminist publications had a key concern with women's history. Sheila Rowbotham's *Hidden from History* (1973) set itself the task of uncovering women's history, with particular reference to trades unionism and socialism, as part of the political project of developing a socialist feminism framed with the object of speaking to 'working class women' and 'transforming women's liberation according to their needs',[17] Socialist feminists did not make much of the earlier feminist history of suffragism, which they considered liberal or bourgeois, so their history was quite selective.[18] The Women's Liberation Conference held at Ruskin College, Oxford, in 1970 was dominated by socialist feminists. Its demands included equality of pay and educational opportunity, twenty-four-hour childcare, free contraception and abortion on demand.[19] These are all relatively socialist issues. Subsequent conferences added other demands: financial and legal independence, the end to discrimination against lesbians and freedom from sexual coercion. These demands represent the fact that non-socialist forms of feminism had arisen to confront the socialist feminist norm. The final Women's Liberation Conference in 1978 was the occasion of heated arguments between socialist and radical feminists. Radical feminism had its roots in the United States, especially in the argument of Shulamith Firestone in *The Dialectic of Sex* (1971) that women's oppression is based on biological difference and can only be ended by a feminist revolution against men. This type of radical feminist argument, which situates women's oppression in pre-history, does not allow for the notion of women's liberation as part of socialism. Its emphases too were different, based on 'consciousness raising' and the validation of women's experiences. Other forms of feminism offered dramatic challenges to the socialist feminist model; black and lesbian feminists formulated theories of 'double oppression' along axes that made white and heterosexual women their oppressors.

The difference in background between the United States and Britain accounts for contrasts of emphasis in feminist literary theory and criticism. Feminist literary theory has sometimes taken the form of an encounter with this or that male theorist. As well as Marx and Engels, Freud, Lacan, Foucault, Bakhtin, Derrida, Deleuze, Habermas are all set to work in feminism. This means that feminist theory is often not really entirely separable from other strands in literary theory, nor are those strands separable from feminism. Even the label 'feminist' is open to question, since it can denote quite different political–theoretical positions, and since not all female scholars or students might think of themselves as feminist, while many men are in one way or another feminists. Feminist literary theory has had more of a life of its own in the United States, where forms of feminism including 'radical' feminism had emphasized the difference of woman more than in Britain. The co-involvement of feminist literary theory and literary-critical practice with other forms of theory and practice should not obscure the massive importance of literary studies for feminism and vice versa. The creation of Departments of Women's Studies which have combined literary and other studies has been only a small part of this relationship. The principal contribution of feminist theory has certainly been in the area of research on women writers, many of whom were neglected. Why they were neglected is a moot point; the claim that writers who turn out to be minor have been rescued from patriarchal literary history is resisted by Germaine Greer in *Slip-Shod Sibyls: Recognition, Rejection and the Woman Poet* (1995), even though Greer had been a founding figure of British feminism. Such doubts cannot erase the centrality of the task of reappraising women's literature, and among feminist publication ventures the Virago Press stands out. Founded in 1973, Virago made available numerous 'lost' works by women authors to a wide readership. Some of these titles proved to be of more interest to specialist researchers than to a general readership, but the point of the venture was a reclamation of history, and vital projects in the triumphant first decade of Virago included for example the republication of Dorothy Richardson's modernist novel series *Pilgrimage* (1915–38), and work by May Sinclair, Winifred Holtby, Sylvia Townsend Warner and many others.

Feminist criticism concentrated on two areas: challenges to the canon which in some cases involved the attempt to identify an entirely female alternative canon; and analysis of the representation of women in literature. Only later did feminism yield gender studies, which concentrated on sexual difference rather than sexual identity, and gay, queer and (occasionally) lesbian studies, which formalized the separation of sexual desire from the comparatively straightforward agenda of feminism. Examples of feminist literary-critical practice from the 1970s are shaped more by an interest in canonical literature than by any advanced theory of reading. Elaine Showalter's *A Literature of their Own* (1977) suggested that the tradition of female writers needed investigating not simply as part of the parade of canonical literature but as documents of women's experience. She credits British women's liberation with the insight that 'a special female self awareness emerges through literature in every period', and argues that a more reliable critical vocabulary must be developed, in an interdisciplinary fashion, to create a systematic history of women's literature as seen through women's eyes.[20] Unlike many US commentators who remain mute about their decision to make English culture the arena of their political critique of literature, Showalter is sensitive enough to attract attention to this constitutive difference in her title ('*their* own') and discusses the comparative states of British and American feminism in her conclusion, arguing that the socialist tradition of British feminism has prevented the emergence of charismatic leaders (as in the suffragist tradition) and that British women writers have not yet responded to feminism as have many American writers (such as Rich, Olsen, Sontag and Piercy). Working-class women have not been represented in literature, she notes. Another key text of American feminist literary criticism is Sandra Gilbert and Susan Gubar's *The Madwoman in the Attic: The Woman Writer and the Nineteenth-Century Literary Imagination* (1979), which discusses mainly British writers alongside some Americans, reserving the bulk of its pages for such staples as Austen, the Brontës and George Eliot. Vital as this gesture was in its time, the silent appropriation of English literature for the discussion of a universal 'female literary tradition' simply reproduces the manner in which English literature had already been adopted as an American tradition and in retrospect appears as much an exercise in the expropriation of cultural capital as it does an exercise in women's liberation; the narrowness of the investigation is somehow alarming. These were comparatively early ventures, however. Looking back on the 1970s, Showalter noted in 'Feminism in the Wilderness' (1981) that feminist literary criticism had started without a theoretical basis and had only recently begun to acquire one. A gap has opened up between feminist critics who wished to embrace 'theory' – Marxism, structuralism, post-structuralism – and those, including Showalter, who preferred to resist the premature codification of feminist literary studies. As Showalter notes, 'While scientific criticism struggled to purge itself of the subjective, feminist criticism reasserted the authority of experience.' Showalter expresses strong doubts about the reliance of feminist criticism on male critical theory: 'the feminist obsession with correcting, modifying, supplementing, revising, humanizing, or even attacking male critical theory keeps us dependent on it and retards our progress in solving our own theoretical problems.' The process is one-sided, the men remain ignorant of feminism, and the feminists end up paying homage to the 'white fathers', making 'Lacan the ladies, man of [the journal] *Diacritics*' and forcing 'Pierre Macherey into those dark alleys of the psyche where Engels feared to tread'. To escape this impasse, Showalter proposes the recognition of 'gynocritics' which will be the theory of female creativity (as oppose to feminist ideology critique). As well as a number of American feminist critics writing on women's literature, French feminism in the form of Kristeva, Luce Irigaray and Hélène Cixous has lent gynocritics momentum. Cixous' 'The Laugh of the Medusa' (1975) had been a suggestive manifesto for a writing based in the woman's body. Linguistics and psychoanalysis have also suggested ways of approaching the feminine. Showalter argues that a gynocritics must concentrate on the analysis of women's culture as a way to avoid problems associated with the other approaches.[21] In effect, Showalter lost the struggle for a gynocritics. Theory had prepared the way to talk about sexual difference, not identity. Barbara Johnson's sophisticated distillation of the complexity of difference in *The Critical Difference* (1980) had already shown another way forward. In literary theory at least, feminism would in general combine forces with 'male' high theory. The specific outcome of that would eventually be 'gender studies', a more subtly inflected version of feminist theory perhaps, but one that also marks a dropping away from some of the earlier, more directly conceived feminist ideals. The more direct outcomes are twofold: first, the thoroughgoing impact of feminist concerns in all branches of 'high theory'; second, and perhaps more in line with the original intentions of women's liberation, a continuing and thoroughgoing appraisal of women's writing, authorship and audience by dedicated specialists who are bringing some of the most recalcitrant episodes of literary history to a broader audience.

*

Politics, whether Marxist or feminist, looked to theory. The adoption of theory was, in the heyday of the 1970s, eclectic. Perry Anderson's account of the political–intellectual state of Britain at this time is one to which many left intellectuals would have assented, and the combination of approximate but bold argumentation and political zeal which characterized this period of theory needs to be grasped in order to explain the sometimes heady speculativeness of the discourse as well as the animus with which 'traditional' scholars and 'opponents of theory' who belonged to different philosophical traditions were treated – and indeed how these traditionalists, where dominant, sought opportunities to discredit the new discourse of theory, a process brought to broader public attention in two famous affairs at Cambridge, one involving Colin McCabe, the other Jacques Derrida. In the first of these, in 1981, a media battle was waged by supporters of theorist Colin McCabe around the refusal of the university to grant him a tenured lectureship in English. Whatever the real merits of the case, this was presented at the time as a battle between theory and tradition. In 1992, the proposal to grant Jacques Derrida an honorary doctorate was opposed by a number of Cambridge dons, whose struggle was perhaps predictably taken up by the media. Whatever the terms of the complaint against Derrida, this again became a debate about theory and tradition, in which the speculative method of Derrida was characterized by opponents as charlatanry, and journalists leapt in to denounce the circularity of what they took to be 'deconstruction'. In reality, while 1981 corresponded to the apogee of the theory wars within Schools and Departments of English, the 1992 spat probably indicated their end. That theory wars only intermittently surfaced in public consciousness in Britain signifies that their effects were mostly confined to the academy. This may have been due not simply to the arcane nature of theory, but to the continued dissociation between theory in general and the political practice which it was intended to inform.

If the general political bent of the background of theory in general was the attempt to form a Marxist theory adequate to present circumstances, the general movement of literary theory can be characterized in terms of the movement from 'work to text', in a phrase popularized by Roland Barthes. It was certainly structural linguistics which gave impetus and validity to this change of stress, but the emphasis on textuality outlasted any attempt directly to adopt the findings of structural linguistics, and even the adoption of any form of structuralism, creating a set of underlying assumptions which have shaped the essence of literary studies to this day. Structuralism in Anglo-American literary studies was not something that developed slowly, became widely adopted, then passed out of fashion, as might be expected. Rather, structuralism arrived relatively suddenly from outside, was not widely adopted as a practice, but was widely referred to as an example, and became a frequent point of reference both for scholarly practice and for theoretical speculation. The impression in Britain was that structuralism arrived suddenly, with the appearance of Jonathan Culler's *Structuralist Poetics: Structuralism, Linguistics and the Study of Literature*, in 1975. In *After the New Criticism* (1980), Frank Lentricchia confirms that in the United States there was a similar impression. Culler's was not the first study of structuralism, nor was this the first discussion of structuralism in the United States. Lévi-Strauss's structural anthropology had made an impact through the 1960s, and the 1966 conference on structuralism at Johns Hopkins had been addressed by Jacques Derrida among others.[22] Yet as Lentricchia notes, Culler's book, and the recognition given it by the award of a the prestigious Lowell prize by the Modern Language Association of America, was a key moment of incursion by the apparently dispassionate discipline of structuralism into the humanist-dominated literary-critical establishment. Lentricchia claims that Culler's centrality at this time in the United States was due to the manner in which he mediated structuralism for a generally conservative audience hostile to French intellectual tradition. 'Culler's book has practically single-handedly mediated (and constituted) our understanding of structuralism, not because his work is more acute than, say, [Fredric] Jameson's, but because his mediation rests on intellectual principles easily recognizable and very dear to the traditionalist.' This has had the effect of 'softening the impact of the new French thought'.[23] Lentricchia's remarks testify to a substantial difference in the academic political climate between the United States and Britain. The appeal of structuralism in the context of the British academic left had already been prepared by the general intellectual climate on the left, especially by the influence of Althusser as mediated by the New Left. By contrast, Fredric Jameson appeared a relatively isolated figure, the tenor of his prose appearing to testify to a lack of generally acknowledged context in the United States. Jameson's *Marxism and Form: Twentieth Century Dialectical Theories of Literature* (1971) had dealt with the new tradition of Hegelian Marxism alongside Sartre. The inclusion of Sartre now seems incongruous, the validity of talking about the Frankfurt School entirely obvious, yet writing in 1971 Jameson is conscious of the resistance from the 'national tradition' of the United States:

> that mixture of political liberalism, empiricism, and logical positivism which we know as Anglo-American philosophy and which is hostile at all points

to the type of thinking outlined here [. . .]. The bankruptcy of the liberal
tradition is as plain on the philosophical level as it is on the political; which
does not mean that it has lost its prestige or ideological potency. [. . .] It is
therefore necessary for those of us in the sphere of influence of the Anglo-
American tradition to learn to think dialectically, to acquire the rudiments
of a dialectical culture and the essential critical weapon which it provides.[24]

It is notable that Jameson sought to introduce formalism via an argument
concerning *Marxism* and form. Of the figures he sought to introduce
to an American public he construed as resistant to them, only one –
Georg Lukács – would be thought of principally as a literary theorist; the
others (Adorno, Benjamin, Marcuse and Bloch) are theorists of culture
who paid varying degrees of attention to literature in the context of
their broader projects. Jameson's emphasis in this volume was on dialectical thought: form was saved for the subsequent volume, *The Prison-
House of Language: A Critical Account of Structuralism and Russian
Formalism* (1972), which dealt with structural linguistics (especially
Saussure and Jakobson), Russian formalism (mostly Shklovsky), and French
structuralism (with emphasis on Lévi-Strauss, Barthes, Greimas and
Derrida). This book is in reality not so much a presentation of structuralism as a critique of it. Structuralism is held to have returned to 'pre-
Marxist and indeed pre-Hegelian conceptual problems with which we no
longer have to concern ourselves'. We must not ignore structuralism, but
commit to 'working our way completely through it so as to emerge, on
the other side, into some wholly different and theoretically more satisfying
philosophical perspective'. On the one hand, linguistics and its formalist and structuralist offshoots offer an alternative to the organic model
which has dominated literary–aesthetic thinking from the Romantics to
the New Critics. As is commonly remarked, the attempt to construe a
literary artefact as if it were like an organism consisting of different parts
linked together to form a functional whole involves an exaggerated or
even entirely incorrect emphasis on the notion of a work as an autonomous entity. In Jameson's account, linguistics, which proposes language
as a model as opposed to the 'work', is the strongest existent counter
to the problems and ideological blindness of the organic model. Yet, as
Jameson notes at the outset, the enabling notion of 'structure' is already
beset with problems. Jameson expresses the matter politely:

the very point of departure for Structuralism – the primacy of the linguistic
model – [. . .] is no less arbitrary for being unique, and the systems of
thought which emerge from it will not themselves be exempt from some

eventual, problematical, and painful reexamination of their own enabling premise.

Jameson goes further, qualifying the role of linguistics in a manner which diminishes its importance from the outset:

> To be sure, when today we say that everything is ultimately historical, or economic, or sexual, or indeed *linguistic*, we mean thereby not so much that phenomena are made up, in their very bone and blood cells, by such raw material, but rather that they are susceptible to analysis by those respective methods.

One further qualification is devastating:

> We find ourselves ultimately before the conclusion that the attempt to see the literary work as a linguistic system is in reality the application of a *metaphor*.

As justification for attention to linguistics, Jameson cites the loss of nature in modernity and the consequent relative autonomy of the representational world which 'the social life of the so-called advanced countries' inhabits, detecting a 'consonance' between 'linguistics as a method and that systematized and disembodied nightmare which is our culture today'.[25]

Jameson's reservations might have had more resonance in the context of Britain than America in terms of the differing political climate *vis-à-vis* Marxism. Yet what is clear from these remarks in Jameson's preface to his short study is that, while it is important to know about structuralism, it is imperative to disavow it and dialectically go beyond it while seeing what its implications are for the mode of thinking – Jameson calls it 'philosophical' – which we have *already* adopted. In other words, Jameson is recommending structuralism to Marxists, or to political critics, not as a science of the text which will provide the ultimate (or final) ground of interpretation, but as a supplement to the kind of dialectical thinking – that is, the attempt to think in terms of the total social process – recommended in his earlier study. Jameson's presentation of structuralism begins with the acknowledgement that starting with language as the ground of analysis is arbitrary. It can be inferred from this that while, on the one hand, structuralism is to be introduced as an antidote to the romantic and New Critical view of the artwork as an organism, on the other hand the view that language can be isolated, and that this isolation can be achieved by treating it as a structure, is quite as flawed in its formalist presumption. Structuralism offers the discipline of structure, New Criticism the organic softness of organism, and we might speculate that this terminological opposition alone has had a certain force of rhetorical persuasion. Yet, as Jameson hints, the two models are not so far apart. Structure, certainly, has its way prepared for it in the discourse of Marxism which famously, in its English-language translated form, refers to entities of social organization (parliament, police) as the superstructure erected on the economic base, and Marxism has as its goal the scientific treatment of society, the exposure of the interrelated totality of social relations, something different from the fragment of social reality which is available within the experience of the individual. Yet in each case the terms 'organism' and 'structure' do not refer to any actual organism or structure. They are terms under which analysis can project a unified object. This unified object is made up of disparate parts. The unity of the object is not wholly the arbitrary projection of the analytical method – it is easy to see why a certain group of entities might be thought of as language and that a half-eaten pork pie would not at a commonsense level belong to this group, just as it is easy to see that a poem which consists of a sequence of words apparently starting at one point and ending at another is also a kind of set. Analysis temporarily supposes that these commonsense unities can be regarded as unities in order to advance analysis, at the same time bracketing (but not forgetting) the question of how far it is possible to regard these apparently unitary ensembles as entities. The terms under which these unities are mapped – organism or structure – do not suggest a singularity; rather, they suggest the manner in which the apparent belonging together of disparate parts can be mapped. This is more complicated than it sounds, as the notion of organism or structure becomes an analogy for the relationship of parts in the supposed totality.

Although the struggle of structuralism against New Criticism has the appearance of a war of opposites, they have in common a problematic central analogy. The notion of organism is invoked by Romantic aesthetics to account for the relationship between differing parts of an artwork. In the way that different body parts – hands, head, heart – fulfil various functions aimed at the overall enabling of the life of the individual organism, so the parts of an artwork, although maybe not like each other, work towards an end which is an expression of the totality to which they belong, not that of any individual part. The articulated ensemble of parts leans towards an end which lies in the relationship of the parts, not in any of the constituent elements. The notion of structure is designed to get away from the idea of individual expression. Any actual or possible individual expression is made possible by its belonging to a system. This system is projected as a totality of relationships of language parts which can be assumed to exist in any given instant of time – they exist synchronically in an imagined given moment, not diachronically, that is, temporally, across a period of time. In fact, the notion of structure is more speculative than the notion of an artwork. It posits a unity where none can be produced. However, its account of the manner in which disparate elements achieve an articulation differs entirely from that of New Critical formalism. Meaning resides not in the articulating totality of the literary work (which here becomes an example of an individual enunciation) but in the difference of each element in the system from any other. Any coding system then relies on a system of differences within an implied totality to achieve its meaning or meaning effect. The notion of structure is an essentially spatial analogy for a process which is certainly temporal, implying a system of purposefully linked elements which together form a functional whole, elements which only have any significance in the totality to which they belong. 'Organism' and 'structure' are in many ways similar, although the former implies some kind of end or intention, while the latter implies only a kind of static, self-supporting body.

The logic of Jameson's position, which I have extrapolated here, surely reflects the assumptions of many who took up the banner of structuralism from political motives, not least the assumption that if the totality of social relationships was, following Marx, the basis on which reality was to be thought through, then language, however potent or significant it might seem, could not be. Yet Jameson's formulation, which lines up linguistics alongside historicism, Marxism and feminism ('when today we say that everything is ultimately historical, or economic, or sexual, or indeed *linguistic*'), expresses in its own moment a lack of confidence in the grand narrative of Marxism, in seeming to refuse it primacy, as if it were no more than one method among others ('phenomena [. . .] are susceptible to analysis by those respective methods').

While Jameson presented structuralism as necessary if problematic for the left, Culler's *Structuralist Poetics* suggested that the full complexity of linguistics could be integrated with existing literary-critical practice without massive strain. Culler certainly performed a great service in providing one of the texts by which 'theory' was able to kick-start itself. His discussion of linguistics covered several key figures – Ferdinand de Saussure, Roman Jakobson, A. J. Greimas, Claude Lévi-Strauss and Roland Barthes – as well as sketching in the work of other linguists influential on structuralism, such as Émile Benveniste. The process of making structuralism safe involves converting it into a reflection of existing critical assumptions by translating its terms into safer-looking equivalents. This is apparent in Culler's treatment of the fundamental distinction in Saussure's work between *langue* and *parole*. For the purpose of analysing language, Saussure says that linguists must pay attention to language and not to individual utterance. *Langue* is the name given to language itself as the structure in which actual utterances achieve significance; *parole* is the term used for individual speech acts. Linguistic analysis will make progress not by dissecting individual utterances but by paying attention to the field of possible utterances which makes possible the individual utterance. Meaning is produced through a system of differentiations. Each sign achieves the attribute or effect of meaning through its difference from all other signs. In order to make this notion of difference hold good it is necessary to insist that the structure, the *langue*, is speculatively projected as synchronic, that is, existing in a moment of time, otherwise it would be necessary to account for the difference between a given sign and *all* signs past, present and even future.

Saussure shifted attention to *langue* as the proper object of linguistics in order to shift the object of language studies to the processes of language, as spoken and written, that were not described by earlier historical approaches, which had tended to be focused on ancient (written) languages ('it is easy, often even amusing, to follow a series of changes', notes Saussure, imputing an element of unscientific amateurism to philological linguistics, in contrast to the 'linguistics that penetrates values and coexisting relations' which 'presents much greater difficulties'[26]). Saussure intended to found a science; the political and metaphysical implications of his work have largely been projected by others. Nevertheless, when Culler claims that the terms *langue* and *parole* are almost commutative with the terms *competence* and *performance* (found in Noam Chomsky's work), he not only adjusts Saussure to a more empiricist context, but also effects a very definite shift in the potential cultural implications of Saussure's model. In essence, Saussure's *langue* exists entirely independently of any individual, and regardless of individual competence.

> But what is language [*langue*]? It is not to be confused with human speech [*langage*], of which it is only a definite part, though certainly an essential one. It is both a social product of the faculty of speech and a collection of necessary conventions that have been adopted by a social body to permit individuals to exercise that faculty. [. . .]
>
> In separating language from speaking we are at the same time separating: (1) what is social from what is individual; and (2) what is essential from what is accessory and more or less accidental.

Language is not a function of the speaker; it is a product that is passively assimilated by the individual. [. . .] Speaking, on the contrary, is an individual act. It is wilful and intellectual.[27]

It is very plain that *langue* exists not only independently of any given speech act, but independently of the linguistic competence of any individual. In Culler's account, both competence and performance are facets of the individual, whose actual performance may fall short of his individual competence:

Someone who has learned English possesses, in his ability to understand sentences that he will never encounter, a competence that outstrips his performance. Moreover performance may deviate from competence; one may, either accidentally or as one's thought changes or deliberately for special effects, utter sentences whose ungrammaticality one would recognize if they were played back. Competence is reflected in the judgement passed on the utterance or in the fact that the rule violated is partly responsible for the effect achieved.[28]

In Saussure, *langue* is a system that exists independently of an individual; the notion of competence shifts the reference to the individual's actual linguistic ability, and to his 'judgement'. The shift from the structure of language to the competence of the individual, which might on its own seem to be an innocuous illustration, in fact proves to be at the centre of Culler's account of structuralist poetics. Just as the ability to construe language is said to depend on the competence of the individual, so too the ability to construe literary works is also said by Culler to be based on individual competence: 'To read a text as literature is not to make one's mind a *tabula rasa* and approach it without preconceptions; one must bring to it an implicit understanding of the operations of literary discourse which tells one what to look for.'[29]

The notion of *langue* also enables a hazy shift from the idea of a single, bounded, national language (such as French) to the possibility that *langue* stands for all that which might be construed as language (including non-linguistic signs and signs notionally 'belonging' to other languages). Perhaps the most remarkable feature of the projection of *langue* as the object of linguistics is its anti-historicism. Linguistics before Saussure had been a largely historical discipline, as linguists would trace grand historical shifts in linguistic features such as grammar and etymology. Saussure did not imagine the synchronic moment of a language as an instant, but as a 'language-state' of a certain 'span of time' in which 'the sum of the modifications which have supervened is minimal'. The *langue* of literature consists of literary 'conventions' which the reader must have mastered. 'Literary competence' is described by Culler as 'a set of conventions for reading literary texts'.[30] On the one hand, Culler stresses that what structuralism might offer to literary study is an account of the enabling structures which make possible both text and interpretation, but on the other he refers to this as an 'internalized competence' which is equated simply with the schooling of the reader. 'The claims of schools and universities cannot be lightly dismissed', Culler warns critics of structuralism:

> To believe that the institution of literary education is but a gigantic confidence trick would strain even a determined credulity, for it is, alas, only too clear that knowledge of a language and a certain experience of the world do not suffice to make someone a perceptive and competent reader. That achievement requires acquaintance with a range of literature and in many cases some form of guidance. The time and effort devoted by generations of students and teachers creates a strong presumption that there is something to be learned [...].[31]

Culler seeks to persuade his readers that structuralism merely confirms the competence of their existing expertise and teaching practice. He suggests that structuralism offers a completion of Northrop Frye's then fashionable work on poetics which suggests that 'the broad laws of literary experience' can be formulated, and that 'there is a totally intelligible structure of knowledge attainable about poetry, which is not poetry itself, or the experience of it, but poetics'.[32] Only a 'slight reorientation' is required to make the transition from Frye's taxonomies to the plane of structuralism. Continuing to close the gap between tradition and structuralism, Culler cites I. A. Richards' pupil William Empson as an example of the closeness of the two strands. His *Seven Types of Ambiguity* is said to show 'considerable awareness of the problems of literary competence and illustrates just how close one comes to a structuralist formulation if one begins to reflect on them'.[33] This account of one element of Culler's version of structuralism flatters the grand professoriat by persuading them that the real implication of structuralism is not to decentre texts, remove the privilege of authors and of elite interpreters, and restore the authority of extra-literary forces, but rather the contrary: this version of structuralism offers a confirmation of the validity of the most recent mode of professorial synthesis (Frye's archetypes) and the impression that the close reading skills which were essential to professorial status (of which Empson's work was held to be the most accomplished example) were in fact themselves intuitively in line with structuralism and not threatened by it at all.

We have examined Culler's text as evidence of a process of mainstreaming structuralism – a process which probably resulted in few converts – and we have emphasized the subtle conversion of ideas with radical potential into confirmation of the validity of existing practices and institutions. However, this is not to say that the deliberately left-wing version of structuralism was necessarily closer to discovering the 'real' implications of linguistics for literary and cultural studies. The basic problem – that there is no more than a possible analogy between the study of cultural objects and the study of language, rather than any simple continuity – is noted both by Jameson and Culler. It should be pointed out too that the trope or concept of 'structure' is used very infrequently by Saussure, even though it is his notion of *langue* which appears to provide the paradigm for the more generalizable use of the term 'structure'.[34] It is not strange that the form of structuralism which took hold in left-wing literary-critical circles might not have been something implied or anticipated by Saussure, but it is in some ways surprising that linguistic structuralism was adopted as a model in the first place. Marxism is basically an analysis of societal change: by contrast, Saussurean linguistics radically rejects historical approaches to language studies. Because it postulates language in a stable state as its object, the anti-historicism of structuralism seems to be dramatically at odds with the Marxist purpose of developing a historical understanding. Moreover, structuralism's emphasis on the system in which articulation takes place seems unpromising for the Marxist task of ideology critique if, as seems implicit in linguistics, what is to be analysed does not include any particular set of claims or effect, ideological or otherwise.

Chapter 5

From Work to Text

The route which structuralism took into French thought has been described in various ways. Seán Burke, who places the 'death of the author' (as an effect of the shift to *langue*) at the centre of his narrative of the impact of structuralism, notes that up to the mid-1950s the impact of structuralism on French thought had been minimal. Foucault, Derrida and Barthes were up until this time immersed in the tradition of French phenomenology, in the form of the influence of the German philosopher Edmund Husserl (1859–1938) as revisited by Jean-Paul Sartre and Maurice Merleau-Ponty.[1] The shift to a focus on *langue* at this time signals what in the French context is thought of as a 'break with the philosophy of the subject' (i.e. with French philosophy from Descartes to the present), a project which is not really symmetrical with any objectives in the Anglo-American context, where the language philosophy of Frege, Bertrand Russell and Wittgenstein had proved a long and effective counter to the subject-centred views of metaphysics, and where literary theory was either socially and pedagogically oriented (Leavis) or already text-based rather than author-based (Richards, Ransom). For this reason, with respect to British and American literary studies, the arrival of the linguistic emphasis in French thought seems at once the exotic report of something that happened long ago and far away, like the aftermath of the Big Bang, at the same time that it has a curious hint of banality, in its discovery that texts are social objects not exhaustively determined in their import by the meaning-intention of their authors.

The importation of linguistics into other aspects of cultural thought took place first in anthropology and psychoanalysis. Just as the process of adaptation to literary studies seems to depend simply on an analogy between linguistic and literary processes, so too the impetus which linguistics gave to certain branches of anthropology and psychoanalysis depended on perceived affinities of method rather than any really rigorously established commutativity of field or of terms, despite claims about the scientific rigour of the linguistic method and an insistence on the validity of the governing term 'structure' – the term which emerges as the most opaque and unanalysable in the whole process.

In an influential series of essays published as *Anthropologie structurale* (1958), Claude Lévi-Strauss set out major claims for the implications of linguistics for anthropological study which also had a major impact on literary theory. These influential essays express a desire for the supposed scientific objectivity of structural linguistics which was soon taken up in other areas of cultural study. They also have the same difficulty in making the parallel a rigorous one, and while on the one hand it is clear that Lévi-Strauss's approach removed anthropology from obvious intellectual dangers, it is absolutely unclear that the device of structure denotes anything more definite than the process of observing regularities (i.e. the stripping out of particularistic data in order to produce observations regarding systemic similarities between disparate cultures). The claim for the scientific validity of structural linguistics is made in terms that literary and cultural studies were to replicate:

> Linguistics occupies a special place among the social sciences [. . .]. It is probably the only one which can truly claim to be a science and which has achieved both the formation of an empirical method and an understanding of the nature of the data submitted to its analysis. [. . .] Structural linguistics will certainly play the same renovating role with respect to the social sciences that nuclear physics, for example, has played for the physical sciences.[2]

The parallels which Lévi-Strauss discovers between kinship systems (an object of anthropology) and language (the object of linguistics) are so general as to call forth a variety of glosses from the author:

> In the study of kinship problems [. . .] the anthropologist finds himself in a situation which formally resembles that of the structural linguist. Like phonemes kinship terms are elements of meaning; like phonemes they acquire meaning only if they are integrated into systems. 'Kinship systems' like 'phonemic systems' are built by the mind on the level of unconscious thought. Finally, the recurrence of kinship patterns [. . .] in scattered regions of the globe and in fundamentally different societies, leads us to believe that, in the case of kinship as well as linguistics, the observable phenomena result from the action of laws which are general but implicit.

[. . .] Although they belong *to another order of reality*, kinship phenomena are *of the same type* as linguistic phenomena.[3]

Lévi-Strauss will modify this in various ways, never to any great degree of elaboration, but this paragraph alone makes clear how profound are the difficulties of extending the analogy. For example, the structure of language can indeed be known only unconsciously to a competent speaker; but a competent social subject can never be wholly unaware of the structure of kinship even if unaware of all its systemic functions. It is not enough to make kinship seem to resemble the phoneme by linking each to the term 'system'. Kinship is said to be an element of meaning, like a phoneme; yet it is plain that while a phoneme is one of a closed set of sounds available for linguistic production, each element of a kinship system exists not merely as part of an arbitrary set of possible differences but is a completely concrete and non-arbitrary social and biological relationship. The final sentence quoted depends on two entirely unanalysed phrases, italicized by Lévi-Strauss, which rest on the assertion of the categories 'orders of reality' and 'type', even though he will insist in a later piece on the necessity of relating language to culture and their common ground in mind.[4] Among the most notable asymmetries between language and kinship is the insistence of linguistics on the arbitrary nature of the relationship between the signifier and the signified. Lévi-Strauss recognizes this at a certain point. While overlooking the fact that a kinship element has no corresponding division as between signifier and signified, he tackles the issue of arbitrariness by explaining that the linguistic sign is not in fact arbitrary *once it has been determined*: 'a linguistic sign is arbitrary a priori, but ceases to be arbitrary a posteriori. [. . .] The arbitrary character of the linguistic sign is thus only provisional.'[5] Lévi-Strauss's objective, of course, is to play down the concept of arbitrariness, as this can have no place in the analysis of kinship but is central to linguistics. Whatever the potential merit of his attempt to persuade linguists to distinguish between the *a priori* and *a posteriori* life of the sign (in relation to some imagined moment of origin), the irony seems notable that, even at this early stage, structural anthropology has to rewrite linguistics in order to free itself of overwhelming conceptual problems created by the attempt to adopt its methods.

The actual process of adapting linguistics to anthropology reveals stark discrepancies even on a cursory examination, and anticipates similar problems in literary theory. However, the reasons why anthropology might benefit from the method of linguistics are quite clear. The introduction to *Structural Anthropology* describes the state of anthropology in the

1950s as divided between ethnographic and historical approaches. The problem for the ethnographic approach (typified by Malinowski) is that it renounces not only historical but virtually all systematic or extraneous knowledge of the society under examination in order to concentrate on the concrete particulars of that society, relying too much, according to Lévi-Strauss, in the instinctive ability of the observer. Lévi-Strauss mocks the 'inner meditation', reliance on 'wonderful intuition', and the 'combination of dogmatism and empiricism' which he found to characterize Malinowski's method, which preferred to observe a single small tribe in isolation without accounting for observable similarities with countless other tribes in the same region.[6] The problem for the historical method (typified by Franz Boas) was that historical information was generally unavailable for the type of pre-literate societies being observed; this meant that any account of the historical evolution of social institutions in such societies was inevitably a speculative reconstruction which rested on narratives of evolutionary progress which draw a false parallel between the development of natural organisms and the development of societies. The structural approach is held to solve the problems in both ethnographic and historical method by concentrating on the unconscious nature of social phenomena. This approach takes its legitimacy from the fact that natives are never able to give observers the justification or rationalization of their social practices. From this Lévi-Strauss concludes that social practices in pre-scientific societies resemble language use in that they are shaped by unconscious forces. The same unconscious forces can be found at work in separate but related societies, thus overcoming the disadvantages of the particularist ethnography of Malinowski; at the same time, focus on the unconscious functional coherence of the social totality avoids the problems of the historical method, in particular its reliance on the conscious expressions of subjects regarding social function and its speculative evolutionary framework.

From this point of view, the appeal of structural linguistics to all forms of cultural analysis becomes clearly visible. Linguistics seemed to have shown that the scientific analysis of cultural phenomena could bracket history and consciousness, and proceed to locate individual acts in terms of a system. Social systems exist *in order to* reproduce themselves, while linguistic systems have no such function: this was only one of the major differences which made the comparison between an individual social action and a phoneme very hard to sustain. Yet this notion of system or structure, when applied to culture, had the advantage that it provided an alternative both to historical, developmental models of literature and to over-individualized close reading. The former concentrated on the history of literary forms without regard to context, and the latter found significance only in the most minute and particular features of the individual work. The idea of structure drew attention to the nature of literary artefacts not as individual acts of expression but as modes of expression which derived meaning not merely from the structure of possible literary works, but from the structuration of all forms of social expression, whether literary or otherwise.

*

Analysis of the structure of the literary work had formed the core of the analytical method developed by the Russian Formalists during the 1920s. Roman Jakobson, Viktor Shklovsky and Vladimir Propp were the leading figures of Russian Formalism, which had its origin in the Moscow Linguistic Circle, a discussion group of philologists led by Jakobson, which was founded in 1915. These linguists developed a marked focus on poetics, and were inspired in part by the poetics of the Russian version of futurism, which, like other types of European modernist poetry, emphasized the autonomy of the word. A similar group, which included Shklovsky, operated in St Petersburg as the Society for the Study of Poetic Language, known as *Opojaz*. An early essay by Shklovsky, 'Art as Technique' (1917), established an essential principle of Formalism, 'defamiliarization' or *ostranenie* as the essence of literary language:

> Art exists that one may feel things, to make the stone *stony*. The purpose of art is to impart the sensation of things as they are perceived and not as they are known. The technique of art is to make objects 'unfamiliar', to make forms difficult, to increase the difficulty and length of perception because the process of perception is an aesthetic end in itself and must be prolonged. *Art is a way of experiencing the artfulness of an object; the object is not important.*[7]

This formulation could almost have been made in the same form by John Crowe Ransom some twenty years later, except that Shklovsky distinguishes the 'artfulness' of the object from the actual object, and goes on to focus on the distinct nature of literary language: 'Poetic speech is *formed speech*, prose is ordinary speech.'[8] The 'literariness' of literature was to be analysed in terms of the 'device', and the function of the device within the system of the work. This emphasis on literary language as a special case of language attracted criticism in the political climate of the 1920s, not only from the revolutionary leader Leon Trotsky, who nevertheless acknowledged the potential scientific merits of this form of inquiry, but from others who flatly rejected 'Formalism', whether in the arts or in criticism, in favour of a political art and criticism which would concentrate less on the formal alienation of the device and more on direct social relevance. The Formalist groups were aware that their method threatened to bracket the social as textually extraneous, but the situation in Russia did not allow for the development of Formalism in that country, although Vladimir Propp's *Morphology of the Folk Tale* (1928) is a successful and influential study from this early period which grounds the structural analysis of narrative in terms of recursive formal features.

The Prague Linguistic Circle which was founded in 1926 included several members of the Russian Formalist circles, not least Roman Jakobson, who, unlike Shklovsky, was a trained linguist. This group was able to pursue its work into the 1930s, unlike the Russians, and was fairly consistently committed to a synchronic view of literature and to the complete synthesis of poetics and linguistics. However, the Czech group extended the range of inquiry of the Russian Formalists beyond the literary text and 'device' and into other aspects of the production and consumption of literary work; they favoured the term 'structuralism'. While Shklovsky had emphasized the phenomenology of literature in terms of the relationship between the mind and the world, Jakobson shifted discussion to the linguistic relationship between the sign and the referent. This shift was prepared for by Russian futurist poetry, which had emphasized the materiality of the sign, but the inflection added by the introduction of linguistics would eventually have its impact on West European literary theory when French structuralism turned to the Prague group and to the work of Jakobson in particular. The insistence that a literary work was a system of signs and therefore not a simple reflection of either the authorial psyche or the objective world was developed by the Prague Circle into an increasingly complex reflection on textuality as the tertium aliquid, non-identical with 'mind' or 'world' and challenging the essence of either pole of the subject–object duality. This thinking has fed a seemingly inexhaustible strand in literary theory to this day. In the longer term, this apparent separation of text and reality would prove to be a strategic move that yielded a greater realism and political specificity; in the shorter term, this essential methodological innovation seemed to its critics to repress social content. The political doubts which accompanied the early development of Russian Formalism and Czech structuralism in the 1920s and 1930s were similar in nature to those which met the project of French structuralism, especially in its British reception. The work of another Russian, which defined itself partly in relation to Formalism but with a greater degree of social specificity, appeared to some in Britain and America to offer a positive model for a politically committed literary theory.

One of the richest expressions of the convergence of structural method and literary criticism came in the work of the Russian Mikhail Bakhtin. His *Rabelais and his World* (1940–6; revised for publication 1965) was long known in its 1968 translation; *Problems of Dostoevsky's Poetics* (1929; 1961–3) was first published in English translation in 1973 (and more widely in 1984); other key works were only available in full translation too late to be part of the main current of the structuralist impact in Britain and America. Of these, the key essay 'Discourse in the Novel' (1934–5) only achieved wide circulation with the 1981 publication of the English translation of *The Dialogic Imagination* (1973). As the dates of composition and of original publication reveal, Bakhtin's work had a troubled history in Stalin's Russia, and ambiguities in his theories may stem from a habitual process of adaptation, much as the music of Shostakovich is thought to have attempted to hold Stalinist criticism at bay. The pattern of publication and translation meant that an intellectual impetus which belonged in substance to the 1930s had its European and American impact only later and in two waves. Moreover, the œuvre itself, and even the basic biographical facts about Bakhtin, have been thrown into confusion by developments in archival scholarship following the demise of the old Soviet Union. Most shocking among these revelations has been the discovery that sections of *Rabelais and his World* were copied word for word and without any attribution from Ernst Cassirer's *The Individual and the Cosmos in Renaissance Philosophy* (1927); furthermore, all references to the German-Jewish scholarship on which the study was heavily dependent had been excised from the text (as a concession to Soviet cultural politics).[9] The necessary reassessment of Bakhtin has become a matter for Russian-reading specialists – it comes too late to be part of the theory movement in general – but the fact that it is occurring at all makes clear the essentially transitory character of the moment of theory – a moment of eclectic and widespread absorption only later to be followed by a period of scholarly consolidation and revision in which a figure for some years central to the project of revising the theoretical basis of English literary studies slowly retreats from view *in the very process* of being rendered more transparent to scholarship and thereby – as Ken Hirschkop puts it – necessarily 'more technical, more difficult, less inspiring'.[10] This is a polite way of suggesting that the Bakhtin who will emerge from the contemporary process of scholarly re-examination will only distantly resemble the figure for whom there was so much enthusiasm in the early years of theory.

Although linked with the Russian Formalist school, Bakhtin's work reflects only elements of formalist doctrine. *Rabelais and his World* uses the work of François Rabelais (*c.*1494–1553) to form an argument concerning the nature of folk and popular culture in the Middle Ages and early Renaissance. Although it is presented in the form of an anthropological inquiry with a strong emphasis on language, of necessity utilizing a 'high' cultural source (i.e. a published literary work), the argument is in essence metaphysical. Bakhtin suggests that there was a permanent opposition between popular and folk culture, on the one hand, and the official culture of Christian power on the other. Popular culture is characterized by laughter and the spirit of carnival. The institutions of the carnival parody authority and official culture by opposing a comic spirit of collective renewal to the tragic spirit of individual fate. Although posited as a reading of the Middle Ages via literature, Bakhtin's argument seems tailored to the Russia of the 1930s, which gave strong official support to the notion of the validity of folk culture. On the one hand, Bakhtin's affirmation of folk culture might have appeared to work as a support of Stalinist doctrines of culture; on the other hand, the celebration of the power of the people in resisting state authority might easily be interpreted as coded opposition to the Stalin regime. In the contrasting political context of America and Britain in the 1970s, *Rabelais and his World* appeared to lend itself to anti-capitalist and feminist criticism, and was one of the principal encouragements to two strands of literary and cultural theory which have continued to play themselves out ever since: the celebration of vernacular culture as a jaunty and spirited riposte to official repression, and the assertion of the body against the word and the subject. Vernacular culture and the body have assumed almost totemic status in recent and contemporary criticism. Each has been the site of considerable theoretical struggle, not least because each tends to appear in the context of a type of conviction politics, in which the validity of the popular or of the body is asserted against a reified 'other' – be it the clerisy, the state or patriarchy. So the vernacular and the body tend to get asserted as a value, and a kind of struggle between good and evil established, which seems to provide a satisfactory symbolic model for some cultural commentators, but not for others who have found the repression thesis insufficiently dialectical – that is, insufficiently able to describe the total process of society, tending to substitute a simple binary designed to explain the loss of nature that ignores the complexity of the process in which society has acted on nature. Although the Frankfurt School and in particular Herbert Marcuse stand behind the intellectual changes which informed the propensity of the American and British left

to criticize culture rather than society and prefer psychological to economic models for explaining oppression, it has been Bakhtin whose
influence has been critical in setting the climate in which these models
acquired increased legitimacy in literary theory.

For all its complexity and (as it turns out, often borrowed) learning,
Rabelais and his World probably appears now to represent something of
a false dawn, not for early modern studies, which have always had reason
to query Bakhtin, but for the political ontology which it appeared Bakhtin
could ground, and which has remained a goal of literary theory ever
since. *Rabelais and his World* argues that 'the framework of modern
culture and aesthetics' has misunderstood and distorted the nature of
'popular character' and folk culture in the Middle Ages and Renaissance,
with the 'element of laughter' having been the most neglected component of this character and culture. The 'boundless world of humorous
forms and manifestations' which 'opposed the official and serious tone of
medieval ecclesiastical and feudal culture' formed a single 'culture of folk
carnival humour'. The main feature of the carnival was its comic mimicry
of 'civil and social ceremonies and rituals'; carnivals embodied 'a completely different, nonofficial, extraecclesiastical and extrapolitical aspect of
the world, of man, and of human relations; they built a second world and
life outside officialdom, a world in which all medieval people participated
more or less, in which they lived during a certain time of the year'.[11]
Carnival was utopian: it established a different order of being in an order
of cyclical time and change. Correspondingly, it established a different
mode of language, 'special forms of marketplace speech and gesture,
frank and free [. . .] a special carnivalesque, marketplace style of expression', found in Rabelais' novel.[12] The validation and celebration of bodily
function in Rabelais also reflects folk culture. The body is not a 'private,
egoistic form' but a universal; 'the material bodily principle is contained not
in the biological individual, not in the bourgeois ego, but in the people,
a people who are continually growing and renewed'.[13] The 'bourgeois
ego', presumably not a feature of feudal society, is anachronistically introduced here to establish a connection with communist rejection of bourgeois
egoism, and would equally serve as a bridge for readers of the 1970s
schooled in the ego psychology of Freud.

Although the politics which, it appeared, could be read off from *Rabelais
and his World* had a popular appeal, and while Bakhtin found supporters
in American academic feminism, Marxists in Britain seem in general to
have resisted the seduction of the carnivalesque in favour of the more
resolutely political Althusserian approach. Terry Eagleton, whose work
in the 1970s both encapsulated and led British Marxist literary theory,

ignored Bakhtin in *Marxism and Literary Criticism* (1976) and *Criticism and Ideology* (1976), and as late as *Literary Theory* made only brief reference to his work. Francis Mulhern included no substantial reference to Bakhtin as late as 1992 in his edited collection on *Contemporary Marxist Literary Criticism.* At the 1982 Essex Conference, Graham Pechey could be found trying to argue a central role for Bakhtin between a receding Marxist formalism and the rising interest in post-structuralism in his 'Bakhtin, Marxism, and Post-Structuralism', which argues that Bakhtin should not be seen as a 'post-formalist' appendage of formalism, but as a modern 'post-structuralist', regardless of his place in the chronology of literary theory.[14] As Eagleton notes, the hope of Bakhtinians was 'to unite the textual, bodily, materialist or sociological concerns of the post-structuralists with a more historical, materialist or sociological perspective'.[15] Why did these hopes for Bakhtin fail to materialize? The work which eventually appeared as *Rabelais and his World* was the culmination of a decade of linguistically based analysis of which the much earlier 'Discourse in the Novel' is the key early document. Had 'Discourse in the Novel' been available throughout the 1970s there is some chance that the reception of Bakhtin might have been different. However, Marxist criticism tended to shun Bakhtin or treat him as an exotic special case. Bakhtin had connections to Russian Formalism, and was commonly supposed to be the actual author of *The Formal Method in Literary Scholarship: A Critical Introduction to Sociological Poetics* (1928; English translation 1985), issued under the name of P. N. Medvedev, and *Marxism and the Philosophy of Language: Fundamental Problems of Sociological Method in the Science of Language* (1929; English translation 1986), issued under the name of V. N. Voloshinov. These apparent connections to a sociological rather than a formalist poetics might have made Bakhtin appear amenable to Marxist literary theory, but it is *Rabelais and his World* itself which must have appeared to those readers to be maddeningly devoid of politics. The argument of that work is ontological, not political. Its loose generalization of the carnivalesque character of the people contrasts dramatically with the complicated discussion of ideological mechanisms which characterized the left at that time. Although Bakhtin's topic belongs to the Middle Ages, this universal folk spirit is said to be still in existence, although suppressed by bourgeois culture. Bakhtin does not introduce any notion of struggle or the development of consciousness, nor appear to allow for it. We might not be surprised by this, since whatever quotient of Marxism appears in Bakhtin it certainly does not amount to a broad endorsement of Leninist vanguardism. Properly understood, Bakhtin's vision of two orders of temporal reality, one cyclical, the other linear and progressive, and their two corresponding realms, one collective and comic the other individual and tragic, takes sides against the Marxist vision of historical progress; its resonance would have been in any case wholly different in the context of the post-revolutionary world of the Soviet Union from among the aspiring revolutionaries of Britain.

Would Bakhtin's early reception have been any different if work in the decade or so preceding the Rabelais text had been available sooner? 'Discourse in the Novel', which dates from 1934–5, only became widely available with the publication of *The Dialogic Imagination* (1981). It represents an invaluable contribution to the theory of the novel as a modern form, and introduces the idea of 'dialogism' – what Julia Kristeva in her glosses on Bakhtin also called 'intertextuality'. This essay aims to theorize the novel in terms that avoid pure formalism and straightforward ideology critique – in terms of what Bakhtin calls a 'sociological stylistics'. Broadly, Bakhtin's claim is that the novel blends together different writing styles which he refers to as 'voices'. While poetry had aimed for a unity of style, the novel did not aim to speak in the voice of the writer but to co-articulate a variety of voices. These voices are thought of not as being invented but as concretely present in society. This plurality of voices is termed 'heteroglossia', and is claimed by Bakhtin to be the evolved essence of the novel form. The excerpt below sets out some of the key claims.

> Any stylistics capable of dealing with the distinctiveness of the novel as genre must be a *sociological stylistics*. The internal social dialogism of novelistic discourse requires the concrete social context of discourse to be exposed, to be revealed as the force that determines its entire stylistic structure, its 'form' and its 'content', determining it not from without, but from within; for indeed, social dialogue reverberates in all aspects of discourse, in those relating to 'content' as well as the 'formal' aspects themselves.
>
> The development of the novel is a function of the deepening of dialogic essence, its increased scope and greater precision. Fewer and fewer neutral, hard elements ('rock bottom truths') remain that are not drawn into dialogue. Dialogue moves into the deepest molecular and, ultimately, subatomic levels.
>
> Of course, even the poetic word is social, but poetic forms reflect lengthier social processes, i.e. those tendencies in social life requiring centuries to unfold. The novelistic word, however, registers with extreme subtlety the tiniest shifts and oscillations of the social atmosphere; it does so, moreover, while registering it as a whole, in all of its aspects.
>
> When heteroglossia enters the novel it becomes subject to an artistic reworking. The social and historical voices populating language, all its

words and all its forms, which provide language with its particular concrete conceptualizations, are organized in the novel into a structural stylistic system that expresses the differentiated socio-ideological position of the author amid the heteroglossia of the epoch.[16]

The first paragraph here underlines that 'Discourse and the Novel' is intended as a riposte to formalism which will not, however, take the route of socialist realism by insisting solely on social content. On the face of it, Bakhtin's account lends itself to claims that the novel is a democratic and liberating form. We should be clear in our own minds that some such account is demanded by the strong association of literature with the modern public sphere since the eighteenth century. It is apparent, too, that 'Discourse and the Novel' seems to give a more politically and socially specific account of the culture it describes than *Rabelais and his World*, which seemed to leave no space for politics or for futurity. Yet reservations about this account of the heteroglossic, dialogic novel are easily arrived at. Most obviously, the unproblematic identification of 'voice', as if a social register were in itself an entity or identity, a speaking subject, seems just wrong. There is hardly any point in resting a complex notion of the rhetoric of fiction on a simplified notion of social 'voice'; indeed, it is easy to see why anyone versed in the notion of consciousness as reified, or reflective of ideology, would resist a notion which appeared to define voice as the product and representative of consciousness, a kind of spontaneous expressive authenticity. In this respect, 'Discourse in the Novel' offers merely a variant of the celebration of 'the people' in *Rabelais*. Further, although readers might have gone to Bakhtin looking for a restoration of social contents, his emphasis, in the final instance, is on the form of the literary work and on the artistic process which has shaped it:

> Every novel, taken as a totality of all the languages and consciousnesses of language embodied in it, is a *hybrid*. But we emphasize once again: it is an intentional and conscious hybrid, one artistically organized, and not an opaque mechanistic mixture of languages [. . .]. *The artistic image of a language* – such is the aim that novelistic hybridization sets for itself. [. . .] An artistic hybrid demands enormous effort: it is stylized through and through, thoroughly premeditated, achieved, distanced. [. . .] The novel demands a broadening and deepening of the language horizon, a sharpening in our perception of socio-linguistic differentiations.[17]

The concept of hybridity, here as in our own time, has the function of naïvely preserving the very concept of identity which it claims to supersede, since the idea of a hybrid plant or animal, which is the basis of the metaphor used here, presupposes the identity of the separate kinds which constitute it. Hybridity is therefore an ineffective metaphor for cultures (which is the underlying, implied stage in Bakhtin's argument here) and even more so for language. Here the presupposition is that within a national language, different registers (defined by lexis, grammar, syntax and so on) can be identified as belonging to groups of speakers (who are projected as if they were individual subjects). It is unlikely that even the most painstaking argumentation could establish that such subsets of 'a' language have the same type of identity as organic kinds – without labouring the point, it is sufficient to say that the key metaphor of dialogization (the hybridization or cross-breeding of linguistic entities) is no more than an illustration of the process by which different social registers are combined. Surprisingly, the notion of a hybrid is static, presupposing a mute combination of which the combined entities are unaware; and indeed this is partly the point. Bakhtin argues that it is the artist who effects this combination in the serious literary novel. This is not, he reminds us, the product of the naïve writer who quite unconsciously writes in numerous incompatible styles, but of the artist who effects a conscious program of maximum self-awareness. While the term 'dialogic' seems to have the connotation of democratic dialogue, it is plain (and not only from the use of the metaphor of hybridity) that no actual dialogue is implied in the notion of dialogism. Bakhtin follows the Formalists (and indeed Kant) in stressing the unity of the work. The argument is concerned to show why it is that the novel is now the pre-eminent modern literary form, even though, in its apparently heterogeneous and even garrulous nature, it lacks the unity of voice of poetry. This lack of unity of voice is what is denoted by the term dialogism, and the mark of artistic success of the novel is found in its realization of this aesthetic goal – in the above quotation described as a 'distancing' or estrangement of language not unlike the quality of language which the formalists claimed for poetry.

Although Bakhtin does not fulfil the kind of political hopes which might have informed the initial interest in his work, the general critical vision in his work has proved indispensable. The presentation of the novel as part of the process of the development of knowledge of 'the era of the Renaissance and Protestantism, which destroyed the verbal and ideological centralization of the Middle Ages' and founded the 'Galilean language consciousness of the kind embodied in novelistic discourse' gives strong theoretical sustenance to the project of studying emergent modern culture (in the manner of Raymond Williams) as opposed to fetishizing poetry as the already-achieved ideal of literary art, even if

Bakhtin's insistence that the novel is high art does not move over into the cultural studies model. The notion of dialogism has tended to be marginal in Britain, where Marxism has demanded more in the way of change than equality of representation, but has found resonance in the United States, where feminism in particular has identified political leverage in the term. In their introduction to a 1991 collection of essays on feminism and Bakhtin, Dale M. Bauer and Susan Jaret McKinstry assert that 'feminists turn to Bakhtin's notion of word and dialogue in order to break down this separation of public rationality and private intersubjectivity'. The issue, they claim, 'is the failure of a masculinized or rationalized public language (what Bakhtin would call the authoritative voice) that is split off in cultural representations from the private voice (Bakhtin's internally persuasive language). A feminist dialogics would bring these two languages together in dialogue.' Dialogism is glossed as 'Bakhtin's theory about encountering otherness through the potential of dialogue'; it is 'central to feminist practice' as it is based on the insight that 'people's responses are conditional, human circumstances are irreducible and contingent'. The object is 'to create a feminist dialogics that recognizes power and discourse as indivisible, monologism as a model of ideological dominance, and narrative as inherently multivocal, as a form of cultural resistance that celebrates the dialogic voice that speaks with many tongues, which incorporates multiple voices of the cultural web'.[18] As an example of the 'individuality and rationalization' of monologic male culture, the authors offer the example of a (male) mass murderer who had been refused admission to the University of Montreal and took revenge on the 'feminism' he blamed for this outcome by shooting fourteen women. This appropriation of Bakhtin is remarkable both as an example of the contrast of contexts (as between the Soviet Union of the 1930s and the America of the 1980s) and as an example of the kind of scavenging process which has characterized some types of academic theoretical performance. Here, the dialogic, a rhetorical feature of the modern novel, is conflated with dialogue, the process of communicative action. Bakhtin's notion of poetry as rhetorically monologic in the manner of the authority structures of the Middle Ages (in contrast to those of modernity) is conflated with the monologism of a masculinized modernity said to repress the carnivalesque and plural feminine. Finally, a critical theory which can at best be supposed to signal some dissent from achieved socialism in the name of democracy is appropriated for an academically based feminist project which makes no reference to socialist ideals and seeks to adapt a European pathos to a social situation which cannot, surely, comprehensively be characterized in terms of the monologism of a psychotic murderer, as if the celebration of one's own benign carnivalesque status could only be ensured by vilifying the evil, monological Other. As Nancy Glazener pointed out in a rebuttal of the American feminist adoption of Bakhtin, the problems of appropriating his work are of a scale that the net effect may run contrary to the aims of the feminist project – for example, it is canonical male authors who, in Bakhtin, are the impersonal and non-monologic site of the coordination of heterogeneous discourses in the dialogic artwork of the novel, a fact which flatly contradicts the feminist identification with discursive hetero-geneity and the carnivalesque body. Glazener points out that 'the con-cept of the anarchically disruptive, diffusely subversive Other, which parts of Bakhtin's work and certain strains of feminist theory have endorsed, is more mystifying than enlightening,' and that 'the myth Bakhtin derives from Rabelais of a larger-than-life folk body, the emblem of a material-based class consciousness for the people, raises more problems than it solves for feminists', since it 'harks back to a golden age in which "the people" were clearly separated from official culture and therefore capable of making their critique from a conceptually pure "outside"'.[19] Even this redaction introduces a problem (the notion that the 'folk' of the Middle Ages were like a collective, critical subject effecting a 'critique' seems to be adopted here rather than rejected) but, more than this, the indirection of this process, in which Bakhtin is criticized in order to make room for reservations about American feminism, leaves unspoken a more funda-mental questioning both of the modelling as a universalized 'feminism' of a certain academic and professional venture, and of the manner in which European theory is appropriated without a full acknowledgment of its origins in the politics of socialism.

*

While Bakhtin found favour with at least some British leftists, French variants of structuralism mostly did not, and while it always seemed that the scientific stance of structuralism ought to find mutual confirmation in the scientific socialism of the Marx–Engels tradition, Marxist theorists in Britain tended mostly to fret about the fact that the confirmation never seemed to arrive. The over-riding contradiction seemed to come around the structuralist desire to analyse a synchronic state of affairs, and the Marxist desire not merely to analyse and describe change, but to bring it about: 'The philosophers have only *interpreted* the world in various ways,' wrote Marx in his famous 'Theses on Feuerbach' (1845); 'the point is to change it' – a slogan which was well known and often cited by British

Marxists in the 1960s and 1970s. Accounts of Marxist criticism in the 1970s tended to make little of the potential of the kind of structuralism practised by Roland Barthes. Despite his evident accomplishment and general influence, Barthes tended to receive only passing acknowledgement from Marxist critics. In the 1970s and 1980s, mention of Barthes was generally accompanied by a warning sign, as in Terry Eagleton's *Literary Theory: An Introduction* (1983):

> Structuralism is best seen as both a symptom of and reaction to the social and linguistic crisis I have outlined. It flees from history to language – an ironic action, since as Barthes sees few moves could be more historically significant. But in holding history and referent at bay, it also seeks to restore a sense of the 'unnaturalness' of the signs by which men and women live, and so open up a radical awareness of their historical mutability. In this way it may rejoin the very history which it began by abandoning. Whether it does so or not, however, will depend on whether the referent is suspended provisionally, or for good and all.[20]

One context of these remarks is obviously the long-standing unease of Marxists about the implications of structuralism (and at this time its co-dependent post-structuralism). Not least, the context is strategic. In the early 1980s literary theory was conceived by many in the context of English studies not as an abstruse inquiry to be conducted by specialists, but as a mode of encouraging political agency among students, who are viewed as potential allies of the working class in revolutionary struggle, part of the collective subject which will be the agent of historical change. English literature was viewed as a key component of the ideological veil which must be shattered by revolutionary consciousness. Academics and students could be part of a political vanguard by participating in revolutionary struggle against the anti-theoretical appropriation of literature by the academy on behalf of the state. Structuralism as a component of Marxism might have been one thing, although at that period Marxist activists, who were generally associated with Trotskyite groups (as was Eagleton), tended to oppose the adoption of Althusser in favour of Leninist praxis. Structuralist literary theory based in linguistics was another matter, however. It was viewed as a threat not simply because its apparent preference for static analysis was at odds with Marxism as both practice and philosophy, but because it presented a seductive alternative to Marxist cultural theory in its state of development at the end of the 1970s. Dissemination of French structuralist work was dependent on translation. Many works of Roland Barthes had been available in translation since the 1960s; from the late 1970s, books by Jacques Derrida became available in English from American sources – most importantly *Of Grammatology* in 1974, *Writing and Difference* in 1978, followed in a wave of intensification by *Dissemination* in 1981 and *Margins of Philosophy* and *Positions* in 1982. The movement towards Derrida was supported by the *Oxford Literary Review*, a dedicated post-structuralist journal, and, with eminent US support in journals such as *Yale French Studies* and *Diacritics*, structuralism in its new post-structuralist guise appeared set to seize the kind of highbrow terrain formerly claimed in the United States by the grand New Critical professors, and indeed some of the most highly regarded of these achieved symbolic if not intellectual integration with post-structuralism in the pages of a widely noted book, *Deconstruction and Criticism* (1979), which gathered five essays by Derrida, Paul de Man, Harold Bloom, Geoffrey Hartman and J. Hillis Miller – the last three Americans being sophisticated rhetorical critics but not really deconstructionists. At the time Eagleton was preparing *Literary Theory*, post-structuralism or deconstruction appeared set to give a fillip to the older style of conservative New Criticism, and simply by virtue of its chicness to challenge the revolutionary novelty of Marxist criticism, especially in its highbrow appeal to the graduate students of the elite universities in both Britain and America, where it appeared to be finding a foothold. Eagleton's claim that structuralism has 'abandoned' language but might rejoin it is glib because it is polemical. The rhetorical aim is to position structuralism outside politics, even though the intellectual aim is to acknowledge that linguistic structuralism might have an implicit if unrealized politics, perhaps in terms of the challenge to ideological reification presented by the alienation-effect of exposing the artifice of signs.

Eagleton's reference to 'social and linguistic crisis' presents changes in thinking about language as a 'crisis' for literary studies by analogy with the crisis of capitalism. This sense of crisis in English studies was in full bloom by the early 1980s. In his 'Introduction' to *Re-Reading English*, subtitled 'The Crisis in English Studies', Peter Widdowson claimed it was time to take stock of 'that area in higher education traditionally referred to as "English" or "Literary Studies", and to redirect it in response to pressing social and political needs'. Theory, led by 'Althusserian structuralism', has questioned 'the assumption that there is a *given* Literature of inherent value'. Although he portrays the defenders of the canon and of pre-theoretical modes of reading as fading and hollow figures, Widdowson nevertheless cautions that the debate around theory in Britain and America is 'by no means as widespread as it should be, nor, despite the barrage of finely-honed theoretical work aimed at their destruction, are those departments reeling as they might be. The power and resistance of such a vested interest is not so easily shaken'.[21] The enemy is intellectually bankrupt but remains unshaken and offers a stiff resistance in defence of his investment in the canon. The rhetoric bypasses any material analysis of what is at stake in this polarized intellectual struggle. It does represent the tone of debate in some English Departments which became deeply internally divided at this time. This happened chiefly at Cambridge and a few other institutions where the curriculum was centrally decided and teachers wishing to teach new materials and approaches felt institutionally obliged to argue the case with their colleagues. In most British institutions, academics had been relatively free to alter that part of the teaching program under their own control, and the denunciations of critically conservative colleagues serve more as a rallying cry than as a portrayal of any sinister reality (Peter Widdowson at the time of publication of *Re-Reading English* was Head of English at Thames Polytechnic and probably had a great deal of control over curriculum).

The context for the discussion of crisis and the insistence on the political nature of English teaching in the early 1980s is of course extra-academic. The vocabulary of 'crisis' refers to current events but draws on classical Marxism. Marx had observed that nineteenth-century capitalism was very irrational in nature. Its planning mechanisms were subordinate to the inexorable logic of the market which resulted in periodic crises. Crisis resulted because the economy was driven by the accumulation of capital, but as capital grew there was a tendency of the rate of profit to fall. As profit fell, capitalist ventures became uneconomic and some would fold, destroying capital and laying off workers. These crises of capitalism, Marx argues, were not accidental but constitutive of an economy based on capital and the expression of its illogical nature. Marxists believed that capitalism could not escape recurrent and deepening crises, and that the capitalist system was always in the process of defending itself against crisis and against the potential political consequences of crisis which put the legitimacy of the system into question and might trigger revolutionary struggle.

To British Marxists at the beginning of the 1980s it seemed that Britain had been passing through a profound crisis for a decade or more. In the period to 1979, Britain had experienced major conflicts between unionized workers and both private and public sector industries. The public sector industries were large and numerous, including at that time coal mining, rail travel, car manufacture, energy, telecommunications, healthcare, water and others. The British economy was already in effect semi-socialist. In large centralized industries unions had gained considerable leverage over wages; strikes were comparatively frequent and industrial efficiency was low. There are different ways of interpreting the politics of this situation. Marxist theory saw trades unions as the principal vehicle of socialist struggle. However, union leaders were seen essentially as bureaucrats dedicated to improving wages and conditions but preserving the status quo. Local union organizers – shop stewards, whether official or unofficial – were able to offer political leadership to workers who otherwise lacked revolutionary consciousness. This at least was the theory of the numerous Leninist revolutionary sects which abounded at this time. A more pessimistic view is that British workers' organizations were in essence reactionary, and were fighting to maintain privileges which had grown up while Britain still benefited from imperialism but which were now slipping away. Unlike the United States, Britain had not been involved in the Vietnam War, which finished in 1973, and did not experience a civil rights movement. However, the attempt to build a civil rights movement by Catholic Nationalists in Northern Ireland had resulted in intercommunal violence with Protestant Loyalists and, following heavy-handed intervention by the British Army, led to a period known in Britain as 'the Troubles', the lasting feature of which was a campaign for Irish independence by the Provisional Irish Republican Army (IRA). Although most of the violence was confined to Northern Ireland, part of this campaign involved bombings on the British mainland by IRA cells, and a political milestone in the struggle was achieved in 1981 when Irish Republican prisoners starved themselves to death as part of a campaign to be treated as political prisoners. Despite the significance of the low-level Irish war, it was the state of the economy which gave the strongest sense of crisis. Constantly rising wages created inflation and further wage demands. The economy was racked by a series of strikes under the Labour government of James Callaghan, resulting in the 1979 'Winter of Discontent', when famously even grave-diggers went on strike, leaving the dead unburied, and uncollected household waste piled up in the streets. Callaghan's government fell and was replaced by the Conservative government of Margaret Thatcher which came in on the ticket of curbing trades union power and reducing the role of the state. Margaret Thatcher was an admirer of General Pinochet in Chile, who had used the army to destroy an elected socialist government and instituted a monetarist economic policy. Like Pinochet, Thatcher too followed the ideas of Milton Friedman and tightened money supply in Britain, with the effect of creating huge increases in unemployment in the early 1980s. I review these facts here in order to underline the reality of political crisis for Marxist theorists of the

1970s and early 1980s, and also to indicate the reasons for the comparatively subdued politics of criticism ever since. Margaret Thatcher took on socialism in the form of trades unions and the Labour Party and beat it. The socialist basis of the economy was partly reversed with a series of privatizations of key publicly owned industries; the unions were defeated in the long-drawn-out miners' strike of 1984–5; and Labour were kept out of power until 1997 with the victory of Tony Blair on a centrist, New Labour platform. Crisis and conflict were followed by defeat for socialists and Marxists, and also for feminists who in any case had tended to subordinate their struggle to that of socialism, and who in Margaret Thatcher were confronted by an icon of female power which sat uncomfortably with left-wing feminist thinking.

The vocabulary of crisis, then, has a large and looming referent in the period in question. The task of communicating politically with students was part of a concrete political task at that time. Peter Widdowson's *Re-Reading English* was published in a series called 'New Accents' which included titles such as Tony Bennett's *Formalism and Marxism* (1979), Dick Hebdige's *Subculture: The Meaning of Style* (1979), Catherine Belsey's *Critical Practice* (1980) and Toril Moi's *Sexual/Textual Politics* (1985). More than the complex works and specialist journals on which they depended, these compact titles were in some ways far more the reality of theory not only for many students at graduate and undergraduate level, but also for hard-pressed academics whose research and teaching commitments made it difficult to work through the extensive (and sometimes untranslated) theoretical literature. Theory claimed to find its place as part of social crisis and political conflict; as the reality of political conflict and socialist revolution receded, so the nature of theory as a generalist activity was altered.

Terry Eagleton's *Marxism and Literary Criticism* and *Criticism and Ideology* (both 1976) set an example for the 'New Accents' series. The former is a short review of Marxist literary theory which takes in Lenin, Trotsky, Plekhanov, Lukács, Brecht and Caudwell, as well as more recent contributions by Lucien Goldmann, Pierre Macherey and Louis Althusser. The latter is an attempt to show how the methods of Goldmann, Macherey et al. can be brought to bear on the ideology critique of English literature. These were useful and generally influential books in their time, but have since taken second place to *Literary Theory: An Introduction* (1983), which has held its place on course bibliographies ever since its publication. There is a strange contrast between the urgent sense of theory as part of the escalating struggle against capitalism of the late 1970s and early 1980s, and the venerable institution which this 1983 volume has now become. It is probable that the date of publication, just before the 1984–5 miners' strike with its destructive effect on socialist confidence and organization, also signals the end of a period of buoyancy for Marxist literary theory. In the longer term this ushered in a period of professionalization of English studies in Britain in which the notion of general English studies as a collective political project was replaced by loyalties to period specialisms. However, the decline in influence of Marxist literary theory was also conditioned by other factors. Even though it falls before the miners' strike, Eagleton's *Literary Theory* already has a defensive aspect to it. Marxist theory itself occupies much less space in the book than might be expected. More than this, the problems of Marxism and the lines of development in Marxist thought which would be pursued in later decades are not acknowledged – Theodor Adorno is not mentioned at all, and Walter Benjamin receives only one reference, although Eagleton had produced a book-length work on Benjamin only two years before. More surprisingly, Michel Foucault receives only a passing mention, a fact which seems astonishing in the light of the subsequent dominance of themes and motifs found in his work in literary studies up to the present day. My next chapter discusses Adorno, Benjamin and Foucault as figures who in many ways arrived after the period of Marxist dominance in literary theory, the first two increasingly discovered as sophisticated alternatives to Althusserian Marxism, the latter as an alternative to Marxism *tout court*, who supplied a model for thinking about culture in terms of institutions while avoiding the limitations of ideological 'false consciousness' and the binary, economistic model of class. It is not a case of criticizing this book for what it missed out or failed to predict, but of interpreting its contents as symptomatic of the state of theory at this time. *Literary Theory: An Introduction* is symptomatic of the end of theory, at least of a certain mode of practice of theory, and surely a reason for its continued viability *as* an introduction is that all of those branches of theory associated with structuralism were already approaching their logical conclusion. Even of those theoretical materials in which there would be a continued growth in interest – in particular Foucault and Derrida – the classic and most influential texts had already been written by the end of the 1970s or early 1980s, even if the process of translation and assimilation was only completed more gradually. Areas where theory was to develop in subsequent decades were arguably those which the very success of Marxism and socialism had tended to marginalize – feminist theory, queer theory and postcolonial theory. Such developments as occurred were largely dependent on ur-theoretical texts, and as developments fell more in the realm of theory than of praxis, but developments they were and notably demonstrated a shift of leadership in theoretical matters away from Europe to the United States (feminism, queer theory) and in the case of postcolonial theory, often under US sponsorship, to writers of non-European descent.

Eagleton's book contains five chapters, covering the rise of English, hermeneutics, structuralism, post-structuralism and psychoanalysis, followed by a brief chapter on 'Political Criticism'. There is no sustained exposition of Marxism, and, perhaps reflecting its continued association in Britain with Marxism and socialism, feminism is not granted a separate chapter. The introduction begins with warnings about the politics of formalism which, as we have seen, were a *locus classicus* of Marxist comment at this time. The section on the 'rise of English' reiterates the criticisms of Arnold and Leavis as ideological defenders of capitalism which had been treated at length by Francis Mulhern's *The Moment of 'Scrutiny'* (1979) and Chris Baldick's 1981 dissertation which was later published as *The Social Mission of English Criticism* (1983) and adds dismissive remarks about New Criticism, which is said to 'convert the poem into a fetish', linking New Critical treatment of poetry to the commodity fetishism described by Marx. The condemnation of New Criticism is worth a moment's pause. It has of course become routine for theory to dismiss New Criticism alongside Leavisism as the twin ideological bastions of cultural ideology, and I have suggested that this view is one-sided. Of course Eagleton must be right to say that New Criticism is socially conservative or at least quiescent, yet as we have seen the philosophical basis of New Criticism does not amount to a mere empiricism but to an ontology of the restoration of nature (i.e. of the particular) in a world dominated by system and money. Marx's theory of the commodity, with which Eagleton makes common cause, looks in two directions. On the one hand, Marx considers the commodity a 'fetish',[22] in the sense that it appears as an immediate reality at the point of purchase but disguises the whole system of exchange of which it is merely a part – it disguises the fact that what appears as a commodity is the objectified labour of the purchaser. To focus on the commodity is to focus on a false immediacy, and fail to understand the social system which produces the commodity as the form of alienated labour. The fetishized commodity therefore becomes a key component of false consciousness. On the other hand, however, Marx directs attention to the system of money not because it constitutes the ultimate reality of the world, but because as a system it denies spirit or man access to the world or nature: the particulars of reality are deferred by the money system and can never be brought back – unless the system of money is destroyed and communism is established. So by different routes, as we have already seen, Marxism shares with New Criticism this ontological model – and the more one sees it the more the very existence of the model looks like a massive ideological bulwark and persistent blockage in thinking – in which the particular must be restored in order to have access to an authentic mode of being. Eagleton follows Lukács (see next chapter) in insisting on the priority of systematic over immediate understanding. Yet the analysis of late capitalist philosophy and culture which for a while in the 1980s acquired the moniker 'postmodernism', and which took its impetus from the rereading of classical German philosophy, made exactly this issue – the possibility or impossibility of the restoration of a masked actuality, its major theme. There is a considerable contrast between Eagleton's bluff assumption that the particular is a fetish and postmodernism's incessant elaboration of the theme of the loss of nature, a theme which British socialists at this time did not consider integral to the philosophy of Marx.

Subsequent chapters of Eagleton's book offer criticism of hermeneutics, reception theory, structuralism and semiotics. According to Eagleton, these movements were 'nails' in the 'theoretical armoury' of the twentieth century, intended to 'fix the literary work once and for all' and deny the possible plurality of meanings of literary texts. Such modes of reading 'are in a real sense guilty': we should instead break with 'the literary institution', break with 'the very ways literature, literary criticism and its supporting social institutions are defined'.[23] Husserl, Heidegger and Gadamer did not have a major direct impact on Anglo-American literary theory and it is odd to find them evoked only to be summarily dismissed. The context, though, is one of political polemic and the aim is to land blows. In a similar vein, Eagleton claims that the 'judicious importation of structuralist concepts is to keep literary criticism in a job' – that is, structuralism is complicit with traditional criticism even, claims Eagleton, in its metacritical function of describing literary institutions – 'the point' he tells us, 'may not be to understand the institution but to change it'.[24] Post-structuralism fares better, as does high feminist theory in the example of Julia Kristeva, but although we are assured that Derrida's deconstruction 'is ultimately a *political* practice',[25] there is more sense here that literary theory is bypassing Marxism than emanating from it, and the rhetorical claim to speak from and for the position of a transcendent 'history' and 'politics' reads differently now in contexts where political hope has either vanished or adopted more local and pragmatic goals, and where the primacy of a progressive history or the priority of collective or administrative politics are rarely acknowledged.

*

The unease of British Marxist theory in the later 1970s and early 1980s is with various theories of textuality and desire that emerged from the French context and were exemplified by the literary journal *Tel Quel*, and by the work of Julia Kristeva, Roland Barthes and Jacques Derrida, among others. Broadly speaking, *Tel Quel* and the individuals partly or strongly associated with it pursued a politicized investigation of desire and textuality, which were conceived of as areas of pleasure and play. This journal existed before the events of May 1968 in France, when a student protest led by anarchists turned into a general student protest, which was attacked by police. The protesters were perceived as victims and received widespread support in France, leading to a general strike involving probably a majority of French workers. What was truly amazing about this event is that it was not organized either by the French General Trades Union (CGT) or the Communist Party (PCF). The demands of students and workers were often revolutionary, although the demands of the CGT and the PCF were not. In the end the strike lost support when President de Gaulle dissolved the National Assembly and threatened to bring in a state of emergency. These radical events left official French communism discredited by its inaction and inability to lead a struggle that had a revolutionary edge and came close to unseating the government. A secondary effect of this was to put Marxist theory on the defensive and create space for a rethink of basic principles. Although the journal *Tel Quel*, edited by the author Philippe Sollers, had not supported the student protest, the events of 1968 pushed it further into radical inquiries into materialism which blended semiology, psychoanalysis, and the residues of Althusserian analysis of the nature of subjectivity. It would be entirely wrong to conflate the disparate figures temporarily or permanently associated with *Tel Quel*, but the themes or terms that this group deployed over a period of time were quite at odds with the materialism of Marxism, which emphasized production and history as the horizons of interpretation. For *Tel Quel* authors, writing (the French term *écriture* is often retained in this context because of its connotations in French theory) is, variously, a site of absence, the trace of the unconscious, a terroristic abyss, a permanent deferral of plenitude, an effacement of the subject, a site of transgression or rupture or pleasure, and an area of play which refuses use value; above all, for the *Tel Quel* authors, writing gives speculative access to, or at least a glimpse of, a beyond of language, an originary *différance* or a pre-symbolic *chora*.

The highly speculative discourse of which *Tel Quel* was for a time a central hub would have seemed romantic and impractical to praxis-oriented Marxist theorists. Yet it was very plain that the new theories of textuality opened doors that Marxism did not. Much of the speculative work around textuality is its own fulfilment, and at worst in Anglo-American contexts generated a kind of epigonism in which imitation of the master or mistress and replication of his or her conclusions became the order of the day. In this respect, these apparently radical versions of theory have been assimilated as a part of the machinery of the reproduction of professional academic life. That said, these theories of textuality have conditioned the assumptions of literary studies in general even where they are not explicitly invoked, not least because a (relatively narrow) selection of these materials have become the stock of theory anthologies and graduate theory courses worldwide. This selection process probably represents a kind of taming of theory, but it is also indicative of an achieved shift in priorities within English as a subject.

The demand for the political responsibility of semiology which was articulated in Britain was also felt by Roland Barthes in France. In a 1974 essay called 'The Semiological Adventure' he recounts the visit of student who wanted him to supervise her dissertation on 'The Ideological Critique of Semiology'. Barthes sees this 'scene' as a sketch of the situation of semiology in the mid–1970s. The scene reiterated the political charge against structuralism that it is a reactionary science complicit with Gaullist technocracy, and situated him (Barthes) as the representative of structuralism whom the student confronted. Barthes notes, though, that in this encounter he was positioned as both inside semiology (an originator of semiology) and outside it (able to participate in its critique), and therefore still able to be addressed in a friendly fashion and not as an adversary. Semiology, says Barthes, was not for him a science, a cause, a school, a discipline or a movement, but an adventure – just what happened to him ('ce qu'il m'advient'). On this occasion, at least, Barthes is willing to reject the demand for political commitment by insisting that he is a product of writing, not the other way round.[26]

Barthes' essays 'The Death of the Author' (1968) and 'From Work to Text' (1971) are key position pieces, not, in fact, because they are elaborately worked through, but because they make available in digestible form governing manœuvres of post-structuralism. 'The Death of the Author' criticizes the emphasis in 'ordinary culture' on the intention of the author and asserts the primacy and autonomy of writing:

Writing is the destruction of every voice, of every point of origin. Writing is that neutral, composite, oblique space where our subject slips away, the negative where all identity is lost, starting with the very identity of the body writing.

Linguistically, the author is never more than the instance writing, just as *I* is nothing other than the instance saying *I*.

A text is not a line of words releasing a single 'theological' meaning (the 'message' of the Author-God) but a multi-dimensional space in which a variety of writings, none of them original, blend and clash. The text is a tissue of quotations drawn from the innumerable centres of culture.[27]

These (and other) lines from 'The Death of the Author' have been repeated so often and in so many contexts that the lines themselves, and not just the essay as a whole, have come to seem canonical, achieving a level of recognition that few theoretical works of any period have accomplished. This is perhaps because this essay graciously synthesizes a variety of speculative approaches in a genial and accessible manner, without obliging the reader to accede to any of the more complicated and specific workings. One strand in Barthes' argument is the literary modernism of Mallarmé which was a key interest of the *Tel Quel* group. Julia Kristeva used the work of Mallarmé as the foundation of her theory of the semiotic *chora*, a hypothetical projection on psychoanalytic lines which is one of the most speculative of the products of this period of theory.[28] Mallarmé is also important for Derrida, whose 'Double Session' published in *Tel Quel* in 1970 uses Mallarmé to work out a model of writing independent of reference and intention.[29] In the English-language context, the notion of impersonality in writing which can be extracted from Mallarmé's work is notably a feature of T. S. Eliot's poetics.[30] 'The Death of the Author' allows for an easy transition from the French to the Anglo-American context, where the intentional fallacy – the mode of interpretation which traces all meaning in a text back to the intention of its author – had no hold on disciples of Eliot and of New Criticism. That 'the subject slips away' in writing acknowledges both the Derridean critique of subject-centred reason and the psycho-analytic critique which locates the conscious ego (the subject) as a prod-uct of unconscious forces, as well as the Althusserian ideology critique which makes of the individual private subject the 'interpellated' product of extra-individual social forces. Barthes does not attempt to synthesize these different schemas (philosophy, psychoanalysis, Marxism, and the fourth mode in which all three are combined, theory), nor does he insist that any of these are accepted. In fact this notion of the disappeared subject is already prepared for in certain texts of modernism – not least Eliot's *The Waste Land* – which thematize authorial absence, and also anticipate the notion of a text 'drawn from the innumerable centres of culture', even if again, here, Barthes alludes beyond modernist literary practice to the dialogism of Bakhtin and the related 'intertextuality' of Julia Kristeva.[31] The title of the essay alludes to the 'death of God' announced by the madman in Nietzsche's *Thus Spake Zarathustra* (1892), thereby appropriating the existentialist theme of the contingency of existence in a world from which God is absent, at the same time that it alludes to the tradition of biblical hermeneutics – which have conditioned literary hermeneutics[32] – and suppose an authorial God whose intentions are expressed in the text of the Bible from which they can be reliably deciphered.

'The Death of the Author' is supplemented by 'From Work to Text', which, perhaps more crucially for literary studies, marks a shift in the way that the literary object is to be conceived. Once again, Barthes elegantly distils the collective tendency of disparate strands of work. Marx, Freud, structural linguistics and structural anthropology have changed the frame of study of the literary object:

> Over against the traditional notion of the work, for long – and still – conceived in a, so to speak, Newtonian way, there is now the requirement of a new object, obtained by the sliding or converting of the old categories. That object is the Text.
>
> The work is a fragment of substance, occupying part of the space of books [. . .]; the Text is a methodological field. [. . .] The work can be seen, text is a process of demonstration, speaks according to certain rules; the work can be held in the hand, the text is held in language, only exists in the movement of a discourse. [. . .] The Text is experienced only in an activity of production.
>
> The Text does not stop at (good) Literature; it cannot be contained in a hierarchy, even in a simple division of genres. What constitutes the Text is [. . .] its subversive force in respect of the old classifications.
>
> The work closes on a signified. [. . .] The Text, on the contrary, practises the infinite deferment of the signified. [. . .] The logic regulating the Text is not comprehensive (define 'what the work means') but metonymic; the activity of associations, contiguities, carryings-over coincides with a liberation of symbolic energy [. . .]; the Text is radically symbolic.
>
> The Text is plural. Which is not simply to say that it has several meanings, but that it accomplishes the very plural of meaning; an irreducible (and not merely acceptable) plural. The text is not a coexistence of meanings but a passage, an overcrossing; thus it answers not to an interpretation, even a liberal one, but to an explosion, a dissemination.[33]

The work is said to be an 'organism' – a favourite metaphor of the New Critics after Coleridge – the text by contrast is a 'network'. The ideas of post-structuralist theory had an immediate and radical impact in some quarters, where they were taken on board in their fullest elaboration and furthest speculative gesture, but it is important not to underestimate the slow-burning effect of the conjuncture of thought which Barthes described here across the field of literary studies. This movement not only liberates literary thinking from the study of works and authors, but allows for forms of inquiry which seek to dislocate meanings other than those intentionally coded by the author, the examination of texts other than those deemed to be great literature, the intertextual analysis of modes of writing which might not even be defined as literature, and many other moves in which the classic object of literary studies is dissolved, extended, abandoned, or revisited from unexpected perspectives. That said, the radical edge of the inquiries of Kristeva, Derrida et al. is not infrequently reduced to a reified gesture or even absent altogether. Yet, as we saw when we examined the work of Raymond Williams, the grounds for the extension of the object of cultural study and the search for legitimizing methods of extending this study were already in place; post-structuralism and its transition – as succinctly summarized by Barthes – met and far exceeded the needs of the Marxist, socialist and feminist scholars who had begun to question the instituting principles of literary studies. It hardly matters that there are easily identifiable problems with Barthes' apparently simplistic metaphor of the 'death' of the author and the corresponding emphasis on subjective readerly pleasure. In his own carefully framed 'What is An Author?' (1969), Michel Foucault allowed that writing is associated with death, and that the author has in effect disappeared, but asserts that the singularity of the author remains active within discourse and does not disappear:

> The name of the author remains at the contours of texts – separating one from the other, defining their form, and characterising their mode of existence. It points to the existence of certain groups of discourse and refers to the status of this discourse within a society and a culture. The author's name is not a function of a man's civil status, nor is it fictional [. . .] The function of an author is to characterise the existence, circulation, and operation of certain discourses within society.[34]

The term 'author-function' might be used instead to examine the discursive and institutional role played by authorships. This approach anticipates the implicit common-sense of literary scholarship in our own time;

authors are understood as brand names, part of the mechanism by which works are marketed, circulated and distributed; authorship is studied as a profession, coming into existence historically, over the eighteenth century, as part of the shift from feudalism to capitalism; and even some authors (such as Shakespeare) are analysed as ideological ciphers, the vehicles of national myth.

I have represented Barthes' essays as key documents in the common sense of literary studies, while suggesting that they strategically embody outward reference to sets of complex arguments (stated elsewhere and by others) which they unobtrusively emblematize (to say they summarize those arguments would be an exaggeration). Yet even to suggest that any dilute version of the death of the author hypothesis would receive general assent goes beyond the facts. Resistance to post-structuralism, though it only rarely seemed well informed, was often scathing, amounting to charges of fraud.[35] However, few writers were prepared to mount a sustained critique of post-structuralist ideas, and some of the few books which appeared on this topic seemed opportunistic and under-researched. One well-researched and considered rebuttal of post-structuralist orthodoxies was Seán Burke's *The Death and Return of the Author* (1992), which featured extended critical accounts of Barthes, Foucault and Derrida. Burke finds the death of the author thesis, in its various manifestations, to be hyperbolic and grounded in a good deal of myth-making (for example, in the misreading of Mallarmé). Barthes is criticized for his projection of the author as the 'God-like' originator of his meanings, which Burke claims is a convenient simplification which does not correspond to thinking about the author in, for example, New Criticism. After all, W. K. Wimsatt and Monroe C. Beardsley had already promoted a widely cited demolition of what they called the 'The Intentional Fallacy' in 1946. Burke dislikes the grandiose claims which accompany the death of the author – across the work of Barthes, Derrida and Foucault these include the deaths of 'God, Man, representation, metaphysics, the book, bourgeois humanism' – and rightly finds Nietzsche and Heidegger behind the fondness for locating changes of an 'epochal' nature in the attempt, shared with Althusserian Marxism, to dislodge 'humanism' – loosely, the philosophical view, evolved in and from the Renaissance, that saw man as the measure of all things.[36]

Burke is shrewd to suggest that the 'author' is a projected construction of post-structuralist theory itself, a postulate of which Barthes et al. cannot rid themselves. Yet once we acknowledge that the author of the literary work is tied to our general way of imagining our individual and collective mode of being (and no vocabulary is right here since it is the vocabulary which is in question – 'human being', 'the subject', 'Man') then surely we cannot escape the fact that our way of mapping our us-ness is indeed conditioned in ways that are not easily grasped. There actually *is* an infinite, sublime, non-human other which sits outside us – which the grammar and syntax of this sentence cannot properly name or even guide us towards. If Marxism projected the idea of an as yet unrealized mode of species being, then post-structuralism began to illuminate, immanently, the limits of our present. To that extent it offered a real stimulus to thought and imagination – even if the metaphor of the death of the author does, of course, imply that the ghostly author will always survive in his or her commemoration. Gone but not forgotten.

While Barthes was essayistic and polemical, Jacques Derrida offered a model of patiently working through the grammar and syntax of texts to demonstrate the limits of language. It was a mode of writing that strongly appealed to English academics of a certain stripe, even if many did not have the philosophical background to really follow what they were reading. Christopher Norris, author of several books on Derrida and deconstruction,[37] switched from English to philosophy to better follow the master, and cautioned the English colleagues he had left behind to take their Derrida one essay at time and to research whichever philosopher he happened to be tackling with great care before moving on. This was good advice, in fact, and most readers of Derrida will admit that it took them some years to catch up. While it is not difficult to paraphrase Derrida's work, it is almost impossible to do so without violating the ethos of that writing and offending professional Derrideans. This is because a central Derridean claim is that language is not underpinned by concepts. In fact Derrida does not make this claim, since that would be to assert a concept, and his work will insist on the notion of the 'trace', a mark made as if by something passing, rather than the more strict correspondence implied by the term 'concept'. The downside of this, in the period of the initial reception of his work, was that the notion spread that Derrida could no more be summarized than Monty Python's Bolton Choral Society and their leader, Superintendent McGough, could succeed in winning the All-England Summarize Proust Competition (they got as far as 'Proust in his first book wrote about the . . .'). The 'Outwork' (or '*Hors D'Œuvre*') to Derrida's *Dissemination* (1972) begins with the words 'This (therefore) will not have been a book,' and goes on to discuss the famous 'Preface' to Hegel's *Phenomenology of Spirit* (1807) and the 'Introduction' to the *Science of Logic* (1812). These are the leading works of the sort of systematic philosophy against which post-structuralism set its face. The 'Preface' to the *Phenomenology* (like the 'Introduction' to the

Science of Logic) rejects the idea of a preface which can properly explain the work which is to follow. Hegel writes:

> It is customary to preface a work with an explanation of the author's aim, why he wrote the book, and the relationship in which he believes it to stand to other earlier or contemporary treatises on the same subject. In the case of a philosophical work, however, such an explanation seems not only superfluous but, in view of the nature of the subject-matter, even inappropriate and misleading. For whatever might be said about philosophy in a preface – say a historical *statement* of the main drift and the point of view, the general content and results, a string of random assertions and assurances about truth – none of this can be accepted as the way to expound philosophical truth.[38]

Derrida uses this statement in Hegel's preface to demonstrate a complex feature of language. Hegel believes that philosophy consists only of its actual exposition and that it cannot therefore be summarized. However, we can detect in this an anxiety about the very nature of linguistic exposition. While we may have the idea that truth (if it exists) or a concept is a static thing, language unfolds through time (if spoken) and through space (if written). Derrida notes the contradiction that the claim that the preface is impossible is made in a preface, and in a nuanced exposition shows how hard it is for philosophy properly to cope with the manner in which writing outruns truth. Language, which is supposed to be identical with truth, turns out to be a kind of supplement. In much of his early and best-known work – published in *Of Grammatology* (1967), *Writing and Difference* (1967), *Voice and Phenomenon* (1967), *Margins of Philosophy* (1972) – Derrida works through the notion that most attempts to describe language have unwittingly subscribed to a metaphysical idea of truth as a transcendent 'present'. Thinking about language always poses a danger to philosophy because language is not identical with truth, nor is it identical with the person who speaks. Language has always been thought of as speech, not as writing, because in writing it is clear that the verbal object is separated from the mental process of the writer. This mental process can be imagined as a pre-linguistic state, as if concepts could exist without language. If we think of language as writing rather than speech, we think of it as a set of signs – 'traces', Derrida writes – which are independent of the writer/speaker, and cannot properly and completely be folded back into any transcendent truth or concept which existed prior to utterance in the mind of the writer/speaker (the subject). This brings us to the reality – uncomfortable for a certain way of thinking – that language as a set of elements outside us (but not exactly a system or structure) contains a level of play, indeterminacy and polyvalency which is at odds with a narrow notion of truth and concept (in which language would denote fixed identities). Derrida attracts our attention to what we would call the non-identity of language and world, if it were not that language as a set of physical traces (such as sound or writing) is not in a binary fashion opposed to world – an opposition which would be metaphysical, i.e. stem from an organizational or pragmatic imperative to think about things in a certain way – but is part of world, making both world and sign the site of a permanent deferral, drift and irrecuperable motion. The false binary opposition of truth and world is essential to the areas of thought which are termed metaphysics, a component of philosophy which stems from the *Metaphysics* of Aristotle, an attempt to identify the concepts which govern the shape and nature of reality. The central claim of Aristotle's *Metaphysics* is that substance (object) and essence (subjective concept) are identical. Put differently, a thing is identical with the account which is given of it – its *logos*. This is the very nub of what Derrida and others will label logocentrism, and is at the heart of the formal metaphysics which held sway in Western philosophy until the High Middle Ages, in the form of the scholastic version of Aristotle as it became formalized by Thomas Aquinas and his followers. Modern philosophy – for example Descartes – sought to break the stranglehold of scholastic thought, but even in the wake of the challenge to Aristotle many metaphysical assumptions persisted, in part because such assumptions seem to be part of the grammatical structure of Western languages. In twentieth-century philosophy, Martin Heidegger, who was acutely aware of these residues and the binaristic subject–object mode which they imposed on thinking, wrote of bringing about the destruction of metaphysics.[39] In a more cautious translation of Heidegger's *Destruktion*, intended to highlight its sense of de-structuring rather than merely destroying, Derrida speaks of 'deconstruction', a term which has wide resonance today as it is liberally used where we might otherwise use the term critique, but which importantly in his work is intended to substitute a notion of 'living on' in metaphysics as opposed to 'destroying' it.[40] Because our thinking is language, or inhabits language, or is the effect of language – no term will really *do* any longer since the forms of such statements embody the essence of metaphysics, the opposition of a knowing subject to a known object via language which is conceived as a medium, a supplementary, tertium aliquid – because our thinking (is) language, a term which must be used under erasure,[41] then we cannot really emerge from a destroyed metaphysics into something new, but can only shake the bars of the cage, so to speak, or look between the blinds.

The essence of deconstruction is to demonstrate or perform this trembling. Here though are the difficulties in what follows, not from Derrida but in a kind of Derridean industry. Derrida's great art is that he executes writing performances which work through the language in its metaphysical aspects, drawing out the figurative nature of the most abstract and philosophical-looking terms, worrying at the metaphysical implications of the most basic ordinary-language structures. As in the discussion of the Preface in 'Outwork', the point is to unfold in a manner both rigorous and creative the anomalies presented by the attempt to speak philosophically even in the work of the most rigorous practitioners. Literary theorists schooled in New Criticism were strongly drawn to this mode of exposition, since it relied on the very kind of sensibility to trope and grammar in which they had been schooled by the literature, especially Romantic poetry, in which they found most value. Moreover, those who were aware of the philosophical implications of New Critical practice (as expounded by Ransom) could easily see that ontology – the science of being – had always been a motivation of their art, even if close reading as such had never done anything to advance the thinking through of 'being' in formal philosophical terms. Derrida's work was performative in exactly the way that New Critical explication was performative. The attraction of Derrida was strengthened by the fact that it was possible to take him in different ways. He could be enjoyed in a straightforward way as a rhetorician. The philosophically inclined, who gravitated to his more weightily philosophical essays, such as those found in *Margins of Philosophy*, found much to endorse in his expositions of the rhetorical nature of philosophy and exposure of raw metaphysical nerve endings. We can add that his writing has a romantic element, is aimed at a sublime beyond which is teasingly exposed (in much the same way that Heidegger often appears to hover on the brink of revelation). There is a psychoanalytic Derrida also, for those so inclined, since a key element in his work links philosophy of the subject to Freud's unconscious (following Lacan), notably in 'Freud and the Scene of Writing' (in *Writing and Difference*). Derrida is not committed to Freudian terms, however, but to a reading of Freud which is participatory and deconstructive – a later volume, *Resistances* (1996), sets clear deconstructive water between Derrida and Freud/Lacan. What Derrida does not do is demand any kind of political assent – although the political implications of his thinking are in part worked out by him in later works – and Derrida's threat to Marx remained muted by his comparative neglect of Marx, at least until the later *Spectres of Marx* (1993), which only really began to show what a full treatment of the metaphysics of materialist philosophy might have looked like. The downside of this attraction was that, like New Criticism, it created a great number of imitators. The impossibility of writing a preface, for example, is replicated in the prefaces of numerous translations and collections of Derrida's work in English, which performatively imitate the master. We are told that Derrida cannot be summarized, translated, paraphrased or in any way anticipated, in terms that imitate and replicate Derrida's own rhetorical working. Derrida's method is attractive and disciplined, although its own claim to be non-conceptual and thereby resist summary – a claim which Derrideans staunchly defend – can become irritating when repeated so often and at such length. Derrida's work does in fact open on to a politics of a certain kind, as we shall see, but part of its initial attraction seems to have been that it didn't actually ask people to believe very much – of a social nature at least. Marxists were suspicious of Derrida. They didn't find a way to make a critique – since in any case the rhetorical and performative method would consign the truth-based notion of critique to the side of Western metaphysics – and in a way the problem of Derrida reception has been that a substantial proportion of his readers have been either fans (immersed in the method) or sceptics (insufficiently immersed), while philosophers, at that time if not more recently, steered clear. Derrida could be seen as a Xeno figure, endlessly producing paradoxes all based on the same discrepancy of language and reality, or as a Sophist, constantly referring arguments of truth to the level of rhetoric. In its most unattractive aspect, Derrideanism can take the form of a new version of Wildean irony. Since any rhetoric is open to deconstruction, any claim can be 'deconstructed' at will by anyone so minded. The rhetorician can in these terms always trump any attempt at substantial discussion, but what is left standing is usually a question of cultural capital and the politics of education – deconstruction has the considerable merit of allowing one to cash in one's own cleverness.

Finally, a note on Julia Kristeva, who deserves more space than I have allowed. A difference between Kristeva and Derrida lies in Kristeva's commitment to psychoanalysis. One of her key early notions, the semiotic *chora*, can be construed as a version of the beyond of language enabling and involved in meaning, though irreducibly prior to it, which is found in Derridean *différance*, but in Kristeva there is a much more material attempt to think about pre-symbolic language and its relationship to the maternal body than anything in Derrida. There is a strand of French feminism – so called outside France although identifications are more complex for those so labelled – which is committed to textual avant-gardism based on projections of the idea of the body which take light from an assumed opposition between patriarchal law and feminine desire. These ideas were played out in various ways in the work of Kristeva, Hélène Cixous and Luce Irigaray. This work has had a continuing general impact on thinking about women and literature, although the uptake has been rather different as between Britain and America, where in Britain the tradition of socialist feminism tended to be of a practical bent, and the understanding was clear that French feminism proceeded from a bourgeois quadrant, while in America a more highbrow and, in social terms, differently rooted version of feminism made more – if still guarded use – of the work of these important if not entirely assimilable figures.

Chapter 6

Enlightenment and Modernity

A major strand in theoretical thought which has had persistent influence throughout the period of high theory until the present day has been the attempt to think about the nature of contemporary society as a perverted product of the Enlightenment. This strand of thought can be traced back to Nietzsche, in philosophy, and to Georg Lukács in the area of literary and cultural theory. Lukács was a Hungarian Marxist whose work pre-dates the struggle over Marxist ideas in the 1970s, and his ideas were heavily drawn upon at that time, being available in important translations issued in London by the Merlin Press. Lukács was admired for his grasp of the Hegelian roots of Marxism, and regarded with mixed feelings for his defence of the bourgeois novel and attacks on modernism.

Lukács' *History and Class Consciousness* (1922) is a classic text of what has now become known as Western Marxism – that strand of Marxism which seeks to restore the philosophical dimension of Marx's work by referring it to Marx's reading of Hegel, a process which in Lukács' early writings involved a certain amount of reconstructive ingenuity, since the key text in this regard – Marx's *Economic and Philosophical Manu-scripts* of 1844 – was not published until 1932.[1] The most important essay in the collection is 'Reification and the Consciousness of the Pro-letariat', in which Lukács describes the process of reification involved in commodification in a reading of Marx inflected by the sociologists Max Weber and Georg Simmel, and profoundly influenced by Hegel. The term reification (*Verdinglichung*) is derived from Marx and desig-nates the manner in which capitalist social relations render consciousness thing-like (re-ification = thing-ification). As a metaphor it is question-able; Louis Althusser, who suggested key modifications to the Marxist theory of ideology in 'Marxism and Humanism' (1963), argued that the then widespread obsession with reification effaced questions of power by exaggerating the role of thingliness in Marx's work. Nevertheless, Lukács' work made both possible and necessary the shift in Althusser's work from an emphasis on ideology as ideas with a conscious influence to ideology as the system or structure of representations which unconsciously shape social relations.[2] Moreover, Lukács' work anticipates the greater part of work on the social determination of consciousness which runs through Adorno and Horkheimer, Michel Foucault, Jean Baudrillard and others.

Lukács utilizes Marx's analysis of the commodity to develop the theory of ideology into a general concept of social reification. Reified consciousness extends into the thought processes of a bourgeoisie structurally incapable of understanding the real nature of social relations. Only the proletariat can grasp the real nature of social relations, when in social revolution it emerges as the collective subject–object of history, and in doing so fulfils the dialectical process described by Marx. On this reading of Marx, which emphasizes the Hegelian component of Marx's thought, only the revolutionary proletariat can, through action, realize the project of critical philosophy in reality, and not just in philosophy.

The reified consciousness which must be shattered by proletarian revolution is analysed by Lukács via Marx's theory of the commodity as found in Book I of *Capital*. Lukács claims that the commodity is 'the central, structural problem of capitalist society in all its aspects', and asks 'how far is commodity exchange together with its structural consequences able to influence the *total* outer and inner life of society'.[3] Lukács constantly refers to the notion of totality throughout this essay as throughout much of his work. The idea of a social totality is of course roundly rejected within the various discourses of postmodernity and of general liberal progressive thought of the last two decades. It sometimes seems to be assumed that the concept of totality is itself an intellectual imposition, a gesture of the mind which misrecognizes the plurality of events in reality, and which itself must be negated at the level of thought. In other words, it is only the tradition of idealism which keeps alive a notion of totality, and we must reject totalizing logic if we wish to be open to otherness and the micrology of diversity in the world. However, Lukács treats totality not as an idealized category of the mind, but as an actually achieved social fact, in a limited but ubiquitous sense – as the commodity and commodity relations. Lukács' concept of totality is based in an analysis of production. He claims that the commodity 'can only be understood in its undistorted essence when it becomes the universal category of society as a whole':

Only then does the commodity become crucial for the subjugation of men's consciousness to the forms in which this reification finds expression and for their attempts to comprehend this process or to rebel against its disastrous effects and liberate themselves from servitude to the 'second nature' so created.[4]

When we only make what we need, things present themselves to us as use values – i.e. as things manufactured for human use. Once we can produce more than we need, things present themselves to us as exchange values – commodities. In Lukács' terms, with the creation of exchange value – of the commodity form – comes a new human horizon which he terms 'second nature'. This has both objective and subjective effects. Things are changed as things:

> This rational objectification conceals above all the immediate – qualitative and material – character of things as things. When use values appear universally as commodities they acquire a new objectivity, a new substantiality which they did not possess in an age of episodic exchange and which destroys their original and authentic substantiality. As Marx observes: 'Private property *alienates* not only the individuality of men, but also of things.'

Consciousness is changed:

> The transformation of the commodity relation into a thing of 'ghostly objectivity' cannot therefore content itself with the reduction of all objects for the gratification of human needs to commodities. It stamps its imprint upon the whole consciousness of man; his qualities and abilities are no longer an organic part of his personality, they are things he can 'own' or 'dispose of' like the various objects of the external world.[5]

These ideas – that things themselves and human consciousness are altered by commodification – will recur in various manifestations of the cultural theory of late capitalism. Lukács himself supplied his own substantial contributions to literary theory in his defence of the realist novel against literary modernism.

Lukács' debate with modernism became very well known in the late 1970s with the publication by New Left Books of the anthology *Aesthetics and Politics* (1977), which also collected together key pieces by Adorno, Benjamin, Ernst Bloch and Bertolt Brecht. In fact, Lukács' various writings on the novel were already comparatively well known in translation. These included the much admired *The Theory of the Novel* (1920), *The Historical Novel* (1955) and other work on realism.

Whatever Lukács' virtues as a literary theorist, it was only his early work which could be read unbracketed, as it were, since association with Stalinist cultural politics left much of the work inflected in ways that did not well match the New Left politics of his readers in the 1970s. For that reason, it is probable that the publication of *Aesthetics and Politics* confirmed the eclipse of Lukács and the beginning of the rise of Adorno and Benjamin as major subjects of New Left interest. That said, even bad theory by Lukács still reads better than more agreeable theory from some other quarters, and his arguments against modernism are worth reprising.

The NLB collection includes an exchange between Lukács and the theorist Ernst Bloch which took place in 1938. Bloch's piece defends the at that time dated aesthetic of expressionist literature against Lukács' attack on it. The discussion is framed in terms of an aesthetic avant-garde art which seeks to embody the isolated experience of the suffering consciousness (expressionist poetry) versus the ability of realist fiction to depict the workings of the social totality and so demystify the one-sided picture presented by immediate consciousness. Bloch and Lukács begin from a commitment to Marxism, so the disagreement between them concerns the politics of aesthetics. Capitalism breaks social reality into fragments, according to Lukács, so the individual will experience reality in a partial and fragmented way. However, capitalism itself constitutes a unity, a totality, albeit one which is not present to consciousness but can only be arrived at intellectually. Therefore a literature which seeks only to reflect and imitate the fragmentation of individual consciousness – such as expressionism or the more contemporary surrealism – is not representing a truth (that reality is fragmentary) but simply fails to make available the reality of capitalist social relations as a totality which lies outside consciousness. As an example, Lukács contrasts James Joyce's *Ulysses* (1922) – which he classifies as surrealist – to Thomas Mann's *The Magic Mountain* (1924), the work of a 'true realist' who analytically presents the bourgeois nature of his characters, thereby making available the nature of social reality. That Lukács and Bloch each take Joyce to be a surrealist in his depiction of consciousness reflects the level of assimilation of Joyce's work at that time and does not reflect the type of view which might be taken today. Lukács agrees with Bloch that there is a need for an aesthetic avant-garde, analogous to the political avant-garde, which will show the way forward for the future. However, Lukács argues that existing avant-gardes such as surrealism cannot fulfil this function, but that future realists can. What is needed is not a rejection of the bourgeois tradition in fiction, but an immersion in it. By embracing modern literary tradition, the full political implications of bourgeois fiction can be recognized, and the grounds of future realism prepared.[6]

As ever with issues regarding literary theory, the dates of this discussion are critical. The late 1930s had seen the fullest reaction of both Stalin and Hitler against modernism in the arts in all its forms, with many avant-gardists silenced or even killed in the Soviet Union, and modernism banned and vilified as Jewish in Nazi Germany. It is probable that the massive hostility to modernism in these states in the 1930s has contributed to a willingness to defend modernism among left-wing critics in later decades. Lukács' position, articulated so shortly before the Second World War, might seem like a road that cannot be taken from any modern perspective. However, his Hegelian vocabulary, in which the falseness of the immediate particular is always opposed to the truth of the general totality, is in fact repeated in numerous subsequent theoretical accounts of the culture of modernity or postmodernity, except in reverse, with the fragmentary and inassimilable defended against the claims of the general. In defence of Lukács, we should note that the idea of totality he deploys is a materialist not an idealist one – to claim that capitalism is a totality, while itself open to question, is not the same as claiming that the world itself is a totality in principle available to consciousness.

Lukács had a major impact on Marxist literary theory in Britain during the 1970s. Less centrally, the work of Theodor Adorno and Max Horkheimer, key figures of the so-called Frankfurt School who took up residence in the United States during the Second World War, as well as the work of their associate Walter Benjamin, were also becoming known in translations issued in London. Adorno and Benjamin have become properly and fully known in the English-speaking world only in more recent decades, having been extensively translated in the United States, but while knowledge of their work has increased among dedicated readers, their general influence has certainly declined. Adorno and Horkheimer are principally known for their collaborative work, *Dialectic of Enlightenment* (1944). This multifaceted work of political, sociological and cultural speculation offers an account of Enlightenment not as a progression towards freedom, but as the increasing subordination of all human beings in modern society to the rule of reason and calculation, with a consequent diminishment, brought about by a kind of psychic mutilation, of individual autonomy. Unlike the type of Marxist theory we have been examining, Adorno and Horkheimer are highly pessimistic about the prospects of revolutionary social change, and generalize their portrait of the totally administered society in such a way that it includes Nazism, American capitalism and Soviet communism. Their work has certainly had a broad influence; alongside Herbert Marcuse, another early Frankfurt associate who similarly attempted to combine psychoanalysis with social and cultural theory, their influence on the New Left in the United States was significant.

Adorno is perhaps given most credit as a theorist of modernist music, although his aesthetic writings range across the whole of music, include essays on literature which fill two volumes, and contain substantial material on other arts and, in particular, on the modern phenomenon which he names the 'culture industry'. Adorno's early training was as a composer, and he studied briefly with Alban Berg. Adorno even published a few compositions in an expressionist vein, but his main emphasis came to be on the theory of modern music, in particular in terms of a defence of the meaningful 'inwardness' of expressionist music (a category which included the first compositional period of Schoenberg) against the reaction against expressionist emotionalism of the 1920s called the 'New Objectivity', which was typified by the music of Hindemith and Stravinsky, which he described in terms of its motoric rhythms, harsh sounds, and empty phrase-making. Adorno associated it with ragtime and jazz, on which composers of 'serious' music sometimes drew albeit in a mediated form. Adorno's work on music of the 1920s and 1930s includes two strands: a defence of the modernism of Schoenberg against that of Hindemith and Stravinsky, realized in *Philosophy of Modern Music* (1948), which draws on an interpretation of the sociology of music that maintains a key place for Beethoven, and a critical denunciation of jazz or light music, in essays such as 'On Jazz' (1937), which views jazz (with reference to the 1920s and 1930s) as the commodified production of industrial modernity. Jazz opposes metrical regimentation, like the time-clock, to a mutilated individual ego which only gestures against the dominant beat through syncopation and soloistic liberties before returning to it and accepting the domination of the social whole. In Adorno's analysis, the development of a culture industry which included the various forms of mass-distributed media was met by the increasingly separate development of a modernist art which eschewed audience and concentrated on developing according to its own inner laws. The result was a distortion of both kinds of art arising from the social conditions of the centralization of social administration which drove the process. In a famous phrase, Adorno calls the dependent (low) and autonomous (high) elements in culture 'torn halves of an integral freedom to which, however, they do not add up'.[7]

While Adorno's commentary on music has been an essential strand in the cultural theory of music, his treatment of mass-market music as a commodity form has tended to attract charges of elitism, even though the 'torn halves' phrase clearly signals what Adorno argues elsewhere: that the inner nature of autonomous, modernist art is also determined by administered culture, since the very division between autonomous and dependent art is the product of the modernization process. The various essays on jazz have aroused suspicion among commentators less versed in Adorno's work, who claim that the substantial African American role in the creation of jazz means that it should be regarded as a serious cultural endeavour. Indeed, eminent supporters of Adorno's theory of serious music have regarded his treatment of jazz as inadequate,[8] even though his early writings on music clearly show that the conceptual basis of his claims against jazz is identical with that of claims against the music of Hindemith (empty, schematically recursive, lacking musical development).[9] Although Adorno's writings on the culture industry have secured a hearing, especially among theorists, and even though the general influence of the Frankfurt School (albeit more directly via Herbert Marcuse) in US culture has been substantial, a major sticking point for many remains the fact that, both as producers and as consumers of art, the ethnic and class groups favoured by liberals and leftists have been generally located on the popular side of culture. Although Adorno was an early and important theorist and researcher of film, radio and television, the very acuteness and acerbity of his insights, often aimed at the over-affirmative celebration of consumer culture emanating from America, sit uncomfortably even with those who regard his analytical assault on consumer culture as a persuasive elaboration of, and journey beyond, basic Marxist principles.

Dialectic of Enlightenment, which combines Adorno's analysis of modernism with Horkheimer's Hegelianism, goes much further than Lukács, whose work had taken the institution of serious literature for granted and gone little beyond the terms of Marx's concept of the commodity in its analysis of commodification. One respect in which this work anticipates a great deal of subsequent theory is in its focus on Enlightenment. Lukács proffered a theory of literature under capitalism; the shift to a theory of culture under intensifying rationalization is of marked significance. In political terms, without being explicit about doing so, it treats the Soviet Union as a case of 'administered society'; in theoretical terms, its basis is a significant doubt about the role of reason in society in general, and in particular about the core Marxist idea of progress defined in terms of the realization of reason through the agency of the proletariat as the subject of history. As the Enlightenment becomes the object of critique, the focus is shifted away from relations of production and the circulation of money, even though labour organization remains central. The result in the text of *Dialectic of Enlightenment* as it was republished in 1947 is a curious generalization of political reference and a peculiar bracketing of its Marxist premises. This unsettling of focus was in part the consequence of the displacement of the Frankfurt School to the United States in the 1930s. In 1947 the House Committee on Un-American Activities interviewed Hans Eisler and Bertolt Brecht, both associates of Adorno, and in the same year alterations were made to the text of *Dialectic of Enlightenment* which removed references to capitalism – so 'capitalism' became 'existing conditions', 'capital' became 'economic system', 'class society' became 'domination' and so on.[10] Jürgen Habermas, as a young graduate student of Adorno and Horkheimer after they returned to Frankfurt University in 1949, regretted that Frankfurt critical theory had become so politically muted and self-centred, and also realized that the critical theory of society on which the cultural analysis of the School was supposed to rest had never been properly articulated. In particular, the emphasis on Enlightenment presented a problem. If capitalism was the object of critique, then a theory of the Soviet Union was missing. If the subjugation of nature by reason was the object, then this must be taking place in both capitalist and non-capitalist society, and reference to the commodity form was not relevant.[11]

'The program of the Enlightenment was the disenchantment of the world; the dissolution of myths and the substitution of knowledge for fancy,' states *Dialectic*, 'yet the fully enlightened earth radiates disaster triumphant.' Knowledge is power over a nature which is to be disenchanted, freed from myth, but 'myth turns into enlightenment and nature into mere objectivity'.[12] Magic was plural, but Enlightenment subjects all to the same domination, which extends from outer nature to inner nature, so that all aspects of the human, now quantified as labour, are subject to rationalizing principles, in a transition which conflates scientific reason and societal rationalization. The whole point about freedom as philosophically described by Marx was that it would entail a shift from the realm of necessity (dependence on nature) to the realm of freedom (independence from need). In a movement which Adorno and Horkheimer described in terms of a kind of dialectical paradox, Enlightenment has brought about not a freedom from the necessity of nature but an absolute subordination to it: 'By taking everything unique and individual under its tutelage, it left the uncomprehended whole the freedom, as domination, to strike back at human existence and consciousness by way of things.'[13] Lukács' analysis of the reification of consciousness returns here in a more speculative mode, and the vengeful things now stand for mute and pre-human nature striking back at humanity by rendering mechanical every aspect of human social relations – work and culture. 'The Culture Industry: Enlightenment as Mass Deception' is the most often cited section of *Dialectic of Enlightenment*. It extends the pessimistic account of Enlightenment into the domain of 'films, radio and magazines' said to 'make up a system which is uniform as a whole and in every part'.[14] The culture-industry product is governed by the creation of 'effect', not by any need to realize the inner logic of the work, which is replaced by a formula; different market categories ensure that there is something for everyone and no one can escape the system; culture is now a branch of administration and its message is subordination of the individual to the social hierarchy; even where its message seems to code individualism, the individual is always returned to the mass in a manner that harnesses the sadistic laughter of the cinema audience; amusement is the prolongation of work; the commodified product of the culture industry is shaped for a distracted audience; the inner freedom to which the subject once aspired has now been replaced by an administratively organized pseudo-individuality. The essay proceeds relentlessly with this type of provocative claim, speculative propositions supported by analytical and polemical consistency if not by always rigorously arguable links. The intensity of this piece, characterized by paratactic leaps, have led to its being sometimes held up as an example of modernist textuality in its own right. A key intellectual thread which recurs throughout this piece is the complete subordination of the particular to the general. The Adorno–Horkheimer account of mass culture and the philosophical aesthetics which accompany it only caught on among English-speaking Marxists to any great extent once the reality of radical and revolutionary politics faded. In terms of literary theory and of any area outside music, Adorno and Horkheimer yield more in the way of speculative satisfaction than they do in terms of any iterable methodology. It is instead the thread of anti-Enlightenment thought which comes to characterize much of the social and cultural theory that succeeds *Dialectic of Enlightenment*. The entry of this line of thinking into literary theory, or more exactly into the practice of literary studies, comes not via Adorno and Horkheimer but via Michel Foucault.

The impact of the work of Michel Foucault on English studies took a long time to develop, yet arguably Foucault is the single greatest influence on the shape and content of literary studies since the breach of theory was opened by the political movements of Marxism and feminism and the intellectual movement of structural linguistics. Foucault wrote very little about literature as such, and in general treated it as a transgressive force as opposed to a discursive norm, implicitly accepting the types of models proposed in France by the *Tel Quel* group, among others. It is ironic that one of Foucault's key legacies has been the treatment of literature as a discourse and as part of discourse, since Foucault himself analysed discourses in the context of science and other social practices in their institutional contexts, and his work on literature in pieces such as 'Language to Infinity' (published in *Tel Quel* in 1963), which emphasizes the excess, terror and defiance of literature, are less influential on literary scholars today than his work on sexuality and the prison. Translations of Foucault's work into English appeared early, as part of a series on the 'Human Sciences' edited by R. D. Laing. *Folie et déraison: histoire de la folie à l'âge classique* (1961) appeared in part as *Madness and Civilisation* (1967); *Naissance de la clinique* (1963) as *Birth of the Clinic* (1973); *Les Mots et les choses: une archéologie des sciences humaines* (1966) as *The Order of Things* (1970); *L'Archéologie du savoir* (1969) as *The Archaeology of Knowledge* (1972). The urgency of translating Foucault was recognized by Penguin, who issued *The History of Sexuality: An Introduction* (1976) in the year of its appearance in France, followed by *Discipline and Punish: The Birth of the Prison* (1977), which had appeared originally in 1975. The first book-length treatment of Foucault seems to have been Alan Sheridan's *Michel Foucault: The Will to Truth* (1980), which was followed by several others, and the two remaining volumes of the *History of Sexuality* received prompt translations in 1985–6.

On the Althusserian left of the 1970s, which might have been expected to at least investigate Foucault, knowledge of his work seems to have been slight. A measure of this may be taken from the basically Althusserian Essex Sociology of Literature conferences which began in 1976. The 1976 Essex Conference on 'Literature, Society and the Sociology of Literature' featured numerous contributions on aspects of Marxist theory but made no reference to Foucault; Stuart Hall's opening 'Critical Survey of the Theoretical and Practical Achievements of the Last Ten Years' concentrated on Raymond Williams and Louis Althusser, while Francis Barker led a workshop designed to rehabilitate Trotsky's literary criticism.[15] Only the most fleeting reference to Foucault can be found until the 'Politics of Theory' conference in 1982, where one paper concentrating on Foucault seems in context and content eccentric, while the first instalment of Toril Moi's *Sexual/Textual Politics* (later a 1985 book) mentions Foucault not at all; the speaker of honour is the Althusserian literary theorist Renée Balibar, while the most forward-looking component is Homi K. Bhaba, making a tentative offering on 'Difference, Discrimination and the Discourse of Colonialism'.[16] Exceptions to the general Althusserian tenor at Essex were few: the rare, high-octane deconstructionist contribution of

Maud Ellmann's 'Floating the Pound' is almost anomalous;[17] otherwise the main growing element on the theoretical horizon is the work of Julia Kristeva, and very much in second place Derrida. It is as if Foucault is barely on the horizon for left theory, even at that 1982 conference where some future strands of theoretical development can be discerned. Another barometer of the reception of Foucault is the very brief, passing reference to his work in Eagleton's *Literary Theory* (1983). In the literary journals, discussions of Foucault were uncommon before the early 1980s; by contrast, the philosopher Jean Baudrillard had published *Oublier Foucault* (*Forget Foucault*) as early as 1977.

This apparently slow uptake of Foucault's work probably has several aspects. To begin with, the role of *The History of Sexuality* in his reception in literary studies is obviously crucial; it evidently had struck no one that earlier works, which appeared in essence to deal with the history of science and of knowledge, had pressing political and cultural implications. Yet even *The History of Sexuality* seems to have taken several years to make its presence felt to the extent that discussions of the body in discourse now have a political or ethical immediacy about which many can agree. It is probable that resistance to Foucault, to the extent that it was not simply a matter of lack of knowledge of his work, was based in the politics of his particular brand of intellectual history. The first major books of 1961 and 1963 deal with the history of psychiatry in particular and of medical science in general, both sciences which, as Foucault later remarked, are 'profoundly enmeshed in social structures', and therefore as much social as scientific.[18] *The Order of Things* (1966) attempts a history of the human sciences in terms which eschew the idea of progressive development in thinking and substitute the idea of shifting epistemes, epochal principles of thought which are the underlying unconscious structure making possible the different sciences of a period, much as the Saussurean *langue* makes possible the individual speech act, or *parole*. These epistemes are of three types denoting three broad periods – the Renaissance, the Classical and the Modern. A key principle for Foucault is that the shift from one episteme to another loosely resembles the 'paradigm shifts' in the natural sciences analysed by Thomas Kuhn in *The Structure of Scientific Revolutions* (1962), although Foucault in fact takes the idea of 'epistemic break' or 'rupture' from Gaston Bachelard. The challenge of this model is that the Enlightenment notion of a gradual progression of reason is entirely bypassed, as is the corresponding notion of progress in social matters. Indeed, Foucault's reading of madness rather romanticizes mental illness by imagining it more as an object of the process of medicalization than as an organic illness; his account of madness, taken in the later context of his work on the prison and on sexuality, tends to offer a model of inverted Enlightenment, in which the disciplinary surveillance and control of the body become intensified in the modern era.

The use of the episteme in *The Order of Things* owes much to structuralism. The strategic advantage of structuralism as deployed in anthropology had been that it did not read social structures in terms of our attempted reconstruction of their development as a narrative of 'social progress', but instead analysed each system in terms of the functionality of its components, grasped by analogy with other similar systems which in turn pointed to an underlying regularity which could be thought of as a structure. The use of structuralism was advantageous in displacing conventional accounts of the human sciences which adopted a standard intellectual history model that projected a slow (and comparatively independent) progress of disciplinary knowledges throughout the ages. Yet the structuralism of *The Order of Things* is too bald, and the construction of vast epochal epistemes uncomfortably resembles Heidegger's approach to the history of thought.[19] Foucault's subsequent book, *The Archaeology of Knowledge* (1969), attempts to correct this by recourse to the term 'archive' and, much more influentially, a model of 'discourse'. Foucault was angry to be termed a structuralist, claiming to use none of the methods and terms of structuralism,[20] yet it is hard to avoid seeing the term discourse as being shaped by structuralist assumptions even though much of Foucault's commentary on his use of the term seems designed to avoid not merely the label, but the problems of structuralism which he recognizes – namely, that structuralism projects a socially abstracted and static object. Since the term 'discourse' has become ubiquitous in modern literary theory and scholarship, the moment of its introduction, and subsequent commentary on it by Foucault, are of intense interest. On the one hand, its structuralist residue and the accompanying post-structuralist commentary make the term internally conflicted in a manner which is interesting to say the least. Yet on the other hand, it seems that what has happened in the practical use of the term is that the process of inquiry associated with it has been dropped – Foucault himself moved on from 'discourse' to 'power' as his attention shifted from linguistic formations to actual social institutions, before moving on in his later work to an ethics of desire. The term discourse in literary academic work now tends to be simply a rubric under which phenomena are allowed to appear, so a discourse of this that or the other topic will be found in certain literary and extra-literary objects, and discursive regularities noted, often critically. This approach has created a great variety of new objects for criticism, more than the abstract notion of boundless 'text' had any prospect of doing on its own; at the same time, the casting of objects as belonging to a discourse defined by any regularity which the observer cares to observe, assembled without necessarily exhausting the possible field of objects, creates the doubt that 'discourses' subject to analysis are simply assemblages of items on which the commentator has seen fit, perhaps for reasons of political disposition, to pass remarks. In that respect, a concept of discourse loosened from its Foucauldian context as a major challenge to dominant models of intellectual history may simply have slipped us into a new academic comfort zone.

The Archaeology of Knowledge defines its task in terms of the need to get rid of notions of tradition, influence, development, evolution, and Hegelian 'spirit', and to question the formalized divisions between recognized discursive genres such as science, literature, philosophy, religion, history and fiction. These apparent unities should be made the object of the analysis of discourses, not treated as being the discourses themselves. Foucault, like Barthes, emphasizes above all the false unity of the book or collection of authorial works (*œuvre*). Against false unities defined by disciplinary names, the physical binding of the book or the conceptual binding of the author name must be set a new openness to discourse (which indeed resembles the 'text' of Barthes and *Tel Quel*):

> We must renounce all those themes whose function is to ensure the infinite continuity of discourse and its secret presence to itself in the interplay of a constantly recurring absence. We must be ready to receive every moment of discourse in its sudden irruption. Discourse must not be referred to the distant presence of the origin, but treated as and when it occurs.
>
> One is led therefore to the project of a *pure description of discursive events* as the horizon for the search for the unities that form within it. This distinction is easily distinguishable from an analysis of the language. [. . .] A language (*langue*) is still a system for possible statements, a finite body of rules that authorizes an infinite number of performances. The field of discursive events, on the other hand, is a grouping that is always finite and limited at any moment to the linguistic sequences that have been formulated. [. . .] The description of the events of discourse poses a quite different question: how is it that one particular statement appeared rather than another?
>
> This description of discourses is in opposition to the history of thought. [. . .] We do not seek below what is manifest the half silent murmur of another discourse. [The proper question is] what is the specific existence that emerges from what is said and from nowhere else?[21]

These statements reveal the fundamental shift which suggested the term post-structuralist as a valid label for Foucault's work. The idea of structure was at odds with the idea of the event. A system does not permit a singularity to emerge. Every possible event is predicted by it. A place is assigned to everything that might happen. The observer, looking only for regularities, will tend to assign particular events to already determined structural unities. It will be seen that in this reference to the discursive event the notion of event, of the singular, is valorized here as in a good deal of the thought of the 1980s which began to be labelled postmodernist, as a gravitation towards 'event' led the move away from structure. We might also note, in literary-theoretical terms, that this notion of reading sensitively in terms of the discursively singular event does, if only at the most abstract level, recall the reading protocols of Ransom's New Criticism, with its anti-systemic, ontological goals. Be that as it may, what we must also note here is the inevitable tension between the implicit demand of the term discourse – that written or spoken artefacts be analysed in terms of groupings and affinities – and the likely outcome that these groupings will become in turn new, governing structures.

> The problem is at once to distinguish among events, to differentiate the networks and levels to which they belong, and to reconstitute the lines along which they are connected and engender one another. From this follows a refusal of analyses couched in terms of the symbolic field or the domain of signifying structures, and a recourse to analyses in terms of the genealogy of relations of force, strategic developments and tactics. Here I believe that one's analogy should not be to the great model of language (*langue*) and signs, but to that of war and battle. The history which bears and determines us has the form of war rather than that of a language: relations of power, not relations of meaning. History has no 'meaning', though this is not to say that it is absurd or incoherent. On the contrary, it is intelligible [. . .]. Neither the dialectic, as a logic of contradictions, nor semiotics, as the structure of communication, can account for the intrinsic intelligibility of conflicts.[22]

To grasp why Foucault's work has been so widely taken up it is better to turn from technical problems associated with the term 'discourse' to the politics associated with his work. In a 1977 interview of remarkable clarity, Foucault articulated the politics of his work in terms of his rejection of Marxism, especially in its highly centralized French form, and his desire to identify more broadly the modes of the exercise of social power beyond the single conflict of class of the Marxist model. Foucault did not make these remarks in terms of the politics of the social movements of this or any later period – the politics of women, sexual orientation, ethnicity – instead his points of reference remain psychiatry and the prison system. His remarks make clear though what Anglophone literary theorists were able to work out for themselves: that the route of substituting 'discourse' and 'power' for 'ideology' and 'capitalism' greatly augmented the analytical means available outside Marxism, especially in terms of Marxism's tendency to understand all forms of oppression as elements of capitalist oppression. It is easy to see why Marxist theorists would have remained hostile to this approach, although the 'threat' presented to Marxism might better be thought of as a constructive one. In the 'Truth and Power' interview, Foucault claims that the real way in which power operated only became visible (in France) after the events of 1968 at a grass roots level. This affirmation of grass roots oppositions, in contrast to the monolith of Communist Party and trades unions, becomes an axiom of post-1968 politics in many quarters. Not only Marxist organization, but basic Marxist concepts are questioned by Foucault. The concept of ideology is faulted for three reasons: (1) 'it always stands in virtual opposition to something which is supposed to count as truth'; (2) 'it refers to something of the order of a subject'; (3) 'it stands in a secondary position relative to something which functions as its infrastructure, as its material, economic determinant.'[23] These remarks on the concept of ideology bring charges that are not easily answered without a good deal of revision of Marx and Engels. The rejection of 'philosophy of the subject' which was a common cry of post-structuralists at that time makes clear, as Foucault elaborates it in this interview, that the 'subject' is the 'spirit' of Hegel, the revolutionary proletariat of Marx, as well as the phenomenological subject of knowledge of Husserl and Heidegger. This knowing subject is of course the principal intellectual target of Foucault at every turn, and in this any difference from the basic anti-humanist principles of Althusser disappears. In place of 'the subject' Foucault calls for a genealogy, 'that is, a form of history which can account for the constitution of knowledges, discourses, domains of objects etc. without having to make reference to a subject which is either transcendental in relation to a field of events or runs in its empty sameness throughout the course of history'.[24] In the latter part of his œuvre, the second and third volumes of the *History of Sexuality*, this anti-humanism brought about a return to a type of ethics which has proved consonant with the spirit of much that has followed in the literary theory of the 1990s. We examine ethics in Chapter 8, but for now I will move on to other aspects of anti-Enlightenment thought in critical theory and to the short-lived but heady speculative buzz surrounding the term 'postmodernism'.

*

The flotation of the terms 'postmodern', 'postmodernism', 'postmodernist' is really a phenomenon of the 1980s. Certainly, the term had been used earlier, if only occasionally, principally by Ihab Hassan in the discussion of innovative fiction after Joyce,[25] and in architecture. The early use of the term should not mask the phenomenon of postmodernism of the 1980s. What is notable about postmodernism is that it has many hallmarks of a speculative commercial attempt. Setting aside any question of the seriousness and integrity of those who employed the term, postmodernism can be viewed as a popularizing and market phenomenon. In effect, it was the brand name under which a number of intellectual currents in cultural practice and theory, philosophy, sociology and a variety of other disciplines came together and were allowed to appear. Postmodernism was unlike Marxism, which had a foundational political thought at its origin as well as a political practice, unlike feminism, which had a clear constituency but a very plural theoretical basis and practice, and unlike deconstruction or post-structuralism, which were associated with very specific theories and practices. Postmodernism by contrast had no central theorist, central constituency, or even a specific domain. The term served greatly positive purposes, in that it was a way for specialized debates and arcane materials to enter the public sphere. Like the kinds of label used by avant-garde art movements such as futurism, the label constituted an effective advertising base and a useful organizing principle for associations, whether artistic or academic, and it came to provide a route between academics and journalists, who made frequent use of the term. Of course, the very fashionability of the term meant that it was prone to all sorts of glib misappropriations. In part, the fall into disuse of the term academically reflects the emptying out of most of its meaning by constant journalistic repetition. Something similar has happened with terms such as 'deconstruct', 'critique', 'ideology', which are used without regard to their *architexte*.[26] Yet while those terms have very specific trajectories, the term postmodernism was already a comparatively empty vessel, the origins of which do not amount to a coherent theory. It is probable that postmodernism has always had more enemies than friends. Marxist commentators, responding to the perceived relativism of the term, produced volumes denouncing postmodernism which were first put to the effort of constructing it. In this respect, these eager critics are reminiscent of Wyndham Lewis, who took it on himself in the 1920s to denounce the spirit of his age as manifested across cultural, philosophical, economic, political and social doctrines, in idiosyncratic surveys such as *The Art of Being Ruled* (1926) and *Time and Western Man* (1927). Lewis had little in common with the Marxist commentators on postmodernism, but like them he put himself to the trouble of constructing the very thing he wanted to denounce. During the high period of postmodernism, the curious were likely to turn to polemical and scholarly works directed against postmodernism in order to find out what it was – works such as David Harvey's *The Condition of Postmodernity* (1989), Alex Callinicos' *Against Postmodernism* (1989), or Christopher Norris' *What's Wrong with Postmodernism* (1990) – useful volumes which seemed to treat postmodernism as a collective cultural phenomenon more seriously than any of its advocates who, by contrast, were mostly content to take responsibility for only one corner of the field. Although postmodernism is exhausted as a term in literary studies and in cultural studies in general, it still circulates in other fields; lawyers and theologians are more likely to be found complaining about postmodernism than anyone in literary studies. This may be because postmodernism in these disciplines designates something slightly different. Since hermeneutic and deconstructive approaches to textuality had already entered literary studies before the postmodernist explosion, these were not usually perceived as part of the postmodernist field. By contrast, postmodernism in the field of law generally refers to Critical Legal Studies, which blends post-structuralist and psychoanalytic methods, while postmodern theology usually designates shifts in biblical hermeneutics which are informed by a range of textual theory including structuralism, post-structuralism and feminism. So the intellectual reference of the term postmodernism in some other fields is much broader than in literary and cultural studies, and this has lent the term persistence in those domains.

Although we have suggested that the term has been hollowed out and was in any case of indeterminate reference, it is important to be clear that certain theories of a definite trajectory were grouped under the heading. A few essays or books actually adopted the term and became part of a small canon of writings on postmodernism. One of these was Fredric Jameson's essay 'Postmodernism: or, The Cultural Logic of Late Capitalism' which appeared in a collection of essays edited by Hal Foster issued in the United States as *The Anti-Aesthetic: Essays on Postmodern Culture* in 1983, and was revised and reissued one year later in London as *Postmodern Culture* (1984). The clarification of emphasis in the later title gives an indication of when the initial moment of the postmodernism publishing phenomenon might be calculated to fall. Jean-François Lyotard's *The Postmodern Condition: A Report on Knowledge* (1979; in English translation, 1984) also became part of this informal canon. To these texts which embraced the name postmodern were added others that did not use it. Strangely, some of the French philosophers recruited to this cause were already well established, and enjoyed a late florescence of interest in their work. This applies especially to the work of Jean Baudrillard, who was born in 1929, and whose earlier work, notably *For a Critique of the Political Economy of the Sign* (1972) was derived from Marxism, but whose later work, from *Symbolic Exchange and Death* (1976), expounded the theory that a hyper-reality of simulacra had replaced the old ontology of sign and deferred world. This pessimistic theory of the mediatized world displayed the influence of the earlier Canadian media theorist Marshall McLuhan, whose work in turn showed the influence of another Canadian cultural pessimist, Wyndham Lewis. Baudrillard's pessimism was strangely at odds with the exciting theoretical vistas his work appeared to open up.

Another established French philosopher who benefited from the postmodern vogue was Gilles Deleuze. Deleuze was born in 1925 and his published work stretches back thirty years before the postmodern boom to a book about David Hume called *Empiricism and Subjectivity* (1953). It is an irony of French 'theory', which was so often summoned to counter Anglo-Saxon empiricism, that its own frame of reference included an interest in empiricism (with its emphasis on what can be verified in experience) as a counter to German systematic philosophy. Deleuze's *Nietzsche* (1965) was a large factor in a resurgence of interest in Nietzsche in France at that time, reflected for example in works of Derrida and Foucault, but it was his collaboration with the psychiatrist Félix Guattari in *The Anti-Oedipus* (1972) and *A Thousand Plateaus* (1980) which are most cited in postmodernist theory. The first of these is a rejection of the normative and repressive aspects of Freud's Oedipus-centred theory of desire in favour of models suggesting atomization and decentralization of power and desire – the molecular, the rhizomatic, micro-multiplicities, deterritorialization, the nomad, and so on. One of the recurrent threads of general postmodernist theory is the celebration of micrologics (which represent the liberating activities of a dominated level that cannot be thought of as individual, since the individual ego already implies a hierarchy) as opposed to macrologics (which are repressive and centralized – capitalist – power, in all its forms). The texts of Deleuze and Guattari are a common reference in this context; at the same time, the form of this reference is not really to the body of Deleuze's work as a whole; really, postmodern theory tries to get away from the centralizing logic of the oeuvre and the repressive organization of systematic thought in order to liberate thinking itself as part of a political process. The mode of postmodernism is very much the essay as opposed to the systematic work or sequence of works, and the two major tomes of Deleuze and Guattari are written as a speculative resource designed to dislodge dominating models.

This brief account of the dominant elements in the constitution of the textual field of postmodernism in the cultural sphere can only be understood with reference to the questions which cause the different elements of the postmodern to be drawn together. In the main, four lines of questioning can be discerned. One is the question of changes in knowledge and ideas since the nineteenth century which is the domain of Lyotard's 'report on knowledge' prepared for the government of Quebec. The second concerns the effects of technology – in particular, media technology – on aesthetic consumption in particular and on social relations in general. The third concerns the changes in relations of production – that is, in the class structure of societies – brought about by the movement from early liberal capitalism to the corporate capitalism of the early to mid-twentieth century and beyond. The fourth regards changes within existing modes of art, including literature, which might be thought to mark a change from the modes of the high modernism of Joyce, Stravinsky and Picasso, say, to some new mode, say those of Alain Robbe-Grillet, Andy Warhol and the Beatles. These four lines of questioning, while they overlap, do not necessarily yield the same periodization. To take the latter, although modernism in the arts insisted on the idea of development as its very rationale, the reality of the arts combines a number of different narratives, within art, within nations, within genres and so on. Periods of change in the arts, even if we agree upon dates – say the Second World War as the major hiatus within the arts – do not necessarily correspond in terms of date to major signposts of changes of structure in any so designated 'late capitalism',[27] which can be pegged to pre-Second World War corporatism or the postwar culture of consumerism. Changes in media technology have more easily dated frameworks, since the introductions of film, gramophone, radio and television are well documented. Even here, differences between nations and the initial slow rollout of such technologies make attempts at dating only of general accuracy. The notion of a postmodern thought able to map a particular period necessarily begins to take second place to the notion that the postmodern consists of a way of thinking about the recent past, or even the present and the future, without too much regard to periodization. Ironically enough, for all its emphasis on micrologics, postmodernist scripts sometimes seem surprisingly mono-narrative in nature, proposing single lines of global development in a manner that would not offend the most conservative cultural historian, being hardly at all inconsistent with the grand cultural narratives of the eighteenth century, such as those found in the work of Johann Gottfried Herder, and not far removed from the phenomenology of Hegel who is nevertheless the *bête noire* of postmodern thought. Since the uneven development process throughout the world has so far meant that half of people currently are said never to have made a telephone call, the strangely global claims of postmodern commentary sometimes jars; it is as if a theorist in the court of the English King Richard I should, by extrapolating from his own immediate surroundings, theorize an imminent future in which all should ride caparisoned horses and live in draughty castles.

Lyotard's *The Postmodern Condition* is subtitled 'a report on knowledge', and defines the postmodern as mapping changes taking place since the end of the nineteenth century, in contrast to those definitions which date postmodernism from the 1950s or 1960s. Lyotard's account has long been a touchstone of accounts of postmodernism in culture, even though it deals very little with questions of culture. Its two principal topics are the history and science of the nineteenth century and their re-narrativization in the twentieth. The nineteenth century is said to be characterized by grand narratives (*récits*) while the twentieth is characterized by the pragmatic, the particular, the local. 'Simplifying to the extreme,' Lyotard writes, 'I define the postmodern as incredulity toward metanarratives.'[28] The emphasis on narrative is accompanied by frequent reference to 'language games' and 'performativity' and citation of the work of J. L. Austin and John Searle, philosophers of language associated with pragmatism; as in the case of Deleuze, the desire to escape systematic philosophy led Lyotard to an interest in the types of empiricism rejected by structuralists. While Lyotard's interest in the 'language game', also pursued in *Just Gaming* (1985), was not widely taken up by others, his siding with postmodern thought against nineteenth-century historicism has formed part of a general movement against Marxism and its Hegelian and Enlightenment origins. Lyotard was part of the backlash in France after 1968 against Marxism, against the centrally organized Communist Party, and against the Hegelian faith in progress of 'Western Marxism'. Like many French radicals he had reacted against the stagnant and centralized French Communist Party (PCF), which seemed to them as bureaucratic as the state. The philosophical authority of the PCF seemed to be drawn from a deterministic version of Marxism which saw progress as inevitable according to a predictive linear narrative.[29] *The Postmodern Condition* demonstrates a dislike too for the technocratic 'systems theory' developed in Germany, with Jürgen Habermas and Niklas Luhmann the principal culprits. Lyotard warns that 'traditional' Marxist theory, based as it is on a unifying narrative of the single 'subject of history',

> is always in danger of being incorporated into the programming of the social whole as a simple tool for the optimization of its performance; this is because its desire for a unitary and totalizing truth lends itself to the totalizing and unitary truth of the system's managers. [...] Everywhere, the critique of political economy (the subtitle of Marx's *Capital*) and its correlate, the critique of alienated society, are used in one way or another as aids in programming the system.[30]

The grand narrative of the progress of spirit is invalid, and with it revolutionary philosophies which relied on this model for their idea of a collective narrative progress. This single progressive (national) history typifies the loss of legitimizing narrative: 'the narrative function is losing its functors, its great hero, its great dangers, its great voyages, its great goal'.[31] Against the lost grand narrative or metanarrative, Lyotard asserts the claims of numerous small narratives or 'micrologies'.

Lyotard's interest in language games has not really been imitated in cultural studies, but his emphasis on narrative pluralism has contributed to a major current in literary theory which emphasizes 'stories', and which opposes the multifarious accounts of the subaltern or marginal to the centralized narrative of Western progress, whether as capitalism or socialism. Lyotard's own contribution to aesthetic debate has not run in this direction, however, but consists of a defence of modernism as a perpetually self-renewing sublime, in a use of terms closely based on Kant's account of sublimity in his *Critique of Judgement* (1790). Lyotard's aesthetic ideas are only briefly touched on in *The Postmodern Condition*, but are treated in many of his works.[32] Unlike other commentators who see postmodern art as a period succeeding that of high modernism, Lyotard remains committed to the aesthetic ideals of modernism which he interprets, in turn, in terms of the product of genius in Kant, where genius is the force which, nature-like, creates according to new rules, and in creating rules creates a new reality, a singularity or event. Lyotard equates the postmodern with the instant in which the modernist in art takes flight, the incipient moment of modernism; his postmodern sublime is like *ein Ereignis* – an event – in the vocabulary of Martin Heidegger.

Despite its odd dependence on classical philosophy, this notion of the 'event' as a singularity defying old rules and creating new ones, which in turn must be superseded, is the logically necessary counter to the structuralist insistence that the individual utterance or artwork is merely a systemically enabled possibility.

A fine writer on art, Lyotard did not supply postmodern theory with a theory of specifically postmodern art. This was to come from various sources, but it was Fredric Jameson's essay 'Postmodernism; or, the Cultural Logic of Late Capitalism' (1983) which was generally agreed to have drawn together the most strands. Jameson's initial foray would eventually result in a book-length work, *Postmodernism* (London: Verso, 1991), but while the initial essay seemed to mark a stimulating beginning, the brick-like amplification of the book seemed already to mark the end of a trajectory. The original essay attempts to create a narrative under which various postwar developments in art, poetry, film, fiction and architecture can be grouped. Jameson's postmodern period, which originates at 'the end of the 1950s or the early 1960s', marks the end of the 'hundred-year-old modern movement', which included among other things abstract expressionism in painting and modernist poetry. The new art is said not to have a single, linear narrative, but Jameson draws out several common threads. A key feature of Jameson's account which has acquired increasingly general circulation is his claim that postmodern art collapses the distinction between high and low art. Adorno's description of modernism hinged on the reality that autonomous and dependent art had different narrative trajectories, even if each was marked by the tragic realization of Enlightenment rationality in a totally administered society. Closer to home in terms of literary studies, Leavis had helped to found literary studies on the basis that modernist works incorporated a sensibility wholly distinct from the commodified language of the formulaic bestseller. Jameson asserts that new modes have emerged in which high and low are combined. In reference to certain currents this has its validity, yet it is easy to find, say, innumerable mass-market literary works which bear little imprint of *Ulysses*, and clusters of works with narrow circulation intended only for the most hard-bitten connoisseur of modernist poetry that are not sold in railway stations. As often in postmodernist theory, the mode here is the essay, and the point is not to represent a totalizing synthesis under which all phenomena can be catalogued, but to allow to emerge important new features. No item in Jameson's essay is very fully or even consistently developed; rather, each constitutes a germ of speculative suggestion, a surprising number of which have been widely replicated. Acknowledging the potential inaccuracy or repressiveness of suggesting the existence of a postmodern aesthetic 'dominant' and admitting to a continuity of modernist and postmodernist, Jameson catalogues a list of postmodernist features. Expressive depth is said to be replaced as an ideal by aesthetic superficiality in a phenomenon Jameson terms 'the waning of affect'. Historical depth is replaced by nostalgia, pastiche replaces parody, as in general an art of surface and loss is substituted for a history which 'remains forever out of reach'. This process is entwined with the 'breakdown of the signifying chain', as theoretically evidenced with reference to the presentation of schizophrenia in the work of Jacques Lacan, which is found to have its aesthetic correlative in the L=A=N=G=U=A=G=E poetry of Bob Perelman. Postmodern aesthetics is said to be characterized by a 'hysterical sublime' of technological deferral. In most of these suggestions, Jameson takes a pessimistic reading of a loss of history and loss of depth of the kind positively advocated by Nietzsche, who commended surface over depth and urged an enabling forgetting of history. Jameson also echoes Baudrillard's notion of the perpetual deferral of the real as simulacra replace signs.[33] Yet strangely, although the essay is mainly pessimistic in outlook, the general reception of postmodernism, which was mediated through this essay among others, seems often to have received these elements in a positive light. Such works are read perhaps more for their attractive eclecticism than for the grand and brooding metanarrative mind which might be thought to steer them.

It did not seem important whether Jameson's essay was right or wrong on any particular; its value was to suggest a field and create a spine to which disparate activities and theories could be drawn. Literature did not entirely need such a fillip, perhaps, since developments in the novel, accompanied by developments in narrative theory, had created a label for the postmodern novel, while the L=A=N=G=U=A=G=E poets in the United States (who now prefer the label 'linguistically innovative poetry'), while not especially favouring the term 'postmodern', later created a similar group effect with their anthology *In the American Tree* (1986). Postmodern poetic theory, as expounded by Charles Bernstein and others, was an impressionistic amalgam of mainstream European theory. Even though Charles Olson followed Ezra Pound's example in producing an extensive body of theoretical prose to accompany and clarify his innovative methods in the 1950s and 1960s, including early use of the term postmodern, an account of poetry which can properly articulate a 'postmodernist' poetics of innovative developments in US poetry since the 1950s, let alone comparative threads in British literature such as the poetry of J. H. Prynne and Drew Milne, yet remains to be written, despite the notable contributions of individual scholars such as Marjorie Perloff and Charles Altieri. Postmodernist fiction, which performed experiments with narrative method little used in earlier periods, more clearly constituted a group and suggested the lines of new theoretical paradigms. As a consequence, a theory of postmodern narrative applied to such writers as Beckett, Alain Robbe-Grillet, Carlos Fuentes, Vladimir Nabokov, Robert Coover and Thomas Pynchon. This list comes from Brian McHale's *Postmodernist Fiction* (1987), which suggested that forms of narrative that in one way or another appeared to reflect on fictionality itself – including fabulation, metafiction and magical realism – could be grouped as postmodernist. Modernist fiction had been *epistemological*: it had asked questions about the knowledge of reality, for example by toying with the degree of the reader's knowledge of the fictional situation. Postmodernist fiction was *ontological*: it foregrounded being in the world as a topic, and McHale catalogued a variety of world structures found in fiction – the 'Chinese box worlds' of John Fowles and Robert Pinguet, the 'tropological worlds' of Marquez and Pynchon, the 'styled worlds' of Gass and Sorrentino. McHale's book reflects a confidence that the American and international novel had produced something on a par with the French *nouveau roman*, and for a time the combination of the theories of Bakhtin and Derrida with this newly grouped and still appearing set of materials looked like the next big thing. But other forces were at work, for with the development of postmodern theory the institutional rhythm of theory reproduction had itself begun to change. Postmodernism may represent the last moment in which any sense of a collective and common culture could raise its head in the realm of literary studies. On the whole, the impression was that not many were prepared to embrace a new canon of (mostly lengthy) postmodernist works, and postmodernist literary studies became a niche rather than an extension of the general field. This was becoming the norm not only in the matter of literature as an object, but also in the theoretical realm. Postmodern theory, which dealt with fashion among other things, was not necessarily doomed to disappear because of its own fashionability. Of course its disappearance is not total, and experts on and keen readers of, say, Deleuze and Lyotard are still to be found. However, while Marxism and feminism had appeared to address a common culture even while denouncing it, and intended in effect to modify that common culture if necessary beyond recognition, accounts of postmodern literature had no such base either in society or scholarship, and neither did proponents of postmodern theory, who had tended to renounce collective struggle and any grand narrative of change.

Chapter 7

PC Wars

The period of PC Wars (later called Culture Wars) in the United States can be firmly dated to 1991, when the expression 'political correctness' first began to be used. Of course, the roots of the PC Wars go back much further – through the history of slavery and the prehistory of patriarchy – and the more immediate roots are found in the politics of the late 1960s, Vietnam, the Cold War, and more straightforwardly in the demographic expansion of student intake on American campuses which was linked to the introduction of speech codes and to curriculum changes in the humanities, especially in literary studies. The PC Wars were a phenomenon brought about not by liberal academics, but by conservative politicians and academics whose strategy was aimed as much at the conservative electorate as at the actual practices in institutions of higher education. As such, it is of intense interest in the institutional history of literary studies, both because it marks an extraordinary extension of literary-theoretical debates into the public domain, and because it marks a kind of reversal of the politics of theory model: instead of left and liberal academics disseminating their ideas in the community, these ideas were instead labelled by hostile commentators and sidetracked. The attack on PC had two targets, curriculum changes in the humanities and campus speech codes. Its success can be measured by the wide dissemination which the term achieved, and by the difficulties of liberal and left academics in making a response of comparable effectiveness.

'PC', of course, stands for 'political correctness'. The term is derived from the context of early twentieth-century communism and refers equally to the culture of the Communist Party before the Russian Revolution and to the period after the revolution including the rule of Stalin. Sections of the American left, like parts of the British left, may have continued to use this term in an ironic fashion, both to acknowledge the necessity of organizing around an agreed line of argument or policy in order to be politically effective, and also as a rueful reminder of the undesirable outcome of this policy of 'democratic centralism' in the history of the Soviet Union. As I note below, responses to the charge of political correctness on the American left sometimes indicate that the cultural prehistory of the term was not known to those so labelled. Be that as it may, the effectiveness of the right's assault – a success to which the widespread dissemination of the term testifies – depended on more than the power to evoke history. Of course, the term is carefully chosen. Because it is related to both pre- and post-revolutionary communism, it serves equally to characterize the culture of a conspiratorial sect striving to achieve power, as well as the actions of a ruthless bureaucracy intent on maintaining its power and suppressing dissent.

In a very straightforward way, the PC Wars constituted a struggle about American identity. In relation to literature, that identity had been secured by the creation of a canon of American literature. That canon, which was only really given form in the 1940s after being given a shove by D. H. Lawrence's *Studies in Classic American Literature* (1923), was already tenuous as an expression of the American polity, did not have the comparatively firm sedimentation of the extensive and shifting English literary canon which it attempted to imitate, and was open to challenge especially on the grounds of its gender and racial bias, its preference for high literature, and its exclusion of other forms of vital document as well as folk and oral cultures. Early key challenges to this canon included Houston A. Baker's *Long Black Song* (1972) and Lawrence Levine's, *Black Culture and Black Consciousness* (1977), which not only attracted attention to black culture (which was in any case far from invisible) but suggested the lines of inquiry which might academically ground African American studies. American identity as an academic literary projection had long been in question by the time the PC Wars started, and this carefully staged conflict marked not so much a defence against the intro-duction of black and feminist studies, which dated back two decades, as an attack. Even in its origins, the 1970s emphasis on identity politics has been construed by leftist commentators as a response to defeat. Todd Gitlin remarks that, in the United States,

> the 1970s were largely a time of defeat for the left, for the working class and the political movements of the 1960s. [. . .] For leftists, the spirit of an insurgent class was no longer available. Instead, they were left with nostalgia, even at some remove, for eras of cogent struggle they knew only

at second or third hand. The general student movement was finished, leaving behind a range of identity based movements, feminist, gay, and race-based, each vigorous, in its own right, yet lacking experiences of everyday practices which would amount to embryonic prefigurations of a reconstituted world.[1]

In recent times the theoretical refinement of gender studies, queer studies and ethnic studies beyond any appeal to political practice or extra-academic audience seems to confirm that the social movements had already become relatively isolated in the universities. Even if this model seems flawed – too based on Marxist and activist expectations – it can hardly have been the case that the political right in 1991 really considered that the cultural pluralization of studies in the humanities constituted a major threat. More likely, the PC Wars were started in part for strategic reasons of reaffirming national identity at the time of the First Gulf War, partly for local reasons, in terms of an attack on public financing of higher education,[2] and perhaps also at a symbolic level by way of confirming a victory which was already in place by refighting the campus wars of the past. It has also been suggested that the 1988 controversy surrounding the concealed Nazi past of the Yale deconstructionist Paul de Man had attracted attention to the shenanigans of theory and may have prompted a new scrutiny of University life.[3]

The conduct of the PC Wars went as high as President George H. W. Bush, who used the occasion of a commencement speech at the University of Michigan in May 1991 to criticize 'political correctness' for replacing 'old prejudices with new ones', stating that 'what began as a cause for civility has soured into a cause of conflict and even censorship'.[4] An article by Richard Bernstein titled 'The Rising Hegemony of the Politically Correct' which appeared in the *New York Times* for 28 October 1990 is thought of as being the first salvo in the PC Wars, and was accompanied by a clutch of books expanding this theme: Roger Kimball's *Tenured Radicals: How Politics Has Corrupted our Higher Education* (1990), Dinesh D'Souza's *Illiberal Education: The Politics of Race and Sex on Campus* (1991), Lynne Cheney's *Telling the Truth: A Report on the State of Humanities in Higher Education* (1992) and Arthur M. Schlesinger, Jr.'s *The Disuniting of America: Reflections on a Multicultural America* (1992), followed in a slightly different vein by Robert Hughes' *Culture of Complaint: The Fraying of America* (1993). Important progenitors of the debate included Allan Bloom's *The Closing of the American Mind* (1987) and E. D. Hirsch's *Cultural Literacy: What Every American Needs to Know* (1987), the latter cast as a kind of primer on common culture. The social basis of these attacks has attracted attention. Lynne Cheney, who wrote her report as the Chair for the National Endowment of the Humanities, is the wife of Dick Cheney, Secretary of Defense under George H. W. Bush and later Vice President under George W. Bush and architect of the Iraq War. D'Souza, an adviser in Reagan's White House and the biographer of conservative evangelical Jerry Falwell, is alleged to have received a $150,000 grant from the conservative Olin Foundation to write *Illiberal Education*.[5] Most intriguing of all is Allan Bloom's connection with Leo Strauss (1899–1973), the political philosopher regarded as the inspiration of present-day neoconservatism.

Lynne Cheney's *Telling the Truth* takes its epigraph from George Orwell's 'The Prevention of Literature' which refers to an attack on 'intellectual liberty and the concept of objective truth'; the epigraph to her first chapter is from Orwell's *Nineteen Eighty-Four*. The evocation of Orwell which becomes a staple of the PC Wars is designed to situate universities as oppressive state powers; the implicit comparison is to the Stalinism of Orwell's Big Brother. Cheney uses her introductory statement to situate herself as the high minded guardian of truth against relativism:

> I want to show how we have come to live in a world where offenses are constantly being redefined. I want to consider the distortions and divisions being wrought by a kind of thinking that denies there is truth and to examine how it is that this postmodern approach has become entrenched and powerful. I want to look at the origins of the radical skepticism of our time; examine its claims to legitimacy; and finally, suggest what we can do to blunt its force and restore truth and reason to a central place in our lives.[6]

The rethinking of culture is cast as a 'postmodern' relativism, threatening the absolutes of truth. Cheney's book is in origin a report to a professional body and necessarily adopts this rhetoric; D'Souza's *Illiberal Education* is more characteristic of the types of anecdotal attack on 'PC', latching on to events such as a 1988 dispute at Stanford University about alterations to the freshman course on 'Western Civilization' which could be cast as an assault on 'Western Civilization' itself. Schlesinger's *The Disuniting of America* argued that multiculturalism was a threat to American national unity:

> Ethnic and racial conflict [. . .] will now replace the conflict of ideologies as the explosive issue of our times.

A cult of ethnicity has arisen both among non-Anglo whites and among nonwhite minorities to denounce the idea of a melting pot, to challenge the concept of 'one people'.

I am constrained to feel that the cult of ethnicity in general and the Afrocentric campaign in particular do not bode well either for American education or for the future of the republic.

With reference to black studies programs which took a loose approach to scholarship in areas such as the history of ancient Egypt, Schlesinger queried the objectivity of new genres of ethnic studies:

The use of history as therapy means the corruption of history as history. [. . .] Even if history is sanitized in order to make people feel good, there is no evidence that feel-good history promotes ethnic self-esteem and equips students to grapple with their lives.[7]

These accounts set the tone for the PC Wars and supplied much of the content and approach of numerous journalistic forays. More interesting than any of them, because it makes a case which is less obviously opportunistic, is Allan Bloom's *The Closing of the American Mind*.

Allan Bloom's *The Closing of the American Mind* (1987) is helpfully subtitled 'How Higher Education Has Failed Democracy and Impoverished the Souls of Today's Students'. The 'Foreword' is by the novelist Saul Bellow, well known for fictional assaults on the nihilism of fashionable beliefs and the censorious nature of campus politics, in works such as *Herzog* (1964) and *The Dean's December* (1982). Bloom was a professor of social thought, influenced in large part by his teacher Leo Strauss, an energetic opponent of the value relativism of modern historicism who advocated a renewed and scrupulous encounter with the major texts of Western rationalism, ancient and modern. *The Closing of the American Mind* echoes Strauss's attacks on value relativism, while Bloom's attack on Romanticism and the elevation of the self recalls Wyndham Lewis's *The Art of Being Ruled* (1926) and *Time and Western Man* (1927).

Bloom's book seems to promise great things, but the confident generalizations about Rousseau and Nietzsche are not matched by very close attention to any actual arguments or texts which might be held to embody the values which he rejects. The centre of gravity in the book is not, as might be expected, the incipient 'political correctness' movement – indeed, the phrase does not appear in Bloom's book. In fact, it is the student movement of the late 1960s in general, and events at Cornell in 1969 in particular. I wish to review these events, briefly, since their connection with Bloom's book illuminates the confused connections between political actualities and the assault on the University and on the ideology of humanities in particular, of which Bloom's book is part of the avant-garde.

Nineteen sixty-nine was the culmination of five years of student activism at Cornell. The activism had focused initially on Vietnam and civil rights, on the one hand, and on the other on general issues of student representation within the university concerning grievances such as restrictions on pot use and laundry charges. In 1968, following the death of Martin Luther King, the administration began to form an Afro-American Studies Institute in response to perceived political demand. Progress was slow, black students on campus protested at the delay, and their activities resulted in disciplinary reprimands against three students. Feelings ran high among students and faculty. Events were brought to a head in April 1969, when an unknown person set a burning cross outside a black girls' co-operative. The symbolism of this prompted a number of black students to occupy a university building in protest. These students were armed with rifles and shotguns, in response, it was claimed, to a perceived threat. Their demands included the withdrawal of the reprimands against the three black students and an investigation of the cross-burning incident. The university administration agreed to these demands; in return, the students ended the occupation and left waving their weapons in the air. Perceiving that these demands had been conceded in the face of a threat of lethal violence, the faculty of the university refused to endorse them. However, a general demonstration by up to 10,000 students led them to reconsider. Consequently, the reprimands were withdrawn and a new representative body was formed for students to air future grievances.[8]

In Bloom's opinion, 'the professors, the repositories of our best traditions and highest aspirations, were fawning over what was nothing better than a rabble. [. . .] The American university in the sixties was experiencing the same dismantling of the structure of rational inquiry as had the German university in the thirties.'[9] As Bloom tells it, the story is one of *La Trahison des clercs – The Treason of the Scholars*, in the title of Julien Benda's 1927 polemic against cultural disintegration. Referring to this incident, Bloom is able to sustain his thesis that scholars have abandoned principle not merely in their ideas but also in their actions, by giving way to armed threats and to the politics of conviction and of the mob. Cornell was a self-policing body and did not invite state police or any other body on to the campus during these events, so the outcome was very much in the hands of the Cornell administration.

In Bloom's narrative, the events of April 1969 are the traumatic confirmation that the professors as a body had abandoned their professed ideal of intellectual autonomy and simply accepted the dictate of the most motivated. The thinkers had ceased to believe in their own reason and had simply given in to believers who acted with more conviction, and hence more authentically, than they could themselves. Certainly, it is easy to understand Bloom's anger that the law was not brought to bear on the armed protesters. However, Bloom's attempt to prove the intellectual links between the Germany of the 1930s and the United States of the 1960s is an unconvincing rationalization of this traumatic primal scene.

Bloom argues that the ideas of Heidegger and Nietzsche, which had contributed to the rise of Nazism, are now influential in the United States. This has come about due to the influx of German émigrés whose impact on the American University has been colossal. However, the rapid uptake of German ideas in America has not recognized the background of Romantic nihilism underlying these ideas. In a striking image, Bloom notes the difference in tone between Louis Armstrong's 1955 rendition of the song 'Mack the Knife' and Lotte Lenya's version of the German-language original, 'Mackie Messer' from Bertolt Brecht and Kurt Weill's musical, *Die Dreigroschenoper*, first performed in Berlin in 1928. Bloom describes this process as 'the astonishing Americanization of the German pathos' in which Weimar Romantic yearning has been replaced by straightforward 'American self-satisfaction', without any sense of the foreignness or difference of the original. Bloom claims that American intellectual and cultural figures such as Mary McCarthy and David Riesman stand in a similar relation to their émigré German mentors such as Hannah Arendt and Erich Fromm, who in their turn depend on a dangerous romantic nihilism: 'Our stars are singing a song they do not understand [. . .]. But behind it all, the master lyricists are Nietzsche and Heidegger.'[10] The German émigrés also imported Freud and Weber, the former convinced of the 'irrational source of all conscious life', the latter of 'the relativity of all values', sources of the contemporary emphasis on 'self' as a value and of the rising generation of intellectuals 'that had been educated in philosophic and scientific indifference to good and evil'.[11] This has been accompanied by a process of rehabilitating the right-wing irrationalists Nietzsche and Heidegger to the ideas of the New Left, while 'most recently professors of comparative literature have gotten heavily into the import business, getting their goods from Paris, where deconstructing Nietzsche and Heidegger and reconstructing them on the Left has been the principal philosophical *métier* since the Liberation'.[12]

This last quotation reminds us that Bloom's story of the end of reason and the end of rights has its centre of gravity in the 1950s and 1960s. It is certainly true that elements of the left have had recourse to Freud, Weber, Nietzsche and Heidegger to make good lacunae and deficiencies in Marx. However, Bloom's narrative is oddly conspiratorial, does not attend to the dynamics of intellectual mediation, and, worst of all, refuses to engage with its direct targets – black studies, feminism, post-structuralism – all of which are painted as too bankrupt to be worth addressing. Yet Bloom's strategy was successful and would pave the way for the later, more crudely framed attacks on PC. By suggesting that his opponents lacked reason or democratic instinct, and by lumping together phenomena of the general culture with specific academic matters, Bloom smoothed out a complex story and allowed a certain stripe of reader to think that difficult matters had been comprehensively addressed.

E. D. Hirsch Jr.'s *Cultural Literacy: What Every American Needs to Know* (1987) was an attempt to address anxieties about the lack of a common culture in a socially and ethnically disunited America. The second issue boasted an 'Updated Appendix', this being the perceived key feature of the book, in the form of a section entitled 'What Literate Americans Know', including '5,000 essential names, phrases, dates and concepts'.[13] Although the list of things-you-should-know meant that the book could be treated as a parlour game, the main part of the text was a serious argument from a Professor of English who had asked himself why his students appeared to lack knowledge of cultural reference points which he thought should be commonplace. The 'cultural literacy' he recommends is not the literacy of wide reading, but consists of 'the network of information that all competent readers possess'. This 'crucial background knowledge possessed by literate people is [. . .] telegraphic, vague, and limited in extent'.[14] We don't need to have read Marx's *Capital*, just know what it is.

'Cultural literacy' is not the same as 'culture' or 'common culture', and Hirsch attempts to steer discussion away from the question of the possibility of a single 'cultural identity' in an ethnically plural state. The key point of Hirsch's proposed programme is to find some sort of general common culture for the United States as a *nation*, independent of ethnicity. His strategy is very different from that of asserting the need for and validity of a core body of American, English or Western literature. Hirsch avoids the idea of a canon, which he knows is contestable because of its ideological nature, in order, if possible, to retain the centrality of the nation.

Cultural literacy is said to be based on a *language* and on *nationality*. The theoretical cornerstone of the organization of this argument around the nation is the assertion that 'every national language is a conscious construct that transcends any dialect, region, or class', and that the nation itself, like the national language, is also a 'conscious construct' and not simply ethnic in nature.[15] Hirsch's approach is pragmatic and functionalist, intended to defuse the accusation that the national culture and language are white. In fact, it doesn't take long to locate omissions in his list of essential names which appear to have a racial slant: Rosa Parks, who famously challenged segregation rules in Alabama, and whose name is a byword for the civil rights movement, is just one glaring omission. However, it is a distraction to attend too closely to individual inclusions and omissions. Hirsch's text is a program for national integration which defines the excluded as the uneducated third, regardless of ethnicity. Integration is now to take place in terms of a functionally defined literacy which makes only passing reference to the literary or to tradition, so as to deflect any possible suspicion of concealed elitism. However, Hirsch's minimal approach seems designed merely to dampen discussions about the nature of literary and cultural tradition which at this time were much more about discovering obscured traditions than codifying the existing ones.

In the wake of these texts which underpinned the general cultural backlash against political correctness came a series of texts designed to defend liberal and leftist academics against these attacks. These works arrived too late to have much effect on the debate outside the institutions, and some commentators ruefully noticed that the left lacked the political astuteness of its opponents, responding with even-handedness to accusations that flagrantly over-interpreted a handful of untypical facts. Indeed, these books are more surveys of the PC Wars than contributions to a lost battle, but for this reason are an interesting barometer in their own right. They include Gerald Graff, *Beyond the Culture Wars* (1992); Michael Bérubé, *Public Access: Literary Theory and American Cultural Politics* (1994); John K. Wilson, *The Myth of Political Correctness* (1995); *Higher Education under Fire: Politics, Economics, and the Crisis of the Humanities* (1995), edited by Michael Bérubé and Cary Nelson; and *PC Wars: Politics and Theory in the Academy* (1995), edited by Jeffrey Williams. At their best these texts offer moments of clarity in their analysis of the social situation of the theoretical base of literary studies. In other moments, a tendency towards self-aggrandizing myth tends to confirm Gitlin's suspicion that forms of cultural studies based on identity politics had lost sight of meaningful political goals.

Surveying the texts which the PC wars generated, it is surprising how little adequate discussion there is of the origin of the term. In *The Myth of Political Correctness* (1995), John K. Wilson goes in for a little myth-making himself by discovering the origin of the phrase to be American, noting that 'everyone agrees that it was used sarcastically among leftists to criticize themselves for taking radical doctrines to absurd extremes', citing commentators who claim it dates back to the American Communist Party in the 1930s or 1940s, or to the Black Power movement of the 1960s.[16] However, Wilson is mistaken. The force of the accusation of 'political correctness' lies in its attempt to link the cultural agenda of present-day liberals to that of the Soviet Union. It seems amazing that anyone so accused did not appreciate this; however, it is also entirely possible that many of those parroting the accusation were unaware of its specific gravity.

Pace Wilson, the term 'political correctness', when used ironically by Marxists, reflects not a criticism of 'absurd extremes', but an awareness of the role of party discipline in revolutionary strategy. Those Marxists who are able to employ any irony in the use of the term are precisely those who are not in a life-or-death revolutionary situation. The irony is a complex one, therefore. It reflects a knowledge of the history of the Bolshevik Party and the Russian Revolution. In the context of the pre-revolutionary Bolshevik Party, and of the pre-Stalin era Communist International, it was essential that party doctrines be rigorously developed and properly understood by party members. The tone of many communications from Lenin and Trotsky reflect the corrective tone of St Paul, trying to influence doctrines and strategies from a distance. However, it is certain that the use of the term 'correct' and its strict binary opposite 'incorrect' reflects not simply a doctrinaire disposition, but the certainty of Marxists at this time that the progress to socialism had been shown by Marx to be scientifically inevitable. Having the (scientifically) correct analysis and therefore the correct strategy was essential to the revolutionary party's role as the 'midwife' of revolution. The notions of 'correctness' or 'incorrectness' feature regularly in the political communications of the Bolshevik leaders, as in the resolution on the 1926 general strike in Britain, produced by Trotsky, Zinoviev and others. Following vituperative attacks on the leaders of the strike, Trotsky et al. declare 'that the Politburo majority has pursued a profoundly incorrect policy on the question of the Anglo-Russian Committee'.[17] This use of the term 'incorrect' signals a disagreement with a policy which has not maximized the revolutionary potential of the British General Strike. The notion of 'correctness' and the term 'correct' are common in Marxist documents of this period, especially in the idea of a 'correct policy'. After the death of Lenin, and with the rise of Stalin, the pursuit of adherence to the 'general party line' and concomitant pursuit of correctness became more a matter of political or bureaucratic control than of revolutionary politics. This process reached its apex in 1937, the year of the Moscow show trials, which were aimed at internal political dissent in general and at Trotsky and his supporters in particular. Trotsky denounced the culture of the Stalinist state in these terms:

> The bureaucratic apparatus does not allow anyone to call things by their real names. On the contrary, it demands from each and everyone the use of a conventional 'communist' language, which serves to mask the truth [. . .]. Mandatory lying permeates the entire official ideology. People think one thing, but say and write another.[18]

This conformism in the use of a bureaucratically determined 'communist' vocabulary was of course part of the object of Orwell's *Nineteen Eighty-Four* (1949), where the traitor Goldstein is a fictionalized version of Trotsky. Despite his betrayal of orthodoxy, Goldstein's treacherous attacks on the state in fact 'contain more Newspeak words [. . .] than any party member would use'.[19]

As Orwell's parody indicates, Stalin's use of political orthodoxy was aimed more at internal opponents than at the defeated capitalist enemy. Trotsky's advocacy of permanent revolution (i.e. of the continued export of the Russian Revolution) was considered ultra-left by Stalin as the defender of the policy of 'socialism in one country'. In any case, however important the use and control of language may have been, Stalin's weapons against Trotskyism did not rely on speech code violations, but took the form of forced confessions, executions and assassinations.

The reform of everyday language had been an important part of Soviet culture in the 1920s. The reforms were aimed at instilling in all the culture of equality which the end of private property had *de facto* achieved. In this respect the Soviet effort differed fairly dramatically from the campus speech codes in the United States with which it is routinely compared. In the Soviet Union, speech codes focused principally on the class basis of certain registers and terms of address. Since the class system of Imperial Russia had been eliminated, it was essential to revise modes of address in order to get people used to the new social equality. The drive for speech-code change came both from party members and from the people, who in most cases adopted it enthusiastically.[20] In American universities, the adoption of speech codes was a desideratum both of administrators and of student activists. The goal of both parties was to combat hate crime and foster civility, against a background where non-white groups were gaining increased access to mainly white campuses. Right-wing critics may have been right to detect a utopian element in the discussion about modes of address. However, it was one thing in the

Soviet Union for these changes to follow the overthrow of the ruling
class; it would have been quite another to hope that reform of speech
codes in the wealthiest universities in the world would lead to social
revolution. Indeed, it seems likely that speech-code reform became more
of an issue in Britain than it ever was in the United States.[21] In Britain
PC language became the butt of endless jokes, which were based on
mostly invented anecdotes but unconsciously revealed that the agenda of
social civility was being taken seriously. In the United States the issue
of access quotas was probably regarded as a more material issue than
speech-code reform.

There is no space here for detailed exploration of affirmative action
policies and the reaction to them. That said, it is plain that affirmative
action shared a context with developments in the study of the humanities, especially of literature. Comparison with the Soviet Union is perhaps
surprisingly illuminating. From 1923 to 1932 the Soviet Union pursued
a policy of affirmative action in order not to look like a Russian Empire
to its numerous non-Russian populations. Nations and individuals were
all considered to have an essential national identity which appeared on
passports and other documents. Only Russia, the central element in the
state, was not treated as a nation. The strategy was to create equality and
political integration; however, the designation by essential nationality
seemed to reinforce nationalism over internationalism and was resented
by Russians. In 1932 the policy was reversed, with local nationalisms
renounced in a 'great retreat' from the cultural reforms of the previous
decade, while the Russian nation and culture was asserted over all others.[22]
The tension between the dominant and subordinate groups, and the
contradiction inherent in asserting local identities *in order to* achieve
supranational social equality, are a notable point of comparison between
the former Soviet Union and some of today's more advanced states. Of
interest to our present discussion is the harnessing of literature to social
goals in the Soviet Union.

Comparison between the recent history of the United States and the
history of the early Soviet Union has the effect of highlighting the objective problems of the role of cultural or ethnic identity in the context of a
state which claims to supersede national and ethnic particularities yet
must also be seen to represent those particularities and must therefore
seem to assert them in the moment in which it claims to transcend them.
It is also clear from the Soviet experience that this has an administrative
dimension: the management of anger about perceived inequalities and
under-representation. It is striking in the Soviet case that classic literature, whether in Russian or national contexts, is very much a tool at the

disposition of state administrators. In the early Soviet Union, the Bolsheviks had allied themselves with avant-gardists, in particular the Proletkult. However, unlike the Proletkult, who thought that the proletariat could form its own literature from scratch, Lenin and Trotsky were themselves staunch defenders of classic literature, believing that it represented the highest achievement of the ages on which socialism could build.[23] In 1932, under Stalin, modernism was abandoned entirely and writers were famously urged to produce works of 'socialist realism' which would celebrate an idealized future and reflect glory on Stalin himself. The words 'correct' and 'truthful' appeared regularly in official reviews of the new socialist realist literature.[24]

When John K. Wilson sneers at the opponents of 'political correctness' that they 'overlook the self-critical origins of the phrase' we would be wrong to detect a rewriting of history so much as a simple lack of knowledge.[25] Such is the difference between the old Soviet Union and the contemporary United States that it is perhaps not surprising that American academic leftists do not respond to the charges of Stalinism levelled against them. However, it is also likely that the defeat of communism and socialism in the United States has meant that many on the American left have had restricted exposure to Marxism and its history. For this reason, some of the texts defending PC – or, more exactly, defending 'theory' against its opponents – showed a marked lack of routine dialectical thinking. Gerald Graff's *Beyond the Culture Wars* (1992) amounts to a partial recantation, as he himself remarks, of an author whose earlier *Literature against Itself: Literary Ideas in Modern Society* (1979) 'made me for while the hero of a war against academic "theory" – until it dawned on me that I was learning more from my adversaries than from my allies'.[26] *Beyond the Culture Wars* includes a confessional element, a common rhetorical strategy in much of the literature generated by the PC Wars. The argument of this book is that academic instructors should 'teach the conflicts' of the PC Wars, rather than allow 'debate' to be suppressed by modular teaching formats which, Graff claims, result in professors teaching their own materials and approaches in isolation. The result, according to Graff, is that the 'debates' between old and new guard are not communicated to students who therefore lack the context that has given these ideas shape. Graff claims that what has taken place is a kind of 'war' at the expense of the 'struggling student' who is denied the information required to participate in the war.

The metaphor of 'war' requires comment. On the face of it, critical differences might be described as a war because of the level of passionate and public debate which they appear to have aroused. There is more to it than this, however, since the reason that passions ran high arose from the fact that the neutrality of the University itself appeared to be put into question. In the Hegelian theory, the state is a neutral body which presides over and regulates conflicts of interest between individuals. In Marxist theory, the state is partisan: the institutions which comprise it – courts, police, army, schools – serve the capitalist class by enforcing the rights of private property and by disseminating capitalist ideology.[27] The University had preferred to think of itself as a body rising above social conflict, rather than as the agent of such conflict. Now its neutrality became challenged, much as the neutrality of the police or of the church might be challenged by traditional Marxists. However, it was neither Marxists nor the working class which had challenged the legitimacy of the humanities in the University, but a spectrum of feminism, black activism and social liberalism. More specifically, the challenge took the form of junior fellow academics articulating the perspectives of extramural activist groups, groups which themselves claimed to speak for whole sectors of the population. These academics transformed these perspectives into new theoretical and curricular practices.

Marx had claimed that history was a succession of class conflicts. Class war was the motor not merely of social change but of social justice. Marx had described class war as the dominant and determining force of social transformation, and his theory does not anticipate the possibility of describing society in terms of *other* binary conflicts. Nevertheless, as early as the 1920s the conservative author and artist Wyndham Lewis loudly lamented what he saw as a growing modern tendency to see society in terms of numerous binary conflicts (of race, sex, generation and of course class). By the 1970s, some feminists and black activists had adopted a stance which saw the interests of women and African Americans as simply opposed to those of the oppressor group, white men. So the notion that society was defined by possibly irreconcilable conflicts of interest – 'wars' – had become an established part of the rhetoric of political activism if not of mainstream politics.

The so-called cultural 'wars', then, are the intra-institutional dimension of social conflicts which are supposed to exist outside the institutions. These conflicts may not simply be temporary disagreements about representation (whether political, professional or semiological) but true wars which can only be ended by the ruin of one or both of the contending parties. The senior professors who found their critical models and curricular preferences under attack were usually white and often male. While one possible defence was to continue to assert the transcendent purpose and value of the Western canon (as did Harold Bloom), many of these old-guard professors probably realized that they had been undermined professionally. Anyone who had previously defended the neutrality of the University and of the Western canon or canon of English literature but was no longer prepared to do so might appear simply never to have noticed some of the most glaring features of the culture they espoused. So as well as being politically compromised, the old guard seemed professionally compromised, since as scholars or close readers they had not noticed the social determinateness of literary history or of the texts themselves.

Graff's account of the reform of his own teaching practice reveals the type of embarrassment which these small-c conservatives faced. Graff explains that he had been accustomed to teaching Conrad's *Heart of Darkness* as 'a universal parable of the precarious status of civilized reason'. Graff himself had been taught that literature embodied 'transcendent concerns' which went beyond politics, and his teaching reflected this. It had never occurred to him 'to ask how a black person might read this story'. Graff's view was changed, we are told, when he read Chinua Achebe's essay 'An Image of Africa: Racism in Conrad's *Heart of Darkness*' (1975). Graff had not previously realized that nineteenth-century race theory was part of Conrad's material and indeed of Conrad's own mind set. Achebe's article opened Graff's eyes to the fact that ideas about race are not simply 'an extraneous or non-literary element of the novel'. Henceforth Graff has assigned this essay to his students, who now include 'black and third world students', albeit, he tells us, in 'pitiful proportions'. By assigning Achebe's essay, Graff believes that he enables his students to 'enter the debate'.[28]

Graff's anecdotal confession documents more than it intends. It testifies, certainly, to the existence of a critical tradition in the United States which has interpretatively privileged the symbolic dimension of texts. So Graff's earlier reading of *Heart of Darkness* had, among other things, reflected the tendency of criticism of American literature in the 1940s and 1950s to argue that the realist dimension of texts was secondary to their symbolic aspect. This move had made possible the establishment of an American Renaissance based on writers who employed symbolism heavily, such as Melville and Poe. It testifies, too, to the paradigm shift in which the mutually supporting critical model and canon were questioned. However, there is more at stake here.

Where Graff asserts that his students are invited to 'enter the debate' we might reasonably wonder what exactly is being debated. Are we asked to believe that there is an ongoing debate between the post-Achebe world and Graff's pre-Achebe universe in which Africa is merely a symbol in Western fictions? If there has been a paradigm shift in the profession and, as a consequence, we have all simply moved on and think differently, then the notion of debate seems to be an ideological fig-leaf chosen to protect the embarrassment of the now-defeated conservatives.

Graff wants to tone down the cultural 'wars' by taming them and transforming them into a 'debate' which can take place within the classroom. It can be observed in passing that the notion of 'debate' already raises many problems, not least concerning access to discussion and the real social outcome of abstract debate. The idea of debate tends to conceal the reality of social conflicts, because it is a form of social conflict mediated in a particular and complicated manner. What is striking about Graff's Conrad/Achebe example is his notion that a debate relevant to his students might be drawn from it. This novel is not by an American and it is not about America. Written by a Polish émigré for British publication, it concerns the late phase of European colonialism. Since it is set after the abolition of slavery in the United States and almost a century after the official ending of the slave trade, this is a different phase of colonialism from that which conditioned slavery. This discontinuity might have alerted Graff to the most blatant insight of all: that *Heart of Darkness* is not a work of American literature at all, and any attempt to construe it as a 'Western' work makes it, also, an object of ethnic or national appropriation.

The liberalized version of PC which was attacked by the right was also a source of despair for traditional and other leftists, and as well as the right-wing attacks it should be noted that other centre and left voices were raised against PC. One contributor to *Higher Education under Fire* reminded his colleagues that the vogue for Nietzsche and Heidegger was politically tainted. The vogue for the:

> Critique of Western rationality [. . .] rooted in Nietzsche and Heidegger, and brought to this country via Foucault and Derrida – [had] been a cause of particular dismay for modern German historians [of which the author is one]. We have looked on in amazement to see intellectual traditions central to the rise of Nazism and fascism become an important component of supposedly critical theory in this country.

Postmodernists should stop going on about the dark side of Enlightenment and 'acknowledge a theme that has been far more prominent in the historiography of Nazism: the dark side of the counter-Enlightenment'.[29] Another warns that the faddish nature of theory, 'the rapidity of its movement and its partial capture by an upwardly mobile fraction of the new middle class within the academy intent on mobilizing its cultural resources within the status hierarchies of the university,' have resulted in a loss of 'any but the most rhetorical connections with the multiple struggles against domination and subordination at the university and elsewhere'.[30] Leftist anti-PC books included Daphne Patai and Noretta Koertge's *Professing Feminism* (1994), which criticized the poor scholarship on many women's studies programmes, while Russell Jacoby's *Dogmatic Wisdom* (1994) and Todd Gitlin's *Twilight of Common Dreams* (1995) criticized the politics of identity movements from a left-wing perspective. The editors of *Mistaken Identities: The Second Wave of Controversy over Political Correctness* (1999) identify the two main leftist criticisms of PC as the accusation that identity politics constitute a new fundamentalism, and concerns about the threat of postmodern relativism to existing cultural, legal and educational institutions. Multiculturalism is found to have an almost threadbare, reactive underpinning:

> For all their multiculturalist talk about 'diversity', many radicals are guided by an implicit moral hierarchy: any culture is better than that of white, European males. They project their ideological aspirations on non-European cultures, characterizing them as uniformly friendly to the environment, non-alienated, pacific, and matriarchal.[31]

While the old left formed in the 1930s contained 'an uneasy mix of trade unionists, immigrants, intellectuals, populist farmers, migrant workers, and the unemployed' and remained universalistic in outlook, the new left of the 1960s found 'an expanding economy, a burgeoning public sector' and above all 'a booming higher education sector that represented the mobility ladder into the middle class'. It was a mixture of 'old leftists, students, Black radicals, environmentalists, peace activists, and counter-culturalists'. The alliance did not last and identity movements inherited the left mantle, promoting a shift in emphasis from universalism to particularism. The themes of social class and the common good have been subordinated to race, gender, culture and sexuality.[32] We might add that Marxism, which could have provided an inbuilt intellectual resistance to the movement into identity politics, had been practically eradicated from humanities departments by the McCarthy era.[33] In an essay bluntly titled 'Marching on the English Department while the Right

Took the White House', Todd Gitlin argues that universalism in US politics had ended with Martin Luther King in 1968. Gitlin identifies a breakdown of the relationship between Jews and black radicals after the latter supported Palestinians in the 1967 Six Day War, followed by outbreaks of black anti-semitism in the 1968–9 teachers' strike, which saw Jewish teachers pitted against black parents. By 1975, Gitlin argues, the old universalist left was thoroughly defeated, 'pulverized':

> Cut off from ecumenical political hopes, the partisans of identity politics became preoccupied with what they might control in their immediate surroundings – language and imagery. [. . .] They spoke confidently of 'disruptions', 'subversions', 'ruptures', 'contestations'. The more their political life was confined to the library, the more their language bristled with aggression. [. . .] While the right was occupying the heights of the political system, the assemblage of groups identified with the Left were marching on the English department.[34]

Some prominent allies of identity politics came to express doubts about the model. Even Henry Louis Gates, one of the foremost African American scholars, wondered aloud whether the ethical universal might return:

> The very notion of an ethical universal – for years dismissed as hopelessly naïve – is beginning to make a comeback in the works of a number of feminist theorists. We had so much fun deconstructing the liberal ideology of 'rights', for example, that we lost sight of how strategically – humanly – valuable the notion proved in, for example, much Third World politics. [. . .] The oppositional style of criticism has failed us, failed us in our attempts to come to grips with an America that can no longer be construed as an integral whole.[35]

In a notable intervention, Richard Rorty, in *Achieving our Country: Leftist Thought in Twentieth-Century America* (1998), was robust in his criticism of the shift from the left's economic focus prior to 1964 and its subsequent cultural focus, a shift accompanied by a transference of allegiance from Marx to Freud:

> This retreat from secularism and pragmatism to theory has accompanied a revival of ineffability. We are told over and over again that Lacan has shown human desire to be inherently unsatisfiable, that Derrida has shown meaning to be undecidable, that Lyotard has shown commensuration between oppressed and oppressors to be impossible, and that events such as the Holocaust or the massacre of the original Americans are unrepresentable.

Hopelessness has become fashionable on the Left – principled, theorized, philosophical hopelessness. The Whitmanesque hope which lifted the hearts of the American Left before the 1960s is now thought to have been a symptom of a naive 'humanism'.

His recommendation is that the left should 'put a moratorium on theory' and 'try to kick its philosophy habit', then 'try to mobilize what remains of our pride in being Americans' in order to realize the state which Washington and Lincoln had envisaged.[36]

*

The attack on PC was the public and largely extra-institutional dimension of debates which had also taken place in the academies. Critics on the right tended to emphasize the nihilist basis of much left theoretical thought, based in Nietzsche and Heidegger, both in different ways tainted by Nazism, and seem really not to have cared at all about the fairly obvious need for civility on campus (the purpose of speech codes) or about the basic scholarly objectivity (let alone ethics) involved in examining curriculum content. The willingness of the right to assert the need for a common national culture begs far too many questions. It is not good enough for a dominant party to assert a culture and insist that it be adopted by others without question or modification. A culture is not a finished project, and certainly does not boil down to a list of texts on a freshman course. A culture considered as national hardly amounts to such if the various parties of the nation cannot agree on it, and in any case important aspects of (for example) civic culture can in principle be agreed on even where other aspects (such as literary studies) become partially subdivided. The left criticisms of multiculturalism (which on the whole avoid the term 'PC') certainly have a valid case to make about the organization and social structure of the American left: in comparison to Europe or even the America of the 1930s, the social basis of socialist struggle is lacking. This was true for a long time. A comparison of Richard Ohmann's *English in America: A Radical View of the Profession* (1976) with Terry Eagleton's *Criticism and Ideology* (also 1976) reveals a massive contrast between Eagleton's confident modelling of a struggle within the discipline of English based on Marxist models (complete with brief worked examples) and Ohmann's meandering and untheorized denunciations of the MLA, the time-serving nature of freshman English programmes, the role of universities in the industrial economy and so on. Yet those who lament the lack of Marxism in America today cannot glance wistfully across the Atlantic for the example of a culture which they would prefer. The revisions to Marxism have come, from within and then, overwhelmingly, from without Marxism itself. The difference between British and American theory at this point tends to be that the British approaches to theory are more conditioned by the residues of Marxism, or at least of socialism, than American approaches which are consequently more speculative.

Chapter 8

Ethics

As we noted in the previous chapter, left and right critics of the theorization of literary studies in the United States did not acknowledge the strong ethical component of theory, preferring to see only a negation of the nation-state or of any residual prospect of socialist struggle. Condemnation of the nihilism of theory did not acknowledge that Foucault and Derrida had both taken a turn into ethics in their later work – Foucault in the last two volumes of *The History of Sexuality*, *The Use of Pleasure* (1984) and *The Care of the Self* (1984), and Derrida in numerous works treating social and political themes with greater or lesser indirection, for example in *From Law to Philosophy* (1990), *The Other Heading* (1991), *Spectres of Marx* (1993) and *The Politics of Friendship* (1994). In the case of each, even had they not developed the ethical aspect of their own work, the ethical uses to which their earlier work might be put would certainly have been found; their work helps to inform developments which are taking place anyway. European socialists, who believe themselves politically superior to American liberals, would probably have a hard time acknowledging it, but key ethical thinking of our time is now conducted in American universities, and of that an important element is taking place in literary studies. This might seem tantamount to saying that the people who work at the wealthiest universities in the wealthiest country in the world have acquired the right to tell the rest of us what to do. Of course, in the area, say, of particle physics the concentration of wealth is central to any research project. In the field of the humanities wealth has a different significance: it can lure academics from other countries – the case of noted postcolonial theorists is the most prominent example of this; it can also be used to buy up research resources, especially, in the humanities, manuscripts and libraries. But it cannot buy up the subject positions which are a key component of cultural inquiry without altering those subject positions in the process. The reasons for America's ethical leadership lie here though: in its purposeful treatment of differences of race, sexual orientation and gender. Class is not another 'difference' of this type even though it is sometimes guiltily thrown into the mix. Nor are 'race' and 'orientation/gender' the same type of difference, as is shown by the quite different ways their treatments have evolved. The ethical advances made in America have come about in two ways. In ethnic studies they have come about because of the history of slavery; in 'orientation/gender' they have come about simply because those questions found an amenable and sophisticated climate free from the preconditioning of socialism. Rich people rarely want to talk about class, and Americans almost never want to discuss socialism; consequently, attempts to wrest class as an issue away from Marxism look perfunctory. Expressing things another way, we should regard the ethical advances I have referred to as entirely disfigured by America's global status and by the class composition of higher education. Yet it is America's global status which gives it a *de facto* position of ethical leadership, and what may be hardest for us to grasp is that the ethical quality of literary studies is of a piece with the international role of the American state, not its antithesis – even though at the level of consciousness many liberal academics are vehemently opposed to many actions of their state. With an eye as much on disfigurement as on ethical substance, this chapter outlines elements of queer studies, as a recent permutation of the study of gender and sexuality, and ethnic studies, which is located in relation to postcolonial theory, the other major ethical strand of literary-theoretical thought which exists in uneasy relationship with the First World university. Finally, in a compacted discussion of the work of Alain Badiou, I ask whether challenges will arise to the functionalism of literary studies – its emphasis on 'what is literature for?' rather than on 'what is literature?'

*

The beginnings of queer theory lie as much in American feminism as anything else. A key early text is Eve Kosofsky Sedgwick's *Between Men: English Literature and Male Homosocial Desire* (1985). Sedgwick was a graduate of Cornell and Yale and taught in American institutions. Sedgwick's influential study is Anglophile, feminist and American, although its subject is a universalized homosociality. In a preface added in 1992 Sedgwick acknowledges the validity of charges that 'she doesn't know much about gay men' and speaks of the 'reckless pleasure' in writing the book which she feels must now be obvious to readers. The argument of the book is that there is a 'potential unbrokenness of a continuum between homosocial and homosexual – a continuum whose visibility, for men, in our society, is radically disrupted. Sedgwick pursues this argument with the stated purpose of examining the alliance between 'feminism and antihomophobia' in 'our society'.[1] This is accomplished through studies of Shakespeare, Wycherley, Sterne, Hogg, Tennyson, George Eliot, Thackeray and Dickens. There is a curious disjunction between the politics of British literary theory in the decade to 1985, bent on expanding the object of literary studies and sternly querying the legitimacy of the canon, and the oddly traditional and Anglophile approach of this study. The references in the quotations above to 'our society' viewed with twenty years of retrospect raise questions. Sedgwick describes the subject of the book as 'a relatively short, recent, and accessible passage of English culture chiefly as embodied in the mid-eighteenth- to mid-nineteenth-century novel'.[2] The period is not so short of course, but this claim begs other questions: why the focus on England? And why assume that novels make a culture accessible? In the 1992 preface Sedgwick claims to be discussing the identity of 'Euro-American gay men', a claim for coverage in no way legitimated by this study and made good on the 'European' side only by discussion of Nietzsche and Proust in a later book, *Epistemology of the Closet* (1990). The potential for criticism of gestures in which gay topics are appropriated by a feminist is acknowledged by Sedgwick, but a resounding silence still surrounds the appropriation of 'English' literature as if this were part of 'our culture', or as if there were such a thing as the even more bizarre confection of Sedgwick's preface, a Euro-American identity of which 'Euro-American gay men' were an identifiable subset (from Rhode Island to Riga via Rochester – Rochester, England, that is). It will be thought by some readers not cricket perhaps to mention this point, but Scottish readers will already have bridled at my omitting to mention that James Hogg is a profoundly Scottish writer. Hogg's Scottishness goes for nothing in Sedgwick's bland generalization about the accessibility of English culture. Her account of Hogg's *The Private Memoirs and Confessions of a Justified Sinner* (1824) is the best-known account of that novel. Her opening paragraph notes that 'one has to admit the native (Scottish) scene and vernacular', but the admission gets no farther than this sentence fragment, and the following article does nothing of the kind. This blindness to the difference of Scotland and its history of independence is the corollary of a freewheeling indifference to Englishness in this whole study. It might be thought that I am insisting unfairly on a dimension of the work which is irrelevant to its main theme, but it seems more than relevant to highlight this glaring silence in a thesis about repression and unacknowledged strategies of identity appropriation. It is certainly not the case that Sedgwick is unaware of the ethical imperatives of inter-pretation. The closing pages of the essay on Hogg broach this subject with a great show of propriety:

> If there is a loss or a danger in my shift of emphasis from the homosexual to the homophobic content of the Gothic, it would lie in the potential blurring, the premature 'universalization', of what might prove to be a distinctly homosexual, minority literary heritage. Feminist critics have long understood that when male-centred critical tradition has bestowed the tribute of 'universality' on a woman's writing, it is often not an affirmation but rather a denial of the sources of her writing in her own, female, specificity. The extra virulence of racism in our culture has minimized the danger of this particular spurious naturalization of the work of writers of color, but the ambiguous, prestigious spectre of 'universality' has neverthe-less exerted a structuring and sometimes divisive effect on the history of at any rate Black American culture. Similarly, a premature recuperation (as being about the entire range of social gender constitution) of a thematic array that might in the first place have a special meaning for homosexual men as a distinctly oppressed group [. . .] would risk cultural imperialism.[3]

Most readers will already have worked out why I have quoted this pas-sage. The last phrase is of course the key. The unacknowledged 'cultural imperialism' by which this text of Scottish literature is assimilated to English literature and then appropriated for a discussion of a quietly universalized 'our culture' would beggar belief in the context of 'Black American culture' (to use Sedgwick's example). The ethical pernicketiness with which the ownership of the text is discussed in relation to sex/gender alignment is in stark contrast to the universalizing imposition of sex/gender identities across national/ethnic boundaries.

We might take Sedgwick's text as an example of New Historicism. The term was first used by Stephen Greenblatt in *The Power of Forms in the English Renaissance* (1982), and has come to define a mode of reading in which a theoretically informed historical attentiveness is substituted for a traditional narrative historicism. It is a non-rigorous, speculative and comparatively freewheeling approach to reading which often draws on Foucauldian ideas about power and discourse, but eschews rigorous theories of society and allows itself a selective approach both to social themes and to selection of texts (literary and non-literary). The label 'New Historicism' perhaps better describes certain critical practices in the field of early modern literature, periods which had been in effect under-theorized since most theory took modern capitalist society and modern (post-Kantian) philosophy as its frame. Sedgwick's important early text of queer theory reflects this kind of freewheeling approach. What is truly striking in it is the mixture of ethical scruple and blindness. This blind-ness is not simply ignorance, but is symptomatic of the institutional state of English studies at that time, elements of which survive today. While reflecting on 'black studies' in her essay on Hogg, Sedgwick ignores the challenge of African American scholars to the dominant role assigned to English literature, and simply uses the theme of homosociality to legitim-ate a trawl (often quite narrative) through well-known canonical texts with a new interpretative bias. In this context, queer theory becomes a legitimation of English studies, especially as conducted in elite universities. More than this, though, Sedgwick's account of her 'reckless pleasure' in composing the book acknowledges something else: that English literature becomes a kind of libidinal playground for US scholars. Sedgwick does go on in her later work to discuss American texts, but the impression is given that lack of implicit attachment to context is an attractive feature of English literature for this type of commentary. The 'cultural imperialism' which Sedgwick acknowledges as a risk in relation to the 'ownership' of gay texts is at stake too in the relationship of US universities to English literature, which is so key a component of American literary studies that the effects of this cultural imperialism for England have yet to be properly articulated on either side of the Atlantic, although a politicized Scottish studies has opened a small breach in the United States and Canada through which English studies may yet enter.

These apparent origins of queer studies in English literature of course do not predict the course of lesbian and gay studies, the extra-mural dimension of these studies, and their gradual professionalization and institutionalization. Although written out of some accounts of queer theory, pioneering work by British academics Jonathan Dollimore and Alan Sinfield in their collection *Political Shakespeare* (1985) was an import-ant part of the movement towards a type of cultural materialism which would investigate the role of subordinate cultures. Queer studies has proved to be a predominantly American phenomenon, not least due to the politicization of American gay men and lesbians during the 1990s against the background of AIDS, and a florescence of subcultural activity around the complexity of gay identities and the problem of bringing different types of same-sex relationship under simple headings such as 'gay' and 'lesbian' – terms which had a political leverage up to a point, but which became administrative and normative once established. For this reason 'queer' was adopted, and whatever its origins (William Burroughs' early autobiographical novel first published in 1985 as *Queer* is an early and bold example of the appropriation of the term normally used as an insult) now serves as the rubric under which questions of gender and sexuality in mind, body and representation are brought into question. Queer now has an uneasy relationship to the conventional 'lesbian and gay' and is not universally accepted – not least because queer embraces instability in a romantic manner that does not have universal appeal.

*

Judith Butler's *Gender Trouble: Feminism and the Subversion of Identity* (1990) is not a work of literary theory but is often cited in feminist and queer literary studies. Its central thesis is that the category of 'women' on which feminism relies might be politically effective in terms of securing the visibility of 'women's issues', but perpetuates the error of conflating gender identity and biological identity, with the effect that heterosexual norms are propagated by a feminist movement which ought to be in the business of challenging them. That it should be necessary to explain this premise might seem remarkable, since the notion that gender is constructed is found in Simone de Beauvoir's *The Second Sex* (1949), which claims that 'one is not born a woman but, rather, becomes one,' and indeed the stirrings of this idea can be traced to Engels' *The Origins of the Family, Private Property and the State* (1884).[4] Interest in Butler's work comes from the fact that she did not simply remind political feminism of this neglected truism, but gave it theoretical articulation in such a way as to thematize it and render it irrepressible. Butler's approach is to revisit the classical positions of the philosophy of the subject and its critique. The frame of reference in *Gender Trouble* is mainly de Beauvoir, Luce Irigaray, Monique Wittig, Lévi-Strauss, Joan Rivière, Freud, Kristeva and, above all, Foucault. The argument finds the notion of 'substance' to have been at fault in the mapping of gender as a subject identity. Butler claims that the phrase 'the metaphysics of substance' is associated with Nietzsche, and although she does not supply a reference for Nietzsche's use of the phrase, the focus throughout is on the linguistic turns which tend to produce the illusion that gender is a substance, a subject and an identity. 'Gender is not a noun,' Butler asserts, but 'is performatively produced and compelled by the regulatory practices of gender coherence'; 'gender is always a doing, though not a doing by a subject who might be said to pre-exist the deed.'[5] The use of 'performative' is derived from the speech act theory of J. L. Austin; the notion of doing as reality and being as myth derives from Nietzsche. While much mockery is made of the idea of substance and the metaphysics from which it is derived, no mention is made of Aristotle, the originator of classical metaphysics, and the task of distinguishing between substance (*ousia*), matter (*hule*) and subject (*hupokeimenon*) is bypassed in a treatment which situates metaphysics as the fall guy, and which sidesteps even the best-known and most sustained treatment of the Aristotelian legacy in the work of Heidegger. On the one hand this is a pity, since in de-essentializing 'gender' Butler advances 'body' as substance, but on the other hand the essence of Butler's contribution has not been to carry through the destruction of metaphysics – by which term is meant not simply the Aristotelian system of the *Physics, Metaphysics, De Anima* and so on, but all of the sedimented legacies of that system in subsequent philosophy (which Derrida cautioned we must 'deconstruct' rather than 'destroy'). The use made of Butler's work in the ethics of recent and contemporary literary commentary has been in the focalization of gender formation in performance – not only in textual matters but also in the forms of social situation routinely depicted in function. 'Gender is an act,' concludes Butler; 'as in other ritual social dramas, the action of gender requires a per-formance that is *repeated*.' The point of these repeated performances is 'the strategic aim of maintaining gender within its binary frame – an aim which cannot be attributed to a subject, but, rather, must be understood to found and consolidate the subject'.[6] For commentary on drawing-room fiction, for example, the foregrounding of the 'way in which bodily gestures, movements, and styles of various kinds constitute the illusion of an abiding gendered self' enables comment on manners to be re-viewed in terms of the repressive mechanisms through which what Butler calls the 'compulsory heterosexuality' is produced and reproduced. It may be that the very eclecticism of Butler's approach has secured her support among different constituencies. Feminists influenced by French theory who had long criticized 'essentialist' feminism; Marxist feminists whose paradigm was the production and reproduction of daily life; Foucauldians who saw identities as the products of (a somewhat abstract) 'power'; Althusserian Marxists who mapped identities as the unconscious effect of symbolic structures; Freudians and Lacanians for whom the ego has never been an essence but a psychic strategy: all of these would find their concerns reflected in Butler's work. At the same time, what these differ-ent intellectual positions find alien or objectionable in each other is also preserved in Butler. Butler's elevation of 'power' in imitation of Foucault seems to promote a new metaphysic which leads away from the material analysis of specific social situations, and the presumption that gender formation is oppressive and violent seems too much a product of various European romantic nihilisms to be of any real political effectivity (here again the charge of elitism against a Yale graduate with a Chair at Berkeley can take root). My own objection is that the attempt to take on metaphysics almost as a sideline operates at too high a level of paraphrase and too readily conflates philosophical metaphysics with a metaphysics of everyday life coded in grammar. In dealing with the admittedly interesting classical philosophical materials, Butler does not question the extent to which metaphysical concepts can be considered to be embodied in daily life as language, grammar or common sense. It is essential to know where we are undertaking a critique of everyday assumptions and where of philosophy. Derrida, in a reading of Émile Benveniste's commentary on Aristotle, had indicated that attempts to treat metaphysics as the unwitting reflection of grammar run into a few problems of their own.[7] Be that as it may, Butler's work, which only infrequently makes use of fiction, can be viewed as an enabling convergence of a variety of strands of the period of theory that can provide a motor for the rereading of large swathes of literary history. It certainly has enabled a renovation of the ethics of reading in a recognition of contents that were previously disguised; more than this, it in general gives leverage and confidence to marginal or subcultural groups for whom the production and policing of gendered identities are issues of concrete rather than speculative oppression. This appears to be essential and important, whatever we think of the details; whether this can lead the way out of a professionalized theory into any form of extra-institutional politics has been generally considered open to doubt.

*

The stimulus to the development of the study of 'Commonwealth literature' was the liberation struggles of British and other colonies in the period beginning in 1960, and the example of the Francophone *négritude* movement associated with Aimé Césaire (Martinique), Léopold Senghor (Senegal) and Léon-Gontran Damas (French Guyana). The movement was an inspiration to African American cultural leaders, and culminated in the International Conference of Negro Writers and Artists held in Paris in 1956, followed by a second held in Rome in 1959. This movement, which had started in the 1930s, offered a universalized notion of negritude as a counter to French colonial racism. Criticisms of it were twofold: that it imitated European cultural forms (the same criticism that was sometimes levelled at the Harlem Renaissance) and that its projection of a universal 'blackness' was based on a too-close inversion of racism, as might indeed have been evidenced by Jean-Paul Sartre's often-cited claim that the negritude movement inverted the poles of the Hegelian subject–object dialectic. The concept of Commonwealth literature arrived a little later, and was developed initially at the universities of Leeds and Kent in England, reinforced by the creation of the Heinemann 'African Writers' series. The idea of Commonwealth literature was politically ambiguous. On the one hand, at a stroke it made essential cultural connections which illuminated the political realities both of colonialism and of decolonization, and provided an educational resource for post-independence countries which could counter the norms of English literature. On the other, it asserted the notion of the British Commonwealth as the unity that continued to bind former colonies, and it privileged Anglophone writing amenable to an educated British readership. For this reason, the very idea of Commonwealth literature tended to reflect structures of colonial power even in the moment that it challenged them, and the complex pressures on writers to conform to the expectations of an international audience reading in English, with the consequent benefits of increased book sales and prestigious invitations, certainly shaped the literatures which it claimed merely to facilitate. Such debates had taken place also in the earlier context of *négritude*, yet those who argued for a rejection of English and French cultural norms did not obviously have right on their side; the governing feature of the globalized world is precisely this internationalization of writing and the hold of metropolitan media centres. The choice for a writer between local or international language and readership is surely a difficult one; but the choice of the local is conditioned by the very existence of the international as a result of the globalization of colonialism, and to opt for the local, whatever the politics of doing so, does not allow for the creation of a thoroughly deconditioned literature. That said, a perhaps unfortunate side-effect of this process of cultural adoption or identification is that 'hybridization', as it is sometimes called, has become a major theme not only of theory but of creative writing itself, which often quite relentlessly focuses on the writer's own dilemmas about national identification both in terms of personhood and in terms of literary affiliation. This theme is certainly exhaustible, but the truth of this cultural moment is surely a key ethical reality of recent history, whether or not the writing and theory which stands as the product of and commentary on this truth can properly embody its reality. It may also be thought that the writers fortunate enough to have international literary careers hardly have the same experience of cultural hybridization as many in the postcolonial world, yet even on this point we should be clear that the distortion created by the adoption of these internationalized writers by the metropolitan centres of New York, London and Paris is of a piece with the movement of global culture generally, and the stories of a detached elite of writers may still have a dialectical kernel of universality.

Despite the early creation of Commonwealth literature as a field for writers and scholars, the period of theoretical activism in the 1970s and early 1980s made very little of it. It was only in the later 1980s that, now as postcolonial literature and accompanied by an emergent body of theoretical writing, this area of activity was given institutional focus in Britain. The belatedness of this emergence seems truly remarkable given the heavy politicization of theory in the 1970s, its supposed international sophistication (in terms of the wide use of French, German and other materials), and its strong emphasis on the ideological function of canon formation. A postcolonial reader edited by British academics called *The Empire Writes Back* which appeared in 1989 was the first indication to many readers that something was indeed afoot, while aficionados of high theory of a Derridean stripe were inducted into a postcolonial critique of the Western Marxist view of history by Robert Young in *White Mythologies: Writing History and the West* (1990). *The Empire Writes Back* took its title from the second of George Lucas' *Star Wars* films. Intended to convey the notion of a reverse movement of literary influence from the colonies to the centre of Empire, the editors blunderingly conveyed the obverse notion: the plot of Lucas' film *The Empire Strikes Back* (1980) concerns the destruction of an attempted rebellion by the military power of the Empire. It is fairly safe to say that the editors of *The Empire Writes Back* did not intend to imply that any attempt at cultural rebellion would be crushed, but quite unconsciously they signposted one of the principal objections that can be brought against postcolonial criticism: that, like the earlier and parentalistic 'Commonwealth literature', postcolonial literature, criticism and theory are a Western construction based in the major metropolitan centres.[8] In Lucas' film, the leading rebel fighter, Luke Skywalker, is cornered by the commander of the imperial forces, the evil Darth Vader, who attempts to woo him over to the dark side. Accused by the reluctant Skywalker of killing his father, Vader chillingly responds 'No, *I* am your father,' at which point Skywalker drops down a service shaft and is blasted helplessly out into space. It is striking that this British projection of the postcolonial took such a scenario as its primal scene.

Robert Young's *White Mythologies* impressed in its own time as the apparent 'conversion' of a dyed-in-the-wool Derridean (Young was an editor of *The Oxford Literary Review*) to an entirely new agenda. This was less than the whole truth: Young's key exhibits included the work of Gayatri Chakravorty Spivak, who was widely known for her introduction to the translation of Derrida's *Of Grammatology* (1976) and becoming known through her collection of essays *In Other Worlds: Essays in Cultural Politics* (1987). Young also discussed the work of Homi K. Bhabha in the form of a number of essays only later collected as *The Location of Culture* (1994). The striking feature of Young's book was not simply the prominence given to otherwise marginal figures (at that time) but the scale of the theoretical narrative in which they were located. Young's introduction strategically positions post-structuralism and not Marxism as the pre-eminent mode of political theory. As Young notes, post-structuralism at that time had been widely criticized by Marxists for its lack of politics and neglect of history. The upshot of *White Mythologies* is that post-structuralism will cast doubt on the narrative of history as a progress led by the industrial working class on which the authority of Marxism rests. Young notes that the founding moment of post-structuralism is not the conflict of May 1968 which is defining for the French left, but the Algerian War of Independence (1954–62), not least because Sartre, Althusser, Derrida, Lyotard and Hélène Cixous were born in or connected to Algeria. This colonial origin of key figures of scare-quoted 'post-structuralism' makes it resistant to French ethnocentrism and aware of questions of social marginality which go beyond class. Marxism in the academic form of the construct of Western Marxism is called to account for its dependence on a model of history derived from Hegel (even where that derivation is repressed), and it is Hegel of course who is the principal object of post-structuralist accounts of the 'subject', whether as consciousness or historical agent. The alternative to Hegelian–Marxist historicism is to be looked for in Edward Said's *Orientalism* (1978), a key text of the emergent post-colonialism (Young does not use this term) which identifies the existence of a 'colonial discourse' that creates an orient rendered mythical in binary terms. Said describes Orientalism both as a massive body of Western learning about the East *and* as an unconscious fantasy of the Other. Said assumes that the colony is entirely possessed by the colonizer, and describes the discourse of Orientalism as if it were a closed totality. The only 'theoretical base' for possible resistance to Orientalism in the West is offered by 'individual experience' in the East.[9] Young argues that Said's model, which opposes discourse to experience, lacks theoretical self-consciousness and requires correction; he suggests that Bhabha's approach can productively transform the stasis of 'Orientalism' by unpacking its 'ambivalence'. According to Bhabha, the focus should not be on the representation of the colonized other within the dominant culture, but on the situation of the discourse *in* the colony in the process of constructing the representation of colonized subjects – a process which is characterized by 'anxiety', 'contradiction', 'ambivalence', 'defence', 'disavowal', 'fetishism', 'fantasy'. As Young points out, each of Bhabha's essays refines this initial position on Said, and the essays themselves create a vocabulary which, in my terms, is transcendental and metaphysical. The fixed terms of psychoanalysis are, as noted above, rolled out in accounts of contexts which they do not strictly anticipate. We might note that Bhabha adopts the rhetorical stance which became a commonplace substitution for politics and argument in the 1990s, of positioning oneself as reasonable and one's target as 'anxious', as if the master-race of left-leaning cultural commentators had tamed and rationalized its unconscious while all others (though perhaps not Others?) were at its mercy, a hermeneutic which amounts less to a method of inquiry than to straightforward dogmatism. As Young notes, the shifting of Bhabha's terminology, which imitates the shifts of Derrida, does not do enough to conceal his static stance: fetishism is succeeded by 'hybridization', 'mimicry', 'paranoia', 'static concepts, curiously anthropomorphized, so that they possess their own desire, with no reference to the historical provenance of the theoretical material from which such concepts are drawn, or to the theoretical narrative of Bhabha's own work, or to that of the cultures to which they are addressed'.[10] It would be hard to formulate this resistance to Bhabha more clearly, but such has been the continued influence of this type of vocabulary in a certain professional academic context that it is worth reviewing Bhabha's work a little further.

The 'Introduction' to Homi Bhabha's collection of essays *Locations of Culture* (1994) is characteristic of postcolonialism's tendency to figure social questions in terms of a romantic sublimity. The 'trope of our times' we are told, is 'to locate the question of culture in the realm of the *beyond*'.[11] 'Our existence' is marked by 'a tenebrous sense of survival, living on the borderlines of the "present"': the scare quotes here remind us that only a pre-Derridean fool would think that one can inhabit the 'present', though we can all apparently agree on the tenebrous nature of the 'beyond' – a term, we are told, which is 'caught so well in the French rendition of the words *au-delà*'. Bhabha works up a metaphysics of terms, a set vocabulary, which is used in essence to dismiss the economic dimensions of social life and privilege the category of 'identity' and the 'subjective'. Deconstruction, of course, does not acknowledge such primitive entities as a stable identity (continuous self-sameness) and certainly not the philosophically bankrupt 'subject', so the foregrounding of these terms allows for the constant reiteration of their conflicted and contradictory nature, in order that the wise might know that while 'we' must seek them 'we' are all located in the very beyondness into which our seeking them ejects us. This discourse produces the internationalized postcolonial reader, equipped with a transferable vocabulary which facilitates moral judgements, academic consensus and interdisciplinary alignments: witness the endless conferences on borders, borderlines, hybridity, migration, etc. Bhabha allows himself the complacent observation that we have moved away from the 'singularities of "class" and "gender" as primary conceptual and organizational categories'. These terms are not, of course, 'singular' but relational; the coded meaning of this sentence is that no one wants to talk about socialism any more. Instead it seems that, whoever or wherever we are, our aspirations for fairer or even safer societies are to be subordinated to our supposed attempts at negotiating 'identities', national, communal, ethnic, racial – all incredibly conflicted, of course, but all amenable to being processed in the same deconstructive and psychoanalytic vocabulary. Bhabha might almost cause us to forget that decolonization, and many of the struggles within post-independence nations, were in fact shaped by Marxism, not only by a politics based on class analysis (which is not the same thing as class *identity*, although the slippage which postcolonial thought introduces might easily lead us to make the category error of thinking so) but also in the framework of a conscious internationalism – again, not an 'identity' but an aspiration and a form of the humanism with which Nietzscheans have so little patience. Robert J. C. Young (not the same Robert Young) settles the matter of the influence of Marxism in quite the other direction: 'With some exceptions, Marxism historically provided the theoretical inspiration and most effective political practice for twentieth-century anti-colonial resistance,' noting that, for example, the Irish struggle is strongly Marxist, and that many post-independence regimes were largely Marxist in character.[12] The theoretical basis of this was Lenin's argument that communists should form alliances with the bourgeoisie in national liberation struggles, aiming to pursue their struggle against the bourgeoisie once independence has been accomplished. Bhabha's discourse assures the postcolonial reader whom it interpellates that we need not deal with socialism; in this discourse, we are already a 'we'. Almost the strangest feature of this discourse is the manner in which its rhetoric settles questions of affiliation and identity in advance by reference to this already-constituted, transcendental we. This is not an accident of expression; this we is probably in the main a certain

English-speaking professional tier, but at the same time it is cast as a
community of the right-minded as surely as any London *Times* editorial
ever could be. This is the same 'we' that utters the collective 'postcolonialist
titter' during the reading of a postcolonial paper at the moment that an
antique piece of racist discourse is produced for analysis. For 'analysis'
read 'judgement', since the analysis tends to be made in advance. We get
this sense from Bhabha's treatment of the collapse of Yugoslavia which
began to unfold in 1991. At the time of publication of Bhabha's book,
ethnically Serbian groups in Croatia had been attempting to seize territory in response to the Croatian declaration of independence from Yugoslavia in 1991. The decision to hold a referendum on independence in
Bosnia in 1992 created further war between ethnic Serbs, Croats and
Bosniacs (Bosnian Muslims) in 1992. These wars, which were in origin
about the desire of ethnic Serbians to remain part of Serbia, turned into
territorial wars in which Serbian groups tended to be dominant due to
support from the Serbian army (which inherited most of the resources
of the former Yugoslav army). One feature of this war was the use of
what became called 'ethnic cleansing', the selective killing and expulsion of
rival groups when territory was seized. This tactic was used on all sides,
although the period of dominance of Serbian forces meant that it was
more closely associated in the international media with Serbia. Fighting
between Croatia and Serbia was especially intense, in part due to inflam-
matory propaganda issued by the nationalist government of Croatia, and
in part due to historical memories of the activities of the Nazi-allied
Croatian militia during the Second World War. A mess for sure, but
Bhabha supplies the judgement of the right-minded in two sentences:

> The hideous extremity of Serbian nationalism proves the very idea of a
> pure, 'ethnically cleansed' national identity can only be achieved through
> the death, literal and figurative, of the complex interweavings of history,
> and the culturally contingent borderlines of modern nationhood. This side
> of the psychosis of patriotic fervour, I like to think, there is overwhelming
> evidence of a more transnational and translational sense of the hybridity
> of imagined communities.[13]

Several things can be said about this. The first is that in a key event
where the question of identity as community and affiliation is in play
with real and not just imagined consequences, all inquiry into the mode
of formation of the identities concerned is entirely absent: Bhabha passes
straight to judgement because the material and imaginary causes of the
Yugoslav wars simply do not interest him. In a sense this is reassuring;

simple moral judgement trumps the endless rhetoric (which Bhabha picks up only a few lines after this quotation) about 'displacement', 'dislocation' and so on, things that are to be looked at in terms of imagined identities, not as material processes. It is worrying that Bhabha has no concern for the history and historical imaginary of the Yugoslav nations, as well as the concrete events, depending on actual events as well as internal propaganda, the interesting process by which certain militant groups can seek and precipitate a wider conflict forcing others to take sides. One reason for his lack of concern is that these processes are hard to access and analyse since they do not make themselves available as literary fodder (although Channel 4 in Britain got itself into hot water by offering a flattering portrait of Radovan Karadzic, a professional psychiatrist and amateur poet who became President of the Bosnian Serbs and is still wanted for war crimes, as a rather interesting example of the poet as a guardian of ethnic consciousness). More than this, though, the reason Bhabha seizes on Serbia and suppresses the historical complexity of the war in Yugoslavia is the unconscious connection with European nationalism. The hollow formulation about the 'literal' as well as metaphorical death of 'interweavings' and 'borderlines' is certainly symptomatic of thinking going wrong, but should only detain us long enough to note that it *has* gone wrong. To cut straight to a rejection of 'nationalism' implies first that 'hideously extreme' nationalisms can easily be known and identified as such, and second that the processes involved in their formation are substantially different from the processes involved for the perpetually romanticized marginalized and migratory other. In the former Yugoslavia, where the recent history concerns German, Ottoman and Hapsburg occupations, as well as the conflict between communists and fascists, affiliation, whether at the level of politics or the more 'tenebrous' level of 'identity' which postcolonialists prefer, is not reducible to 'psychosis' as Bhabha suggests. The term 'psychosis' is introduced to remind us that all this dwelling on identity is to be conducted in a liberal and pluralistic fashion; 'we' are not to arrive at the violent conclusions of militant nationalists. But the history of decolonization, and the still active history of the postcolonial world, has been largely shaped by militant nationalists; the Serbs are wheeled out to unconsciously settle 'us' into more imaginary priorities.

Like Said and Bhabha, Gayatri Chakravorty Spivak, the leading figure in postcolonial theory, privileges colonial discourse as the object of theory. Spivak's work combines elements of Marxism, feminism and deconstruction; freewheeling and occasional in nature, it avoids overarching theoretical claims, although the vocabulary and concerns are consistent enough. Born in Calcutta, Spivak is a Cornell graduate who at the time of writing teaches at Columbia; her work, and accounts of her work, focus in part on herself as a teacher, in part on the dilemmas of the 'subaltern', a term derived from Gramsci which denotes all groups subordinated along lines of race, caste, class, gender and so on. That thread in Spivak's work which celebrates the good fortune of her status as a successful academic includes an often noted essay, 'French Feminism in an International Frame' (1981). The main section of the essay is a critique of the cultural limitations of Julia Kristeva's *On Chinese Women* (1974), which Spivak uses to suggest that the privileged doctrines of French 'high feminism' might encounter problems in being applied to a different national political situation (in this case, the situation of Chinese women). This might seem unremarkable, in that criticism of Kristeva's book has been almost universal, but it is plain from the drift of Spivak's remarks that she is using this occasion to broach her views on the confining limits of US higher education. In this essay, Spivak repeatedly laments her own 'victimage', which she described in terms of her education – an English degree in Calcutta, a PhD at Cornell, a commitment to feminism as 'the best of a collection of available scenarios', and finally a move into highly theorized 'international feminism'.[14] There is usually nothing more uninteresting than the well-off complaining about their bad luck, but this apparent narcissism (which eventually yields a book title, *Outside in the Teaching Machine*) can be viewed as a materialist attempt to consider the modalities under which information is generated and distributed in a globalizing society. At the heart of Spivak's work is a critique of administrative language – especially imperialist administrative language – in its cultural dimension, by someone who herself is an enabler of cultural administration at the centre of a new empire. Spivak has asked questions about how to look outside the grid of given knowledge (which constitutes her 'victimage') in the graduate department of an elite university, and how as a feminist to go beyond the set objects of feminism, at that time, to 'Third World' subaltern subjects who do not have a voice (that she can access) and who cannot be simply mapped according to existing tenets of Western feminism:

> As soon as one steps out of the classroom, if indeed a 'teacher' ever fully can, the dangers rather than benefits of academic feminism, French or otherwise, become more insistent. Institutional changes [*sic*] against sexism here or in France may mean nothing or, indirectly, further harm for women in the Third World. This discontinuity ought to be recognised and worked at.[15]

As set out in this 1981 essay, the question seems a materialist or at least pragmatic one, and the emphasis on the teaching situation is quite typical of leftists and feminists of the period. However, the danger signs are there in the universalizing not simply of the 'West' but of the generalized and collectivized 'Third World Woman', as well as in the tincture of pathos surrounding the 'victimage' of the inquirer.

Spivak's essay 'Can the Subaltern Speak? Speculations on Widow Sacrifice' (1985) is an account of the Hindu practice of *sati* in which a widow throws herself on the funeral pyre of her husband.[16] Spivak points out that the British banned the practice, and claims that in doing so they prohibited what they regarded as a crime and an offence to Christianity, but did not allow the woman a position from which to speak. In *sati* it is patriarchy which assigns the woman a position; with the prohibition of *sati* it is imperialism which assigns her position. The critic cannot speak for her but can only produce the analysis of the enunciative subject position allowed her or, in this case, denied her. This claim is made in terms derived from European high theory, and here is the tension in this mode of postcolonial discourse. On the one hand it seeks to mark 'heterogeneity' and 'discontinuity'; on the other, the vocabulary of 'Europe', 'Other', 'West', 'subject', is entirely dependent on Western philosophy. Spivak's principal reference is to Foucault. The essay includes a discussion of a well-known interview between Foucault and Deleuze which appears in the translated collection *Language, Counter-Memory, Practice* (1977). Spivak develops Foucault's use of the episteme with reference to his account of the redefinition of madness at the end of the eighteenth century in his study *Madness and Civilization* (1961). This 'epistemic violence' is similarly at work, claims Spivak, in the 'heterogeneous project to constitute the colonial subject as Other'.[17] Spivak does warn against the sort of terminological absolutism which she finds in Foucault, whose 'too simple notion of repression' allows him to introduce an exaggerated governing term which 'fills the empty place of the agent with the historical sun of theory, the Subject of Europe'.

> This S/subject, curiously sewn together into a transparency by denegations, belongs to the exploiters' side of the international division of labor. It is impossible for French intellectuals to imagine the kind of Power and Desire that would inhabit the unnamed subject of the Other of Europe.[18]

In terms of this Subject, the subaltern woman disappears: 'Between patriarchy and imperialism, subject-constitution and object-formation, the figure of the woman disappears, not into a pristine nothingness, but into a violent shuttling that is displaced figuration of the "third-world woman".'[19] Spivak's piece plays a risky game. French anti-subjective philosophy is introduced only to be critiqued; but its contents live on in the form of a discussion which absolutely distances colonizing Subject from colonized Other. That the British, normally accused of extreme empiricism, should be found at the apex of the 'European' Subject is perhaps surprising, and it is not hard to produce reservations about Spivak's whole model. However, the mode of Spivak's work, which weaves through the grandiose vocabulary of French high theory to approach areas which are academically remote (at least in terms of the norms and expectations of literary studies) has several strategic advantages. First, as an American or, in effect, international academic, Spivak is aware of the dangers of assuming an administrative stance towards her proposed objects which would merely contribute to the continuation of imperialism by indirect means; second, Spivak works against simple models of Third World representation, which might for example solicit authentic native representation as a replacement for inauthentic colonial representation; third, Spivak continues to work against the US identity politics with which she undoubtedly once found herself surrounded – her essay on the *suttee* is a rebuttal of the type of individualist and self-centred discourse associated with much American feminist literary criticism, and her emphasis on the complexity of class and gender positioning resists easy assignments of racial or ethnic identity. Perhaps the downside of Spivak's focus on the British Empire is that, while she has certainly set an enviable example of intellectual finesse in that area, in the context of the United States she has unintentionally reinforced a tendency to see the world through the eyes of English writing, and perhaps encourage a morally easy focus on slightly more remote British history and a corresponding avoidance of politically sensitive and linguistically challenging topics in more recent American history.

*

Postcolonial theory in its origin was centred on very few figures, although the field of postcolonial literary studies has grown rapidly, and anthologies of postcolonial theory contain a good deal that goes beyond Said, Bhabha and Spivak. That said, I would like to shift the focus to a corresponding development in the United States: ethnic studies. The correspondence is not really a simple one; not least, an asymmetry is suggested by the prominence of the term 'ethnic' which postcolonial criticism worked so hard to avoid because of its intractable administrative connotations. Ethnicity is an invention, of course. Werner Sollers claims that

> ethnicity is not so much an ancient and deep-seated force surviving from the historical past, but rather the modern and modernizing sense of a contrasting strategy that may be shared far beyond the boundaries within which it is claimed. It marks an acquired modern sense of belonging that replaces visible, concrete communities whose kinship symbolism ethnicity may yet mobilize in order to appear more natural. [. . . I]t is not a thing but a process – and it requires constant detective work from readers.[20]

Ethnicity is the form under which the effects of recent history appear. The conquest of America and slavery are only part of the history of colonialism, and it is not accidental that ethnic studies have looked to postcolonial theory for many terms and themes. Equally, postcolonial studies were in their inception influenced by the example of African American culture. There are examples of modern constructed ethnicities in the nineteenth century. Italian national identity (which many Italians do not believe exists even today) was a co-ordinated response to Austrian imperial rule. Black or African American identity was a similar construct, as post-emancipation Northern and Southern blacks insisted on their common ethnicity, against an earlier practice of emphasizing their difference.[21] The transatlantic slave trade is the most extreme form of cultural dispossession imaginable; ethnicity is the mode of acknowledging this reality, and all of the problems which appear with ethnicity are not problems that lie within the concept itself; the 'falseness' of ethnicity is simply the reality of the form which catastrophe has adopted.

Ramon A. Gutierrez, founder of the Department of Ethnic Studies at University of California, San Diego, describes the emergence of ethnic studies as a discrete discipline in US universities in the early 1990s in terms of a struggle for resources. According to Gutierrez, the impulse for the inclusion of ethnic topics in university curricula in the first instance came from demands made by 'young women and men of African, Mexican, Native American and Asian ancestry'. These students 'demanded that scholars from minority communities be hired to teach the history and culture of minorities in the United States' and that 'the study of ethnicity be removed from [. . .] departments of sociology and anthropology, where race and ethnicity were pathologized, problematized and exoticized.' The shift in emphasis from civil rights to black power which took place over the 1960s saw a development of student demands 'for separate centers, programs, and departments devoted to the study of African, Asian, American Indian, and Mexican culture and history'. As

Gutierrez tells it, whether created as dependent programs of study, as autonomous departments, or even, as at the University of California, Berkeley, as an umbrella Department of Ethnic Studies, ethnic studies were engaged in a struggle for resources against a background of uneven scholarly performance and the scepticism of some university administrators. Gutierrez' own Department of Ethnic Studies at UCSD was an attempt to make, not ethnicities, but ethnic studies as such the object of study, although, as Gutierrez acknowledges, ethnicity has tended to be studied in the context of the United States, and principally with reference to 'African-Americans, Asian-Americans, Chicanos/Latinos, and Native Americans'.[22]

Gutierrez' remarks offer a potted history of the subject, but do not do justice to what is ethically imperative in ethnic studies, which do not really arise from the spontaneous demand of students, but reflect an ideology of ethnic identity which is in part an administrative fiction, in part a performative fact, and in part an obscure question of ethical responsibility to history. Ethnic studies is a consequence of slavery; although ethnic studies include other ethnicities, their origin certainly lies in African American culture and theory, which set an example and reference point for others. Slavery removed slaves from their cultures, which survived only in traces in language, gesture, music and social relationship. Modern slave descendants will often know that they are part of this history, but know that its relationship to their identity is obscure, since the history itself is obscure. History and present are refracted through cultural modes which are the domain of the historically victorious power – the white man. These modes are in some cases only broadly related to the traditional African modes, which in any case can only with difficulty be accessed by African Americans in any other than an anthropological manner. Those who choose to analyse this dilemma will find it hard to leave behind the white or Western modes of thought in which they have learned to think things; those who choose to research it will have to transform traditional materials of anthropology into something relevant; those who choose to answer the call of ethnicity will have to assess carefully their attitude to modern artistic forms and resources. All of these questions were addressed in African American thought and culture, not least in the novel, especially by Richard Wright and Ralph Ellison, and in a body of literary theory which insisted on the validity of oral and biographical materials, and critically developed analogies between literature and music in order to illuminate the existence of specifically African American trends and to capitalize on the existence of the one really original predominantly African American form, jazz.

What has proved interesting in the United States in recent decades has been the aspiration of other groups to this kind of cultural ethnic identity. These comparatively more recent ventures have found the ground better prepared, but have also inherited a high degree of theoretical complexity arising from their belatedness. There is in other words no naïve way forward. The dilemma of Native American literature is the most peculiarly pressing in US culture today. Arnold Krupat's *Ethnocriticism: Ethnography, History, Literature* (1992) situates early American Indian literature at the junction between ethnography and criticism, and connects the term to multiculturalism (a term of long use in British social administration) and cosmopolitanism. In *The Turn to the Native* (1996), Krupat contrasts postcolonial and Native American literature on the grounds that native people are still colonized in an apparently irreversible way. Krupat characterizes the project of 'Native American writers today' as an act of translation of existing cultural and linguistic contents into English:

> Even though contemporary Native writers write in English and configure their texts in apparent consonance with Western or Euramerican literary forms – that is, they give us texts that look like novels, short stories, poems, and autobiographies – they do so in ways that present an 'English' nonetheless 'powerfully affected by the foreign tongue'.[23]

Most Native writers are not fluent speakers of indigenous languages, and the invocation of an oral tradition underlying the literary is an invention of these writers. Krupat might have added that not all Native American authors set themselves such cultural goals, and that in any case the very idea of Native American may be diluted by lines of descent in ways that render the notion of the Native writer and the Native audience highly problematic. The Anishinaabe novelist and scholar Gerald Vizenor has recourse to the figure of the trickster, as found in Native literature and worldwide, as the archetype of a survival strategy in the face of domination: 'Native survivance is a sense of presence, but the true self is visionary. The true self is an ironic consciousness, the cut of a native trickster.' A creative theorist as well as a novelist, Vizenor uses his essays as vehicles of 'resistance, not tradition'. While post-structuralist pathos insists on absence, natives who have so frequently disappeared in fact must insist on presence:

> Natives have resisted empires, negotiated treaties, and, as diplomatic strategies, embraced the simulations of absence to secure the chance of a

decisive presence in national literature, history and canonry. Native resistance to dominance is an undeniable trace of presence, but even these memories of survivance in a constitutional democracy are cast as narratives of absence and victimry.[24]

This subaltern most definitely intends to speak. Vizenor's collection of essays *Fugitive Poses* (1998) focuses on the figure of the '*indian*', the invented scapegoat, whose disappearance conceals the presence of the native. The framing vocabulary is deconstructive:

> Native identities are traces, the *différance* of unnameable presence, not mere statues, inheritance, or documentation, however bright the blood and bone in museums. Native identities must be an actuation of stories, the commune of survivance and sovereignty.[25]

In a different vein, Elizabeth Cook-Lynn notes the difference between Native people and 'Third Worldists':

> What Third Worldists, then, have in common is the question of what their fictive mythmaking has to do with the reality of their postcolonial conditions as *nations* of people. For those writers who are called American Indians, the question of whether the myth of nationhood is a cultural force is often unanswerable in their works.[26]

For Native people, the question of authentic identity has often come to the fore in a manner which tends to stall the cultural project rather than carry it forward, as Sidner Larson notes in *Captured in the Middle* (2000):

> There are also other vitally important issues that remain strongly suppressed and are never discussed. The more common subjects have tended to orbit around a long-standing 'authenticity' debate that is still firmly grounded in blood quantum, wherein an individual must usually prove one-quarter Indian blood and the higher the percentage of Indian blood the more authentic the individual is considered to be. Lately, however, the debate has also branched into discussions of whether the content of Indian writing is authentic, which opens up the new problem of who is qualified to judge.[27]

According to Larson, the authenticity debate merely masks discussion of 'more tangible problems, such as genocide' and 'the *American Holocaust*' which American Indian scholars are said to mention rarely. Larson searches for a pragmatic and historically responsive mode of Native

literature and criticism, suspecting the 'double talk' of high theory imitators such as Vizenor, and noting that the demand for ethnic studies came
from the universities and placed ethnic scholars suddenly in positions of
great responsibility without much support for development, with the
result that such scholars have become 'combative' or 'transient' or simply
left academia.[28]

The work of Native scholars and writers offers intriguing insights into
the relationship between a (culturally mediated) 'people', academic institutions, literary producers, and the colossal burden which is literary theory
in all of its dimensions. This historical cultural nexus is in effect at the
ethical cutting edge of literary-theoretical discussion today. At the same
time, Native American theory and writing struggles to rise to its occasion. The difficulties are of course objective, the product of the attempt
to respond to a historical burden. Sidner Larson is rare in this context
as a philosophical pragmatist who is intent both on asserting the realities
of genocide against the finessing of questions of authenticity, and on
being sufficiently outward-oriented, as his references to Rwandan genocide show, to grasp that questions for Native Americans are really global
questions – not Native, not American, but having in their scope the
many histories of displacement, dispossession and extermination which
are the stuff of history and the real referent of culture.

However, it would be wrong to argue that ethnicity itself constitutes
the truth of history rather than its distortion and transitory effect. The
'multiculturalism' with which Krupat associates his ethnocriticism is very
much an administrative policy which depends on the perspective of the
state. As Larson notes, it is universities which have called for ethnic
studies rather than students who have spontaneously demanded them.
Multiculturalism promotes and administers ethnic difference; British
administrators and politicians who for decades have insisted on the validity and practice of multiculturalism have now begun to question it, in
the light of terrorist attacks in London by radicalized, often British-born
Moslems. This is a reminder that ethnicity and its accompanying notion
of ethnic culture are, in one of their aspects, pragmatically developed
administrative notions which hark back to the colonial period. Colonial
states were often mapped in such a way as to group together ethnically
affiliated groups which, while they had no history of nationhood in their
own right, equally had no aspiration to nationhood with the other
ethnicities with which they were grouped. Colonial administrators could
manipulate ethnic rivalries in a divide and rule strategy. We could of
course look back through British and French history for examples of this,
but we need look no further than the present, where in Iraq the policy

of exploiting the rivalry of different groups, while initially in the interest of Iraq's new administrators, has now created traumatic civil war. The war in Iraq is of a piece with events in former Yugoslavia and Rwanda, in that in each case conflict arises between officially different ethnicities within the same borders. Whether in America, Yugoslavia or Iraq, connections of kinship between different ethnicities, which in one climate or context are normal and accepted, become traumatic points of conflict as contexts change. A further challenge to ethnic mapping are the universalistic beliefs which transect ethnicities. The modern liberal state is the product of an Enlightenment that conferred abstract equality on everybody and began to treat religions as the product of superstition, although it also grounded the notion that a people had its own cultural history. Universalism goes back further, however, to St Paul's insistence that Christianity was a matter for Gentiles as well as Jews, and to the Moslem notion that the *umma* transcends nation and race. Christ urged faith in God, not war against the occupying power. The situation of Jews in the Holy Land was not dissimilar to that of other colonial and postcolonial nations today; it is for this reason that Joyce's *Ulysses* equates Dublin with Jerusalem, England with Rome, Bloom with Christ, Nationalists with Zealots – as a reflection on how to cope with the cultural and linguistic implications of conquest. Christianity and Islam challenge ethnicity and transect it. How the promotion of ethnic cultures is to sit with already accomplished universalism and its spiritual internalization is part of the problem for an ethnopoetics, of course, and it is crystal clear that ethnic culture is the mediation of historical defeat of one kind or another; but universalism too grows out of defeat and ethnic studies in their most self-conscious form have to make their reckoning with historical and current examples of ethnic conflicts as the product of administrative processes designed to facilitate domination.

*

This study began by making reference to Matthew Arnold and his review of the function of the literature of a subordinated people in relation to their conquerors. In the transition from Arnold to Vizenor it appears that much less has changed than might at first have been supposed. Throughout this, the social function of literature has remained perpetually in view. In his recent acclaimed study *The Singularity of Literature* (2004), Derek Attridge asserts that what is needed to 'complement the instrumentalist achievements of recent criticism' is 'a mode of attention to the specificity and singularity of literary writing'.[29] I suggest that literary studies may need to seek further means to reflect and act on its most fundamental processes if it is to move beyond, or at least independently alongside, the powerful vogue of ethical-instrumentalist criticism. Since literary studies tend to professional closure and conceptual repetition, it seems likely that the impetus to transformation will come from outside literary studies. The period of theory drove literary studies ever more deeply into the Other of French theory, in a fruitful way in which the very strangeness of the new theoretical idioms, and their complex and transformative relationship to German thought and classical philosophy in general, served as a mirror of recognition to literary studies, fulfilled political requirements, and crucially constituted a kind of authority which, because in essence discontinuous with the field of literary studies, could be embraced without any awkward Oedipal rivalry. French theory itself entered into the dynamics of professional productivity as it was seized upon in part to meet political needs, but in part to meet the University's demand for ever-differentiated scholarly product. Any attempt to suggest that France might again be the motor of academic change in English-speaking countries might for this reason be met by the suspicion of academic-productive motives, more so because in France, after the deaths of Baudrillard, Foucault, Lyotard and Derrida, the public intellectual is often stated to be in short supply. Scepticism about novelty will be increased if there seems little intuitive connection between existing patterns of literary theory and the newcomer, and more so if the newcomer appears to have been there for some time, quietly ignored. So it is with some hesitation that I conclude with an account of the work of French philosopher Alain Badiou. It will be interesting to see how far Badiou's work can be taken up into the mainstream of literary theory, beyond the professional interest of specialists who have made his work their domain. Badiou's key works include *Being and the Event* (1988), *Manifesto for Philosophy* (1989), *Conditions* (1992), *Ethics* (1993) and *Logics of Worlds* (2006). Until recently almost none of his work has been translated, although a recent translation of his magnum opus, *Being and the Event*, and convenient volumes of essays have made some headway towards his international adoption, and interest from literary theorists such as Thomas Docherty and Andrew Gibson has made inroads into his reception in literary studies.[30]

Badiou's *Short Manual of the Inaesthetic* (1998) has the following epigraph:

> By 'inaesthetic', I mean a relationship of philosophy to art which, positing that art is itself a producer of truths, does not claim in any fashion to make

it an object of philosophy. Contrary to aesthetic speculation, the inaesthetic describes the strictly intra-philosophical effects which are produced by the independent existence of certain works of art.[31]

The notion that philosophy and art are separate processes is central to Badiou's thought, but quite contrary both to decades of literary theory, which have constantly made literature the object of philosophy, and also to modern philosophy, which since the time of Hegel has aspired to the condition of poetry, while poetry has taken on certain of the functions of philosophy. Only certain poets, whose work resembles a truth process, have been treated as quasi-philosophers, but since Nietzsche, philosophers such as Heidegger and Derrida have *envied* the idiom of poetry. Badiou acknowledges the existence of what he terms an 'age of poets', but claims that it is over. The 'age' ran from Hölderlin via Mallarmé, Rimbaud, Trakl, Pessoa and Mandelstam to Celan – a canon which is Badiou's own. These poets embodied the uncertainty and disorientation of their age; that age is now over. These poets have in common their acceptance of the dismissal (*destitution*) of the object, that is of the notion of objectivity, and their poetry is characterized by the attempt to go beyond subject–object relations and open a way to being. Badiou describes such poetry as in essence 'de-subjectifying'. The thought of Heidegger, described in *Being and the Event* as the last universally recognized philosopher, took sustenance from his blending of the properly philosophical critique of the object with its poetic dismissal. Since the age of the poets is over, it is now necessary for philosophy to detach itself from poetry. Disorientation can now be *conceptualized*, and Heidegger was in any case wrong in his strictures on modernity to oppose the knowledge of mathematics to the truth of poetry, favouring the latter against the technologization of his age, since fundamentally poetry (Mallarmé is cited) recognizes its affinity with mathematics in that it has blindly perceived that mathematics, like poetry, lacks an object. According to Badiou's account, this means that the poets of the age of poetry, on whom Heidegger relies to distinguish between a scientific language oriented towards instrumental knowing and a poetic-philosophical language oriented to the truth of being, the question forgotten since the Greeks, are already undermined by poetry's own identification with mathematics, which tends to confirm that poetry and mathematics have a similarly 'pure' or objectless modality, undermining the opposition between them which Heidegger constructs.[32]

Badiou's thought is mapped in terms of large structures. Hitherto, he states, the connection between art and philosophy has been articulated in three ways: the didactic (Plato), in which art is at the service of truth; the romantic (Badiou includes Philippe Lacoue-Labarthe and Jean-Luc Nancy, whose joint volume *L'Absolu littéraire* [1978] is continuous with romantic thought), in which art alone is capable of truth; and classicism (Aristotle), in which art is not related to truth, but is concerned to transfer desire to an object. The three main strands of modern thought correspond to the didactic, the romantic and the classical: they are Marxism (Brecht), where art remains didactic; hermeneutics (Nietzsche, Heidegger), where the philosopher–artist approaches being through the reading of the poem; and psychoanalysis (Freud, Lacan), where the art-work is treated as imaginary investment. These models are all exhausted, and a new one must be brought into being in which art is itself a truth process (not a representation) and satisfies the conditions of being both 'immanent' ('rigorously coextensive with the truths it gives') and 'singular' ('these truths must not be found anywhere but in art'). It is a philosophical novelty to regard art as a truth process and a considerable effort of reformulation is called for. Philosophy cannot produce truth; it is always the elaboration of a category of truth. There are only four truth processes – art, science, politics and love – each of which produces a form of 'subject' as a merely local configuration (and not as the transcendental subject of old).[33] The task of philosophy in relation to art is to show that it produces truth as opposed to opinion (*doxa* – the distinction is Platonic). The question of today, states Badiou, is: 'is there anything but opinion, that is to say, one will excuse (or not) the provocation, is there anything other than our "democracies"?'[34] The 'democratic materialism' of the present day, which recognizes only the existence of bodies and languages and excludes truths, is opposed by the carefully named 'materialist dialectic' of *Logic of Worlds*, which purports to locate 'eternal truths' in art. Badiou's own writing on literature can only begin to show what a radical revaluation of the literary called for in these arguments would mean; whether the ethically dominated modes of current literary theory will be amenable to such a radical reversion of principle seems unlikely, but remains to be seen.

Notes

Introduction

1 See esp. Roy Harris, *Saussure and his Interpreters* (Edinburgh: Edinburgh University Press, 2001).

Chapter 1

1 See the invaluable 'Introduction' to Alan Bacon, ed., *The Nineteenth-Century History of English Studies* (Aldershot: Ashgate, 1998), esp. pp. 5–9.

2 See e.g. Chris Baldick, *The Social Mission of English Criticism, 1848–1932* (Oxford: Clarendon Press, 1983).

3 Matthew Arnold, *On the Study of Celtic Literature and Other Essays*, intr. Ernest Rhys (London: Dent, 1976), pp. 4–5.

4 Quoted ibid., pp. 6–7.

5 Ibid., p. 7.

6 Ibid., p. 8.

7 Ibid., pp. 110–11.

8 *Culture and Anarchy*, ed. and intr. J. Dover Wilson (Cambridge: Cambridge University Press, 1960), pp. 45, 47, 48.

9 Matthew Arnold, 'The Study of Poetry' (1880), in *Selected Criticism of Matthew Arnold*, ed. and intr. Christopher Ricks (New York and Scarborough, Ont.: New American Library, 1972), p. 171.

10 See e.g. Walter Benjamin, 'Paris, the Capital of the Nineteenth Century', in *Selected Writings*, vol. 3: *1935–1938*, ed. Howard Eiland and Michael W. Jennings, trans. Edmund Jephcott, Howard Eiland et al. (Cambridge, Mass, and London: Harvard University Press, 2002), esp. pp. 38–9.

11 *Selected Writings of Walter Pater*, ed. and intr. Harold Bloom (New York and Scarborough, Ont.: New American Library, 1974), pp. 59, 60.

12 Ezra Pound, 'The Serious Artist' (1913), in *Literary Essays of Ezra Pound*, ed. and intr. T. S. Eliot (London: Faber & Faber, 1954), p. 41.

13 Ibid., pp. 42–7.

14 F. R. Leavis, 'Mass Civilization and Minority Culture', in *For Continuity* (Cambridge: Minority Press, 1933), p. 13.

15 Ibid.

16 Ibid., pp. 16, 18, 21, 22.

17 Ibid., p. 38.

18 Edgell Rickword, review of *The Art of Being Ruled*, *The Calendar of Modern Letters* 3: 1 (Oct. 1926), pp. 247–50.

19 Wyndham Lewis. 'The Dithyrambic Spectator: An Essay on the Origins and Survival of Art', *The Calendar of Modern Letters* 1: 2 (April 1925), pp. 93–4.

20 'Comments and Reviews', *The Calendar of Modern Letters* 1: 2 (April 1925), p. 153.

21 T. S. Eliot, *The Sacred Wood: Essays on Poetry and Criticism* (London: Methuen, 1960), pp. 47–59.

22 'Commentary', *The Criterion* 7 (April 1924), p. 231.

23 Wyndham Lewis, 'The Values of the Doctrine behind Subjective Art', *The Criterion* 6: 1 (July 1927), pp. 9–13.

24 *The Criterion* 6: 2 (Aug. 1927), p. 98.

25 See David Ayers, *English Literature of the 1920s* (Edinburgh: Edinburgh University Press, 1999).

26 See Francis Mulhern, *The Moment of 'Scrutiny'* (London: NLB, 1979), pp. 22–5.

27 In *A Selection from Scrutiny*, vol. 1, ed. F. R. Leavis (Cambridge: Cambridge University Press, 1968), pp. 166–74.

28 *New Verse* 31–2 (Autumn 1938), p. 2.

29 See Edgell Rickword, 'Straws for the Wary: Antecedents for Fascism', *Left Review* 1: 1 (Oct 1934), pp. 19–25; Montagu Slater, 'The Purpose of a Left Review', *Left Review* 1: 9 (June 1935), pp. 359–65.

Chapter 2

1 Quoted in I. A. Richards, *Science and Poetry* (London: Kegan Paul, Trench, Trubner, 1926), p. 1.

2 Ibid., pp. 6, 7.

3 Ibid, p. 48.

4 For Ezra Pound's most sustained discussion of imagism, still sometimes overlooked, see his 'Vorticism', in *Gaudier-Brzeska: A Memoir* (1916; Hessle: Marvell, 1960), pp. 81–94, and for the 'objective correlative' see T. S. Eliot, *Selected Essays* (London: Faber & Faber, 1951), p. 145.

5 Richards, *Science and Poetry*, pp. 25–6, 67 (emphasis in original).

6 *Principles of Literary Criticism* (1924; repr. with two new appendices, London: Kegan Paul, 1926), p. 98. Coenaesthesia is the 'perception of one's whole bodily state arising from the sum of somatic sensations' (*OED*).

7 Richards, *Science and Poetry*, pp. 34–5, 33.

8   Ibid., pp. 60, 61, 64–5.
9   Richards, *Principles of Literary Criticism*, p. 35.
10 Richards, *Science and Poetry*, p. 67.
11 Richards, *Principles of Literary Criticism*, p. 32.
12 Ibid., p. 35.
13 'Introduction to the Torchbook Edition' of 'Twelve Southerners', *I'll Take My Stand: The South and the Agrarian Tradition*, intr. Louis D. Rubin, Jr., biographical essays by Virginia Rock (New York: Harper, 1962), p. xvii.
14 'Twelve Southerners', *I'll Take My Stand*, pp. xxiii–xxiv, 3, 4–5, 10, 14, 50, 166.
15 See Alexander Karanikas, *Tillers of Myth: Southern Agrarians as Social and Literary Critics* (Madison, Milwaukee and London: University of Wisconsin Press, 1969), pp. 171–88. See also John M. Bradbury, *The Fugitives: A Critical Account* (1958; New Haven, Conn.: College and University Press, 1964); Mark Jancovich, *The Cultural Politics of the New Criticism* (Cambridge: Cambridge University Press, 1993).
16 Michel Henry, *Marx I: Une philosophie de la réalité* (Paris: Gallimard, 1976), pp. 280–367 at p. 280.
17 Walter Benjamin, *Selected Writings*, vol. 3: *1935–1938*, ed. Howard Eiland and Michael W. Jennings, trans. Edmund Jephcott, Howard Eiland et al. (Cambridge, Mass., and London: Harvard University Press, 2002), pp. 101–33. I prefer this more literal translation of the title to the better-known one of the earlier translation.
18 Originally 'The Psychologist Looks at Poetry'. *The World's Body* (New York and London: Scribner, 1938), pp. 146, 156.
19 Ransom, *The New Criticism* (Norfolk, Conn.: New Directions, 1941), p. xi.
20 Ibid., p. 89.
21 Richards, *Science and Poetry*, p. 3.
22 Ibid., p. 25.
23 See Jacques Derrida, *Of Grammatology*, trans. Gayatri Chakravorty Spivak (Baltimore and London: Johns Hopkins University Press, 1976), pp. 30–65.
24 Ransom, *The New Criticism*, p. 5.
25 Ransom, *The World's Body*, pp. x–xi.
26 Ibid., p. 329.
27 Ibid., p. 347.
28 Ransom, *The New Criticism*, pp. 45, 111.
29 Cleanth Brooks, Jr., and Robert Penn Warren, eds., *Understanding Poetry: An Anthology for College Students* (New York: Henry Holt, 1938), p. iv.
30 Ibid., p. ix.
31 See Paul de Man, *The Resistance to Theory* (Minneapolis and London: University of Minnesota Press, 1986), pp. 3–20.
32 See e.g. Theodor Adorno, 'Commitment', in *Notes to Literature*, vol. 2, ed. Rolf Tiedemann, trans. Shierry Weber Nicholsen (New York: Columbia University Press, 1992), pp. 76–94.

33 On this topic, see Gerald Graff, *Professing Literature: An Institutional History* (Chicago and London: University of Chicago Press, 1987), p. 145, for the argument that the New Criticsism was under pressure 'to measure up to the institutional criteria set by its scholarly opposition, which was still in control of literature departments'.

34 John Guillory, *Cultural Capital: The Problem of Literary Canon Formation* (Chicago and London: University of Chicago Press, 1993), pp. 134–75.

35 Ibid., p. 14.

36 See Trevor Ross, *The Making of the English Literary Canon: From the Middle Ages to the Late Eighteenth Century* (Montreal and Kingston: McGill-Queens University Press, 1998); Jonathan Brody Kramnick, *Making the English Canon: Print-Capitalism and the Cultural Past, 1700–1770* (Cambridge: Cambridge University Press, 1998); Richard Terry, *Poetry and the Making of the English Literary Past, 1660–1781* (Oxford: Oxford University Press, 2001).

37 See Graff, *Professing Literature*, pp. 211–16.

38 In William C. Spengemann, *A Mirror for Americanists: Reflections on the Idea of American Literature* (Hanover and London: University Press of New England, 1989), p. 19.

39 'American Writers and English Literature', ibid., p. 135.

40 See Harold Bloom, *The Anxiety of Influence: A Theory of Poetry* (Oxford: Oxford University Press, 1973).

41 Frank Lentricchia, *After the New Criticism* (London: Methuen, 1980), pp. xiii, 5.

42 Northrop Frye, *Anatomy of Criticism: Four Essays* (Princeton: Princeton University Press, 1957), p. 11.

43 Ibid., pp. 24–5.

44 Ibid., p. 16.

45 Documented in Richard Macksey and Eugenio Donato, eds., *The Languages of Criticism and the Sciences of Man: The Structuralist Controversy* (Baltimore: Johns Hopkins University Press, 1970).

46 Frye, *Anatomy of Criticism*, p. 133.

47 Ibid., pp. 6, 12.

48 Ralph Ellison, *Shadow and Act* (New York: Vintage, 1972), p. xix.

49 Ibid., p. 24.

Chapter 3

1 Karl Marx, 'Preface' to *A Contribution to the Critique of Political Economy*, trans. S. W. Ryazanskaya (1859; London: Lawrence & Wishart, 1981), pp. 20–1.

2 Karl Marx and Friedrich Engels, *The German Ideology* (New York: Prometheus Books, 1998), p. 42.

3 Ibid., pp. 50, 67–8.

4   Ibid., p. 90.
5   For a convenient history of the School, see Norma Schulman, 'Conditions of their Own Making: An Intellectual History of the Centre for Contemporary Cultural Studies at the University of Birmingham', *Canadian Journal of Communication* (online), 18: 1, 1993, available at http://www.cjc-online.ca/viewarticle.php?id=140.
6   Richard Hoggart, *Speaking to Each Other*, vol. 1: *About Society* (London: Chatto & Windus, 1957), pp. 11–27.
7   Richard Hoggart, *The Uses of Literacy: Aspects of Working Class Life, with Special References to Publications and Entertainment* (London: Chatto & Windus, 1957), p. 17.
8   Ibid., p. 17.
9   Ibid., p. 309.
10 Ibid., p. 105.
11 Ibid., p. 272.
12 Hoggart, *Speaking to Each Other*, vol. 1, p. 255.
13 Ibid.
14 Cf. *Culture and Society 1780–1950* (1958 Harmondsworth: Penguin, 1963), pp. 287–90, where Williams is similarly critical of the terms 'mass', 'public' and 'man in the street' as terms which need to be grasped in terms of our 'experience' of them, i.e. in terms of their immanence.
15 Hoggart, *Speaking to Each Other*, vol. 1, pp. 256–7.
16 Ibid., pp. 257–9.
17 On this topic see e.g. Chris Baldick, *The Social Mission of English Criticism, 1848–1932* (Oxford: Clarendon Press, 1983), p. 63; Tom Steele, *The Emergence of Cultural Studies 1945–65: Cultural Politics, Adult Education and the English Question* (London: Lawrence & Wishart, 1997), pp. 33–47.
18 See Steele, The Emergence of Cultural Studies, pp. 72–81.
19 Raymond Williams, *The Politics of Modernism* (London: Verso, 1989), p. 162 and as quoted in Steele, *The Emergence of Cultural Studies*, p. 15.
20 See Steele, *The Emergence of Cultural Studies*, pp. 98–116.
21 See Williams, *Culture and Society*, pp. 262–71.
22 Ibid., p. 266.
23 Ibid., p. 273.
24 Ibid., p. 17.
25 Ibid., p. 48.
26 Ibid., p. 96.
27 Ibid., pp. 244, 246.
28 Raymond Williams, *Politics and Letters: Interviews with New Left Review* (London: NLB, 1979), pp. 100, 119–20.
29 Raymond Williams, *The Long Revolution* (London: Chatto & Windus, 1961), pp. ix–xi.
30 Ibid., pp. 29, 31, 38–9.
31 Ibid., p. 41.

32 Ibid., pp. 46, 48–9, 61–3.
33 Ibid., pp. 67–8.
34 Walter Benjamin, *Selected Writings*, vol. 3: *1935–1938*, ed. Howard Eiland and Michael Jennings, trans. Edmund Jephcott, Howard Eiland et al. (Cambridge, Mass., and London: Harvard University Press, 2002), p. 33.
35 Williams, *The Long Revolution*, p. 71.
36 Williams. *Politics and Letters*, p. 139.
37 Ibid., p. 159.
38 Ibid., p. 163.
39 Ibid., pp. 169–70.
40 See John Eldridge and Lizzie Eldridge, *Raymond Williams: Making Connections* (London and New York: Routledge, 1994), pp. 4–6.
41 Williams, *Politics and Letters*, p. 168.
42 Ibid., p. 172.

Chapter 4

1 Dates shown are dates of translation: *Pour Marx* (Paris: Maspero, 1965) as *For Marx* (London: Allen Lane, 1968); with Étienne Balibar, *Lire 'le Capital'* (1965; Paris: Maspero, 1969) as *Reading Capital* (London: NLB, 1970); *Lénine et la philosophie* (Paris: Maspero, 1969) as *Lenin and Philosophy: and Other Essays* (London: NLB, 1971).
2 See Althusser, *For Marx*, pp. 21–31.
3 Perry Anderson, 'Components of the National Culture,' *New Left Review* 50 (July–Aug. 1968), pp. 3–4.
4 Ibid., pp. 42–3. Quoted from Louis Althusser, 'Freud et Lacan', *La Nouvelle Critique* 161–2 (Dec.–Jan. 1964–5), p. 107.
5 See Althusser, 'Ideology and Ideological State Apparatuses', in *Lenin and Philosophy*, pp. 127–86.
6 See Pierre Macherey, *A Theory of Literary Production*, trans. G. Wall (London: Routledge & Kegan Paul, 1978), pp. 82–93.
7 Terry Eagleton adopted this phrase as the title of his collection, *Against the Grain: Essays 1975–1985* (London: Verso, 1986).
8 C. B. Cox and A. E. Dyson, eds., *The Twentieth Century Mind: History, Ideas and Literature in Britain*, vol. 3: *1945–1965* (London: Oxford University Press, 1972), pp. 440–63.
9 Anderson, 'Components of the National Culture', p. 51. Quoted phrases are from F. R. Leavis, *Education and the University: A Sketch an English 'School'* (London: Chatto & Windus, 1943), p. 33.
10 Perry Anderson, *Considerations on Western Marxism* (London: NLB, 1976), p. 49.
11 Ibid., p. 103.
12 Tony Cliff's *State Capitalism in Russia* (1955; London: Pluto, 1974) was the set text of this argument.

13 See e.g. Judith Hole and Ellen Levine, *Rebirth of Feminism* (1971; New York: Quadrangle, 1975), p. 17.

14 See ibid., pp. 113–14.

15 Juliet Mitchell, 'Women: The Longest Revolution', *New Left Review* 1: 40, pp. 2–65.

16 Juliet Mitchell, *Women's Estate* (Harmondsworth: Penguin, 1971), p. 96 (emphasis in original).

17 Sheila Rowbotham, *Hidden from History: 300 Years of Women's Oppression and the Fight against It* (1973; London: Pluto, 1977), pp. 168–9.

18 See Barbara Caine, *English Feminism 1780–1980* (Oxford: Oxford University Press, 1997), pp. 260–3.

19 See Micheline Wandor, ed., *The Body Politic: Writings from the Women's Liberation Movement in Britain 1969–1972* (London: Stage 1, 1972), p. 2.

20 Elaine Showalter, *A Literature of their Own: British Women Novelists from Brontë to Lessing* (Princeton: Princeton University Press, 1977), p. 8.

21 Elaine Showalter, 'Feminist Criticism in the Wilderness', in Elizabeth Abel, ed., *Writing and Sexual Difference* (Brighton: Harvester, 1982), pp. 10, 17–35.

22 See Richard Macksey and Eugenio Donato, eds., *The Languages of Criticism and the Sciences of Man: The Structuralist Controversy* (Baltimore and London: Johns Hopkins University Press, 1970).

23 See Frank Lentricchia, *After the New Criticism* (Chicago: University of Chicago Press, 1980), pp. 103–5.

24 Fredric Jameson, *Marxism and Form: Twentieth Century Dialectical Theories of Literature* (Princeton: Princeton University Press, 1971), p. x.

25 Fredric Jameson, *The Prison-House of Language: A Critical Account of Structuralism and Russian Formalism* (Princeton: Princeton University Press, 1972), pp. vi–ix.

26 Ferdinand de Saussure, *Course in General Linguistics*, intr. Jonathan Culler, ed. Charles Bally, Albert Sechehaye and Albert Reidlinger, trans. Wade Baskin (London: Peter Owen, 1974), p. 101.

27 Ibid., pp. 9–14.

28 Jonathan Culler, *Structuralist Poetics: Structuralism, Linguistics and the Study of Literature* (London and Henley: Routledge & Kegan Paul, 1975), p. 9.

29 Ibid., pp. 113–14.

30 Ibid., p. 118.

31 Ibid., pp. 120–1.

32 Northrop Frye, *Anatomy of Criticism: Four Essays* (Princeton: Princeton University Press, 1957), quoted ibid., p. 119.

33 Culler, *Structuralist Poetics*, p. 125.

34 See Roy Harris, *Saussure and his Interpreters* (Edinburgh: Edinburgh University Press, 2001), p. 4.

Chapter 5

1   Seán Burke, *The Death and Return of the Author: Criticism and Subjectivity in Barthes, Foucault and Derrida* (1992; 2nd edn. Edinburgh: Edinburgh University Press, 1998), pp. 11–13.

2   Claude Lévi-Strauss, *Structural Anthropology*, trans. Claire Jacobson and Brooke Grundfest Schoepf (Harmondsworth: Penguin, 1972), pp. 31, 33.

3   Ibid., p. 34, emphasis in original.

4   Ibid., pp. 67–72.

5   Ibid., pp. 93, 94.

6   Ibid., pp. 12, 13.

7   In Lee T. Lemon and Marion J. Reis, eds., trans. and intr., *Russian Formalist Criticism: Four Essays* (Lincoln and London: University of Nebraska Press, 1965), p. 12 (emphasis in original).

8   Ibid., p. 23 (emphasis in original).

9   See Ken Hirschkop and David Shepherd, eds., *Bakhtin and Cultural Theory* (1989; rev. edn. Manchester and New York: Manchester University Press, 2001), pp. 1–13.

10 Ken Hirschkop, *Mikhail Bakhtin: An Aesthetic for Democracy* (Oxford: Oxford University Press, 1999), p. vii.

11 Mikhail Bakhtin, *Rabelais and his World*, trans. Helene Iswolsky (1968; Bloomington: Indiana University Press, 1984), pp. 4–6.

12 Ibid., p. 10.

13 Ibid., p. 19.

14 See Francis Barker et al., eds., *The Politics of Theory: Proceedings of the Essex Conference on the Sociology of Literature July 1982* (Colchester: University of Essex, 1983) pp. 234–45.

15 Terry Eagleton, *Literary Theory: An Introduction* (1983; 2nd edn. Oxford: Blackwell, 1996), p. 200.

16 Mikhail Bakhtin, *The Dialogic Imagination: Four Essays*, ed. Michael Holquist, trans. Caryl Emerson and Michael Holquist (Austin: University of Texas Press, 1981), p. 300.

17 Ibid., p. 366 (emphasis in original).

18 Dale M. Bauer and Susan Jaret McKinstry, eds., *Feminism, Bakhtin and the Dialogic* (New York: State University of New York Press, 1991), pp. 1, 2 , 4.

19 Nancy Glazener, 'Dialogic Subversion: Bakhtin, the Novel and Gertrude Stein', in Hirschkop and Shepherd, *Bakhtin and Cultural Theory*, pp. 157, 160.

20 Eagleton, *Literary Theory*, p. 122.

21 In Peter Widdowson, ed., *Re-Reading English* (London and New York: Methuen, 1982, pp. 1, 2, 4.

22 I here set aside the question marks against the anthropological basis of this metaphor. See e.g. Robert Young, *White Mythologies: Writing History and the West* (London and New York: Routledge, 1990) pp. 144, 208 n. 4.

23 Eagleton, *Literary Theory*, pp. 77–8.
24 Ibid., p. 107.
25 Ibid., p. 128.
26 Roland Barthes, *Œuvres Complètes*, vol. 3: *1974–1980*, ed. Eric Marty (Paris: Seuil, 1995), pp. 36–40.
27 Roland Barthes, 'The Death of the Author', in *Image Music Text*, ed. and trans. Stephen Heath (London: Fontana, 1977), pp. 142–8.
28 See Julia Kristeva, *Revolution in Poetic Language*, intr. Leon S. Roudiez, trans. Margaret Waller (New York: Columbia University Press, 1984), pp. 25–30.
29 In Jacques Derrida, *Dissemination*, trans. Barbara Johnson (London: Athlone, 1981), pp. 173–286.
30 See Maud Ellmann, *The Poetics of Impersonality: T. S. Eliot and Ezra Pound* (Brighton: Harvester, 1987).
31 Kristeva, *Revolution in Poetic Language*, pp. 59–60.
32 On this topic see Hans-Georg Gadamer, *Truth and Method*, trans. Weinsheimer and Marshall (New York: Continuum, 1998), pp. 173–84.
33 Roland Barthes, 'From Work to Text', in *Image Music Text*, pp. 155–64.
34 Michel Foucault, 'What is an Author?', in *Language, Counter-Memory, Practice: Selected Essays and Interviews*, ed. and intr. Donald F. Bouchard, trans. Donald F. Bouchard and Sherry Simon (Oxford: Blackwell, 1977), pp. 123–4.
35 See e. g. Peter Washington, *Fraud: Literary Theory and the End of English* (London: Fontana, 1989).
36 Burke, *The Death and Return of the Author*: on Barthes, see pp. 20–9; on Wimsatt and Beardsley, see pp. 138–9; on Nietzsche and Heidegger, see pp. 113–14, 117–19; and on the proliferation of epochs, see p. 173.
37 Christopher Norris, *Derrida* (London: Fontana, 1987); *Deconstruction and the Interests of Theory* (London: Pinter, 1988); *Deconstruction: Theory and Practice* (London: Methuen, 1982); *The Deconstructive Turn: Essays in the Rhetoric of Philosophy* (London: Methuen, 1983).
38 G. W. F. Hegel, *Phenomenology of Spirit*, trans. A. V. Miller (Oxford: Oxford University Press, 1977), p. 1; quoted in Derrida, *Dissemination*, pp. 9–10.
39 See Martin Heidegger, *Being and Time*, trans. Macquarrie and Robinson (Oxford: Blackwell, 1962), pp. 41–9.
40 For a discussion of this term see Jacques Derrida, 'Letter to a Japanese Friend', in Peggy Kamuf, ed., *A Derrida Reader: Between the Blinds* (New York and London: Harvester, 1991), pp. 269–76.
41 On 'under erasure' see its originating exposition in Martin Heidegger, 'On the Question of Being' (1955), in *Pathmarks*, ed. William McNeill (Cambridge: Cambridge University Press, 1998), pp. 310–11.

Chapter 6

1 For a brief discussion of the discovery of this text and reference to its effects on Lukács, see Karl Marx, *Early Writings*, intr. Lucio Colletti, trans. Rodney

Livingstone and Gregor Benton (Harmondsworth: Penguin, 1975), 'Introduction', pp. 7–18.

2　See Louis Althusser, *For Marx*, trans. Ben Brewster (1969; London: Verso, 2005), pp. 231–6.

3　Georg Lukács, *History and Class Consciousness*, trans. Rodney Livingstone (London: Merlin, 1971), pp. 83–4.

4　Ibid., p. 86.

5　Ibid., pp. 92, 100.

6　See Theodor Adorno et al., *Aesthetics and Politics* (London: Verso, 1980), pp. 9–59.

7　Letter of March 1936, in Theodor W. Adorno and Walter Benjamin, *The Complete Correspondence 1928–1940*, ed. Henry Lonitz, trans. Nicholas Walker (Cambridge, Mass.: Harvard University Press, 1999), p. 130.

8　See e.g. Max Paddison, *Adorno, Modernism and Mass Culture: Essays on Critical Theory and Music* (London: Kahn & Averill, 1996).

9　See 'Gebrauchsmusik' (1924), in Theodor Adorno, *Gesammelte Schriften*, vol. 19, ed. Rolf Tiedemann (Frankfurt am Main: Suhrkamp, 1984), pp. 445–7; 'Die stabilisierte Musik' (1928), in *Gesammelte Schriften*, vol. 18 (1984), pp. 721–8.

10　See Rolf Wiggershaus, *The Frankfurt School*, trans. Michael Robertson (Cambridge: Polity, 1994), p. 401.

11　See ibid., pp. 541–3.

12　Theodor Adorno and Max Horkheimer, *Dialectic of Enlightenment*, trans. John Cumming (London: NLB, 1979), pp. 3, 9.

13　Ibid., p. 41.

14　Ibid., p. 120.

15　See Francis Barker, John Coombes, Peter Hulme, David Musselwhite and Richard Osborne, eds., *Literature, Society and the Sociology of Literature: Proceedings of the Conference Held at the University of Essex July 1976* (Colchester: University of Essex, 1977).

16　See Francis Barker et al., eds., *The Politics of Theory: Proceedings of the Essex Conference on the Sociology of Literature July 1982* (Colchester: University of Essex, 1983).

17　See Francis Barker et al., eds., *1936: The Sociology of Literature*, vol. 1: *The Politics of Modernism. Proceedings of the Essex Conference on the Sociology of Literature July 1978* (Essex: University of Essex, 1979), pp. 190–213. This piece was later published in the deconstructionist journal, *The Oxford Literary Review* 3: 3 (1979), pp. 16–27, confirming its real provenance.

18　Michel Foucault, 'Truth and Power', in *Power/Knowledge: Selected Interviews and Other Writings 1971–1977*, ed. Colin Gordon, trans. Colin Gordon et al. (New York and Hemel Hempstead: Harvester, 1980), p. 109.

19　See Paul Rabinow, 'Modern and Counter-Modern: Ethos and Epoch in Heidegger and Foucault', in Gary Gutting, ed., *The Cambridge Companion to Foucault* (Cambridge: Cambridge University Press, 1994), pp. 197–213.

20 See 'Foreword to the English Edition', in Michel Foucault, *The Order of Things: An Archaeology of the Human Sciences* (London: Tavistock, 1974), p. xiv.
21 Michel Foucault, *The Archaeology of Knowledge*, transl. A. M. Sheridan Smith (1972; London: Tavistock, 1974), pp. 25, 27–8 (emphasis in original).
22 Foucault, 'Truth and Power', p. 114.
23 Ibid., p. 118.
24 Ibid., p. 117.
25 Ihab Hassan, 'POSTmodernISM', *New Literary History* 3: 1 (1971), pp. 5–30.
26 For this term, see Gérard Genette, *Introduction à l'architexte* (Paris: Seuil, 1979).
27 See e.g. Daniel Bell, *The Coming of Post-Industrial Society* (New York: Basic Books, 1973); Ernest Mandel, *Late Capitalism* (London: Verso, 1975).
28 Jean-François Lyotard, *The Postmodern Condition: A Report on Knowledge*, trans. Geoff Bennington and Brian Massumi (Minneapolis: University of Minnesota Press, 1984), p. xxiv.
29 For this context, see Jean-François Lyotard, *Political Writings*, trans. Bill Readings and Paul Geiman (Minneapolis: University of Minnesota Press, 1993).
30 Lyotard, *The Postmodern Condition*, pp. 12–13.
31 Ibid., p. xxiv.
32 See esp. 'The Sublime and the Avant-Garde', in *The Lyotard Reader*, ed. Andrew Benjamin (Oxford: Blackwell, 1989), pp. 196–211.
33 See Fredric Jameson, 'Postmodernism: or, The Cultural Logic of Late Capitalism', *New Left Review* 146 (1984), pp. 53–92.

Chapter 7

1 See Todd Gitlin, 'The Anti-political Populism of Cultural Studies', in Marjorie Ferguson and Peter Golding, eds., *Cultural Studies in Question* (London, Thousand Oaks and New Delhi: Sage, 1997), p. 28.
2 See Ernst Benjamin, 'A Faculty Response to the Fiscal Crisis: From Defense to Offense', in Michael Bérubé and Cary Nelson, eds., *Higher Education under Fire: Politics, Economics, and the Crisis of the Humanities* (New York and London: Routledge, 1995), pp. 52–71.
3 Jim Neilson, 'The Great PC Scare: Tyrannies of the Left, Rhetoric of the Right', in Jeffrey Williams, ed., *PC Wars: Politics and Theory in the Academy* (New York and London: Routledge, 1995), p. 65.
4 Quoted in John K. Wilson, *The Myth of Political Correctness: The Conservative Attack on Higher Education* (Durham, NC, and London: Duke University Press, 1995), p. 8.
5 Neilson, 'The Great PC Scare', p. 72.
6 Lynne V. Cheney, *Telling the Truth* (1995; New York: Simon & Schuster, 1996), pp. 20–21.

7   Arthur M. Schlesinger, Jr., *The Disuniting of America: Reflections on a Multicultural America* (New York and London: Norton, 1992), pp. 10, 15, 74, 93.

8   All details from Irving Louis Horowitz and William H. Friedland, *The Knowledge Factory: Student Power and Academic Politics in America* (1970; Carbondale and Edwardsville: Southern Illinois University Press, 1972), pp. 267–79.

9   Allan Bloom, *The Closing of the American Mind: How Higher Education Has Failed Democracy and Impoverished the Souls of Today's Students* (London: Penguin, 1988), p. 313.

10 Ibid., pp. 151–2.

11 Ibid., pp. 150–1.

12 Ibid., p. 226.

13 E. D. Hirsch, Jr., *Cultural Literacy: What Every American Needs to Know* (1987; with rev. appendix, New York: Vintage Books, 1988). Quoted text from front cover.

14 Ibid., pp. 2, 26.

15 Ibid., pp. 82–83.

16 Wilson, *The Myth of Political Correctness*, pp. 4–5.

17 *Leon Trotsky on Britain*, intr. George Novak (New York: Monad, 1973), p. 253.

18 Leon Trotsky (1937), quoted in Vadim Z. Rogovin, *1937: Stalin's Year of Terror*, trans. Frederick S. Choate (Oak Park, Mich.: Mehring Books, 1998), p. 142.

19 George Orwell, *Nineteen Eighty-Four* (Harmondsworth: Penguin, 1954), p. 16.

20 Richard Stites, *Revolutionary Dreams: Utopian Vision and Experimental Life in the Russian Revolution* (New York and Oxford: Oxford University Press, 1989), pp. 131–5.

21 John Molyneux, 'The "Politically Correct" Controversy', *International Socialism Journal* 61 (Winter 1993), available at http://pubs.socialistreviewindex.org.uk/isj61/molyneux.htm.

22 See Terry Martin, *The Affirmative Action Empire: Nations and Nationalism in the Soviet Union, 1923–1939* (Ithaca and London: Cornell University Press, 2001), e.g. pp. 17–18 , 405–6, 412; David Brandenberger, *National Bolshevism: Stalinist Mass Culture and the Formation of Modern Russian National Identity, 1931–1956* (Cambridge, Mass., and London: Harvard University Press, 2002), pp. 77–94.

23 See Vladimir Lenin, 'On Proletarian Culture' (1920), *Lenin on Literature and Art* (Moscow: Progress Publishers, 1967), pp. 166–8; Leon Trotsky, 'Class and Art' (1924), in *Trotsky on Literature and Art*, ed. and intr. Paul N. Siegel (New York: Pathfinder, 1972), pp. 63–82.

24 See Jeffrey Brooks, *Thank You, Comrade Stalin! Soviet Public Culture from Revolution to Cold War* (Princeton: Princeton University Press, 2000), pp. 106–25.

25 Wilson, *The Myth of Political Correctness*, p. 5.

26 Gerald Graff, *Beyond the Culture Wars: How Teaching the Conflicts Can Revit-alize American Education* (New York and London: Norton, 1992), p. viii.

27 See 'Critique of Hegel's Doctrine of the State', in Karl Marx, *Early Writings*, intr. Lucio Colletti, trans. Rodney Livingstone and Gregor Benton (Harmondsworth: Penguin, 1975), pp. 57–198.

28 Graff, *Beyond the Culture Wars*, pp. 25–30.

29 Jeffrey Herf, 'How the Culture Wars Matter: Liberal Historiography, German History, and the Jewish Catastrophe', in Bérubé and Nelson, eds., *Higher Education under Fire*, pp. 154–5.

30 Michael Apple, 'Cultural Capital and Official Knowledge', in Bérubé and Nelson, eds., *Higher Education under Fire*, p. 98.

31 Cyrill Levitt, Scott Davies and Neil McLaughlin, eds., *Mistaken Identities: The Second Wave of Controversy over 'Political Correctness'* (New York: Peter Lang, 1999), p. 8.

32 Levitt et al., *Mistaken Identities*, pp. 8–9.

33 See Richard Ohmann, 'English and the Cold War', in Noam Chomsky et al., *The Cold War and the University: Toward an Intellectual History of the Postwar Years* (New York: New Press, 1997), pp. 73–105.

34 Levitt et al., *Mistaken Identities*, pp. 162–4.

35 Henry Louis Gates, 'Good-bye Columbus? Notes on the Culture of Criticism', in David Theo Goldberg, ed., *Multiculturalism: A Reader* (Oxford and Cambridge, Mass.: Blackwell, 1994), pp. 212–13.

36 Richard Rorty, *Achieving our Country: Leftist Thought in Twentieth-Century America* (Cambridge, Mass., and London: Harvard University Press, 1998), pp. 36–7, 91–2.

Chapter 8

1 Eve Kosofsky Sedgwick, *Between Men: English Literature and Male Homosocial Desire* (New York: Columbia University Press, 1985), pp. 1–2, 20.

2 Ibid., p. 1.

3 Ibid., p. 115.

4 Judith Butler, *Gender Trouble: Feminism and the Subversion of Identity* (New York and London: Routledge, 1990), pp. 8, 36.

5 Ibid., pp. 24–5.

6 Ibid., p. 140.

7 Jacques Derrida, 'The Supplement of Copula: Philosophy before Lin-guistics' (1971), in *Margins of Philosophy*, trans. Alan Bass (New York and London: Harvester Wheatsheaf, 1982), pp. 175–205.

8 See e.g. Aijaz Ahmad, *In Theory: Classes, Nations, Literatures* (London and New York: Verso, 1992), pp. 43–71.

9 Robert Young, *White Mythologies: Writing History and the West* (London and New York: Routledge, 1990), p. 134.

10 Ibid., p. 146.
11 Homi K. Bhabha, *The Location of Culture* (New York and London: Routledge, 1994), p. 1.
12 Robert J. C. Young, *Postcolonialism: A Historical Introduction* (Oxford: Blackwell, 2001), p. 169.
13 Bhabha, *The Location of Culture*, p. 5.
14 In Gayatri Chakravorty Spivak, *In Other Worlds: Essays in Cultural Politics* (New York and London: Routledge, 1988), p. 134.
15 Ibid., p. 150.
16 References are to the revised and greatly expanded version in *A Critique of Postcolonial Reason: Toward a History of the Vanishing Present* (Cambridge, Mass., and London: Harvard University Press, 1999), pp. 244–311.
17 Ibid., p. 266.
18 Ibid., pp. 254, 254n., 265.
19 Ibid., p. 304.
20 Werner Sollors, ed., *The Invention of Ethnicity* (New York and Oxford: Oxford University Press, 1989), pp. xiv–xv.
21 See Judith Stein, 'Defining the Race', in Sollors, *The Invention of Ethnicity*, pp. 77–104.
22 Ramon A. Guttierez, 'Ethnic Studies: Its Evolution in American Colleges and Universities', in David Theo Goldberg, ed., *Multiculturalism: A Reader* (Oxford and Cambridge, Mass.: Blackwell, 1994), pp. 156, 158, 164–5.
23 'Postcolonialism, Ideology and Native American Literature', in Amrijit Singh and Peter Schmidt, eds., *Postcolonial Theory and the United States: Race, Ethnicity and Literature* (Jackson: University Press of Mississippi, 2000), p. 77 (from *The Turn to the Native* [1996]).
24 Gerald Vizenor, *Fugitive Poses: Native American Indian Scenes of Absence and Presence* (Lincoln and London: University of Nebraska Press, 1998), p. 23.
25 Ibid., p. 37.
26 Elizabeth Cook-Lynn, *Why I Can't Read Wallace Stegner and Other Essays: A Tribal Voice* (Madison: University of Wisconsin Press, 1996), p. 89.
27 Sidner Larson, *Captured in the Middle: Tradition and Experience in Contemporary Native American Writing* (Seattle and London: University of Washington Press, 2000), pp. 41, 42.
28 Ibid., pp. 47–8.
29 Derek Attridge, *The Singularity of Literature* (London and New York: Routledge, 2004), p. 13.
30 See Thomas Docherty, *Alterities: Criticism, History, Representation* (Oxford: Clarendon Press, 1996); Andrew Gibson, *Beckett and Badiou: The Pathos of Intermittency* (Oxford: Oxford University Press, 2007).
31 Alain Badiou, *Petit manuel d'inesthétique* (Paris: Seuil, 1998), p. 7.
32 This account summarizes Alain Badiou, *Manifeste pour la philosophie* (Paris: Seuil, 1989), pp. 49–58.

33 See Alain Badiou, *L'être et l'événement* (Paris: Seuil, 1988), pp. 23–4 on generic procedures and truth, and pp. 429–30 on subject.

34 This paragraph paraphrases *Petit manuel d'inesthétique*, pp. 9–29. The quotation appears on p. 29. See also Alain Badiou, *Conditions* (Paris: Seuil, 1992), pp. 93–107. For a development of Badiou's thought on the immersion of ethics in 'opinion' (*doxa*), see Alain Badiou, *L'éthique: Essais sur la conscience du mal* (Paris: Hatier, 1993).

Selected Bibliography

Abel, Elizabeth, ed. *Writing and Sexual Difference*. Brighton: Harvester, 1982.

Adorno, Theodor W., and Walter Benjamin. *The Complete Correspondence 1928–1940*. Ed. Henry Lonitz, trans. Nicholas Walker. Cambridge, Mass.: Harvard University Press, 1999.

Adorno, Theodor, Walter Benjamin, Ernst Bloch, Bertolt Brecht and Georg Lukács, *Aesthetics and Politics*. London: Verso, 1980.

Adorno, Theodor, and Max Horkheimer. *Dialectic of Enlightenment*. Trans. John Cumming. London: NLB, 1979.

Ahmad, Aijaz. *In Theory: Classes, Nations, Literatures*. London and New York: Verso, 1992.

Allen, Sandra, Lee Sanders and Jan Wallis, eds. *Conditions of Illusion: Papers from the Women's Movement*. Leeds: Feminist Books, 1974.

Althusser, Louis. *For Marx*. Trans. Ben Brewster. London and New York: Verso, 2005. First publ. in Eng. 1969.

—— *Lenin and Philosophy*. Trans. Ben Brewster. London: NLB, 1971.

—— and Étienne Balibar. *Reading Capital*. Trans. Ben Brewster. London: NLB, 1970.

Anderson, Perry. *Considerations on Western Marxism*. London: NLB, 1976.

Arnold, Matthew, *Culture and Anarchy*. Ed. and intr. J. Dover Wilson. Cambridge: Cambridge University Press, 1960.

—— *On the Study of Celtic Literature and Other Essays*. Intr. Ernest Rhys. London: Dent, 1976.

—— *Selected Criticism of Matthew Arnold*. Ed. and intr. Christopher Ricks. New York and Scarborough, Ont.: New American Library, 1972.

Ashcroft, Bill, Gareth Griffiths and Helen Tiffin, eds. *The Post-Colonial Studies Reader*. London and New York: Routledge, 1995.

Attridge, Derek. *The Singularity of Literature*. London and New York: Routledge, 2004.

Bacon, Alan, ed. *The Nineteenth-Century History of English Studies*. Aldershot: Ashgate, 1998.

Badiou, Alain. *Conditions*. Paris: Seuil, 1992.

—— *L'éthique: Essais sur la conscience du mal*. Paris: Hatier, 1993.

—— *L'être et l'événement*. Paris: Seuil, 1988.

—— *Logiques des mondes*. Paris: Seuil, 2006.

—— *Manifeste pour la philosophie*. Paris: Seuil, 1989.

—— *Petit manuel d'inesthétique*. Paris: Seuil, 1998.

Bak, Hans, ed. *Multiculturalism and the Canon of American Culture*. Amsterdam: Vu University Press, 1993.

Baker, Houston A. *Long Black Song: Essays in African American Literature and Culture*. Charlottesville: University Press of Virginia, 1972.

Bakhtin, Mikhail. *The Dialogic Imagination: Four Essays*. Ed. Michael Holquist, trans. Caryl Emerson and Michael Holquist. Austin: University of Texas Press, 1981.

—— *Problems of Dostoevsky's Poetics*. Trans. Caryl Emerson. Manchester: Manchester University Press, 1984.

—— *Rabelais and his World*. Trans. Helene Iswolsky. Bloomington: Indiana University Press, 1984.

Baldick, Chris. *The Social Mission of English Criticism, 1848–1932*. Oxford: Clarendon Press, 1983.

Barker, Francis, John Coombes, Peter Hulme, Colin Mercer and David Musselwhite, eds. *1936: The Sociology of Literature*, vol. 1: *The Politics of Modernism. Proceedings of the Essex Conference on the Sociology of Literature July 1978*. Essex: University of Essex, 1979.

—— eds. *1936: The Sociology of Literature*, vol. 2: *Practices of Literature and Politics. Proceedings of the Essex Conference on the Sociology of Literature July 1978*. Essex: University of Essex, 1979.

Barker, Francis, Margaret Iverson and Jennifer Stone, eds. *The Politics of Theory: Proceedings of the Essex Conference on the Sociology of Literature July 1982*. Colchester: University of Essex, 1983.

Barker, Francis, John Coombes, Peter Hulme, David Musselwhite and Richard Osborne, eds. *Literature, Society and the Sociology of Literature: Proceedings of the Conference Held at the University of Essex July 1976*. Colchester: University of Essex, 1977.

Barthes, Roland. *Elements of Semiology*. Trans. Annette Lavers and Colin Smith. New York: Hill and Wang, 1968. First publ. 1964.

—— *Image Music Text*. Ed. and trans. Stephen Heath. London: Fontana, 1977.

—— *Mythologies*. Trans. Annette Lavers. London: Paladin, 1973.

—— *Œuvres Complètes*, vol. 3: *1974–1980*. Ed. Eric Marty. Paris: Seuil, 1995.

Baudrillard, Jean. *For Critique of the Political Economy of the Sign*. St Louis, Mo.: Telos, 1981.

—— *Symbolic Exchange and Death*. Intr. Mike Gane, trans. Iain Hamilton Grant. London: Sage, 1993.

Bauer, Dale M., and Susan Jaret McKinstry, eds. *Feminism, Bakhtin and the Dialogic.* Albany: State University of New York Press, 1991.

Bauman, Zygmunt. *Legislators and Interpreters: On Modernity, Postmodernity and Intellectuals.* Cambridge: Polity, 1987.

Bell, Daniel. *The Coming of Post-Industrial Society.* New York: Basic Books, 1973.

Benjamin, Walter. *Selected Writings,* vol. 3: *1935–1938.* Ed. Howard Eiland and Michael W. Jennings. Trans. Edmund Jephcott, Howard Eiland et al. Cambridge, Mass., and London: Harvard University Press, 2002.

Bercovitch, Sacvan, and Myra Jehlen, eds. *Ideology and Classic American Literature.* Cambridge: Cambridge University Press, 1986.

Bernstein, Charles, ed. *The Politics of Poetic Form: Poetry and Public Policy.* New York: Roof, 1993.

Bérubé, Michael. *Public Access: Literary Theory and American Cultural Politics.* London and New York: Verso, 1994.

Bérubé, Michael, and Cary Nelson, eds. *Higher Education under Fire: Politics, Economics, and the Crisis of the Humanities.* New York and London: Routledge, 1995.

Bhabha, Homi K. *The Location of Culture.* New York and London: Routledge, 1994.

Bloom, Allan. *The Closing of the American Mind: How Higher Education Has Failed Democracy and Impoverished the Souls of Today's Students.* Foreword by Saul Bellow. 1987. London: Penguin, 1988.

Bloom, Harold. *The Anxiety of Influence: A Theory of Poetry.* Oxford: Oxford University Press, 1973.

Bloom, Harold, Paul de Man, Jacques Derrida, Geoffrey H. Hartman and J. Hillis Miller. *Deconstruction and Criticism.* New York: Continuum, 1999. First publ. 1979.

Bradbury, John M. *The Fugitives: A Critical Account.* New Haven, Conn.: College and University Press, 1964. First publ. 1958.

Brandenberger, David. *National Bolshevism: Stalinist Mass Culture and the Formation of Modern Russian National Identity, 1931–1956.* Cambridge, Mass., and London: Harvard University Press, 2002.

Brantlinger, Patrick. *Crusoe's Footprints: Cultural Studies in Britain and America.* New York: Routledge, 1990.

Breton, André. *Manifestes du surréalisme.* Paris: Gallimard, 1962.

Brooks, Cleanth, Jr., and Robert Penn Warren, eds. *Understanding Poetry: An Anthology for College Students.* New York: Henry Holt, 1938.

Brooks, Jeffrey. *Thank You, Comrade Stalin! Soviet Public Culture from Revolution to Cold War.* Princeton, NJ: Princeton University Press, 2000.

Burke, Seán. *The Death and Return of the Author: Criticism and Subjectivity in Barthes, Foucault and Derrida.* 2nd edn. Edinburgh: Edinburgh University Press, 1998. First publ. 1992.

Butler, Judith. *Gender Trouble: Feminism and the Subversion of Identity.* New York and London: Routledge, 1990.

Butler, Judith. *Subjects of Desire: Hegelian Reflections in Twentieth-Century France.* New York: Columbia University Press, 1999. First publ. 1987.

Butler, Judith, John Guillory, and Kendall Thomas, eds. *What's Left of Theory? New Work on the Politics of Literary Theory. Essays from the English Institute.* New York: Routledge, 2000.

Callinicos, Alex. *Against Postmodernism: A Marxist Critique.* Cambridge: Polity, 1989.

Cheney, Lynne V. *Telling the Truth.* New York: Simon & Schuster, 1996. First publ. 1995.

—— *Telling the Truth: A Report on the State of the Humanities in Higher Education.* Washington DC: National Endowment for the Humanities, 1992.

Chomsky, Noam, Laura Nader, Immanuel Wallerstein, Richard C. Lewontin, Richard Ohmann, Howard Zinn, Ira Katznelson, David Montgomery and Ray Siever, *The Cold War and the University: Toward an Intellectual History of the Postwar Years.* New York: New Press, 1997.

Chun, Lin. *The British New Left.* Edinburgh: Edinburgh University Press, 1993.

Collini, Stefan. *Absent Minds: Intellectuals in Britain.* Oxford: Oxford University Press, 2006.

Cook-Lynn, Elizabeth. *Why I Can't Read Wallace Stegner and Other Essays: A Tribal Voice.* Madison: University of Wisconsin Press, 1996.

Culler, Jonathan. *Structuralist Poetics: Structuralism, Linguistics and the Study of Literature.* London and Henley: Routledge & Kegan Paul, 1975.

Daly, Mary. *Gyn/Ecology: The Metaethics of Radical Feminism.* London: Women's Press, 1979. First publ. 1978.

de Man, Paul. *The Resistance to Theory.* Minneapolis and London: University of Minnesota Press, 1986.

de Saussure, Ferdinand. *Course in General Linguistics.* Intr. Jonathan Culler, ed. Charles Bally, Albert Sechehaye and Albert Reidlinger, trans. Wade Baskin. London: Peter Owen, 1974.

Deleuze, Gilles. *Empirisme et subjectivité.* Paris: Presses Universitaires de France, 1953.

—— *Nietzsche.* Paris: Presses Universitaires de France, 1965.

Deleuze, Gilles, and Félix Guattari. *Capitalisme et schizophrénie: L'Anti-Oedipe.* 2nd edn. Paris: Éditions de Minuit, 1973.

—— *Capitalisme et schizophrénie 2: Mille Plateaux.* Paris: Éditions de Minuit, 1980.

Derrida, Jacques. *A Derrida Reader: Between the Blinds.* Ed. Peggy Kamuf. New York and London: Harvester, 1991.

—— *Dissemination.* Trans. Barbara Johnson. London: Athlone, 1981.

—— *Margins of Philosophy.* Trans. Alan Bass. New York and London: Harvester Wheatsheaf, 1982.

—— *Of Grammatology.* Trans. Gayatri Chakravorty Spivak. Baltimore and London: Johns Hopkins University Press, 1976.

—— *The Other Heading: Reflections on Today's Europe.* Trans. Pascale-Anne Brault and Michael B. Naas, intr. Michael B. Naas. Bloomington: Indiana University Press, 1992.

—— *The Politics of Friendship.* Trans. George Collins. London: Verso, 1997.

—— *Specters of Marx: The State of the Debt, the Work of Mourning, and the New International.* Trans. Peggy Kamuf, intr. Bernard Magnus and Stephen Cullenberg. New York and London: Routledge, 1994.

—— *Writing and Difference.* Trans. and intr. Alan Bass. London and Henley: Routledge & Kegan Paul, 1978.

Docherty, Thomas. *Alterities: Criticism, History, Representation.* Oxford: Clarendon Press, 1996.

D'Souza, Dinesh. *Illiberal Education: The Politics of Race and Sex on Campus.* New York: Free Press, 1991.

Dworkin, Dennis. *Cultural Marxism in Postwar Britain: History, the New Left and the Origins of Cultural Studies.* Durham, NC, and London: Duke University Press, 1997.

Eagleton, Terry. *Criticism and Ideology: A Study in Marxist Literary Theory.* London: NLB, 1976.

—— *The Function of Criticism: From the Spectator to Post-Structuralism.* London: Verso, 1984.

—— *Literary Theory: An Introduction.* Oxford: Blackwell, 1996. First publ. 1983.

—— *Marxism and Literary Criticism.* London: Methuen, 1976.

Eldridge, John and Lizzie Eldridge. *Raymond Williams: Making Connections.* London and New York: Routledge, 1994.

Eliot, T. S., *The Sacred Wood: Essays on Poetry and Criticism.* London: Methuen, 1960. First publ. 1920.

Ellison, Ralph. *Shadow and Act.* New York: Vintage, 1972.

Ellmann, Maud. *The Poetics of Impersonality: T. S. Eliot and Ezra Pound.* Brighton: Harvester, 1987.

Empson, William. *Seven Types of Ambiguity.* Harmondsworth: Penguin, 1972. First publ. 1930.

Engels, Friedrich. *Selected Writings.* Harmondsworth: Penguin, 1967.

Erlich, Victor. *Russian Formalism: History – Doctrine.* 4th edn. The Hague, Paris and New York: Mouton, 1980.

Fekete, John. *The Critical Twilight: Explorations in the Ideology of Anglo-American Literary Theory from Eliot to McLuhan.* London, Henley and Boston: Routledge & Kegan Paul, 1978.

Ferguson, Marjorie and Peter Golding, eds. *Cultural Studies in Question.* London, Thousand Oaks and New Delhi: Sage, 1997.

Ffrench, Patrick. *The Time of Theory: A History of Tel Quel (1960–1983).* Oxford: Clarendon Press, 1995.

Fink, Leon, Stephen T. Leonard and Donald M. Read, eds. *Intellectuals and Public Life: Between Radicalism and Reform.* Ithaca and London: Cornell University Press, 1996.

Foucault, Michel. *The Archaeology of Knowledge.* Trans. A. M. Sheridan Smith. London: Tavistock, 1974. First publ. in Eng. 1972.

—— *The History of Sexuality,* vol. 1: *An Introduction.* Trans. Robert Hurley. Harmondsworth: Penguin, 1981.

Foucault, Michel. *Language, Counter-Memory, Practice.* Trans. Donald F. Bouchard and Sherry Simon. Oxford: Blackwell, 1977.

—— *The Order of Things: An Archaeology of the Human Sciences.* London: Tavistock, 1974.

—— *Power/Knowledge: Selected Interviews and Other Writings 1972–1977.* Trans. Colin Gordon, Leo Marshall, John Mepham and Kate Soper. Hemel Hempstead: Harvester, 1980.

Frye, Northrop. *Anatomy of Criticism: Four Essays.* Princeton: Princeton University Press, 1957.

Furedi, Frank. *Where Have All the Intellectuals Gone? Confronting 21st Century Philistinism.* London and New York: Continuum, 2004.

Gadamer, Hans-Georg. *Truth and Method.* Trans. Joel Weinsheimer and Donald G. Marshall. New York: Continuum, 1998.

Gascoyne, David. *A Short Survey of Surrealism.* London: Cass, 1970. First publ. 1935.

Genette, Gérard. *Introduction à l'architexte.* Paris: Seuil, 1979.

Gibson, Andrew. *Beckett and Badiou: The Pathos of Intermittency.* Oxford: Oxford University Press, 2007.

Gilbert, Sandra M., and Susan Gubar. *The Madwoman in the Attic: The Woman Writer and the Nineteenth-Century Literary Imagination.* New Haven and London: Yale University Press, 1979.

Goldberg, David Theo, ed. *Multiculturalism: A Reader.* Oxford and Cambridge, Mass.: Blackwell, 1994.

Goldmann, Lucien. *Towards a Sociology of the Novel.* Trans. Alan Sheridan. London and New York: Tavistock, 1975.

Gouldner, Alvin W. *The Future of Intellectuals and the Rise of the New Class: A Frame of Reference, Theses, Conjectures, Arguments, and an Historical Perspective on the Role of Intellectuals and Intelligentsia in the International Class Contest of the Modern Era.* London and Basingstoke: Macmillan, 1979.

Graff, Gerald. *Beyond the Culture Wars: How Teaching the Conflicts Can Revitalize American Education.* New York and London: Norton, 1992.

—— *Literature against Itself: Literary Ideas in Modern Society.* Chicago: Elephant, 1995. First publ. 1979.

—— *Professing Literature: An Institutional History.* Chicago and London: University of Chicago Press, 1987.

Graff, Gerald, and Reginald Gibbons, eds. *Criticism in the University.* Evanston, Iee.: Northwestern University Press, 1985.

Guillory, John. *Cultural Capital: The Problem of Literary Canon Formation.* Chicago and London: University of Chicago Press, 1993.

Gutting, Gary, ed. *The Cambridge Companion to Foucault.* Cambridge: Cambridge University Press, 1994.

Harris, Roy. *Reading Saussure: A Critical Commentary on the Cours de Linguistique Generale.* London: Duckworth, 1987.

—— *Saussure and his Interpreters.* Edinburgh: Edinburgh University Press, 2001.

Harvey, David. *The Condition of Postmodernity: An Inquiry into the Origins of Cultural Change.* Oxford: Blackwell, 1989.

Hegel, G. W. F. *Phenomenology of Spirit.* Trans. A. V. Miller. Oxford: Oxford University Press, 1977.

Heidegger, Martin. *Pathmarks.* Ed. William McNeill. Cambridge: Cambridge University Press, 1998.

Henry, Michel. *Marx I: Une philosophie de la réalité.* Paris: Gallimard, 1976.

Higgins, John. *Raymond Williams: Literature, Marxism, and Cultural Materialism.* London: Routledge, 1999.

Hirsch, E. D. *Cultural Literacy: What Every American Needs to Know.* New York: Vintage Books, 1988.

Hirschkop, Ken. *Mikhail Bakhtin: An Aesthetic for Democracy.* Oxford: Oxford University Press, 1999.

Hirschkop, Ken, and David Shepherd, eds. *Bakhtin and Cultural Theory.* Manchester: Manchester University Press, 2001.

Hoggart, Richard. *Speaking to Each Other,* vol. 1: *About Society.* London: Chatto & Windus, 1970.

—— *Speaking to Each Other,* vol. 2: *About Literature.* London: Chatto & Windus, 1970.

—— *The Uses of Literacy: Aspects of Working Class Life, with Special References to Publications and Entertainment.* London: Chatto & Windus, 1957.

Hole, Judith, and Ellen Levine. *Rebirth of Feminism.* New York: Quadrangle, 1975. First publ. 1971.

Hollinger, David A. *Postethnic America: Beyond Multiculturalism.* New York: Basic Books, 1995.

Holquist, Michael. *Dialogism: Bakhtin and his World.* London and New York: Routledge, 1990.

Holub, Robert C. *Reception Theory: An Introduction.* London and New York: Methuen, 1984.

Horowitz, Irving Louis, and William H. Friedland. *The Knowledge Factory: Student Power and Academic Politics in America.* Carbondale and Edwardsville: Southern Illinois University Press, 1972. First publ. 1970.

Hulme, T. E. *Speculations: Essays on Humanism and Art.* Ed. Herbert Read. London, Henley and Boston: Routledge & Kegan Paul, 1936. First publ. 1924.

Inglis, Fred. *Raymond Williams.* London: Routledge, 1995.

Jagose, Annamarie. *Queer Theory: An Introduction.* New York: New York University Press, 1996.

Jameson, Fredric. *Marxism and Form: Twentieth Century Dialectical Theories of Literature.* Princeton: Princeton University Press, 1974. First publ. 1971.

—— *Postmodernism: or, The Cultural Logic of Late Capitalism.* London: Verso, 1991.

—— *The Prison-House of Language: A Critical Account of Structuralism and Russian Formalism.* Princeton: Princeton University Press, 1972.

Jancovich, Mark. *The Cultural Politics of the New Criticism*. Cambridge: Cambridge University Press, 1993.

Kant, Immanuel. *The Critique of Judgement*. 13th edn. Trans. James Creed Meredith. Oxford: Oxford University Press, 1991.

—— *Critique of Pure Reason*. Trans. and ed. Paul Guyer and Allen W. Wood. Cambridge: Cambridge University Press, 1997.

Karanikas, Alexander. *Tillers of Myth: Southern Agrarians as Social and Literary Critics*. Madison, Milwaukee and London: University of Wisconsin Press, 1969.

Kauffman, Linda S., ed. *American Feminist Thought at Century's End: A Reader*. Cambridge, Mass., and Oxford: Blackwell, 1993.

Kimball, Roger. *Tenured Radicals: How Politics Has Corrupted our Higher Education*. New York: HarperCollins, 1990.

Kramnick, Jonathan Brody. *Making the English Canon: Print-Capitalism and the Cultural Past*. Cambridge: Cambridge University Press, 1998.

Kristeva, Julia. *About Chinese Women*. Trans. Anita Barrows. New York: Boyars, 1977.

—— *Desire in Language: A Semiotic Approach to Literature and Art*. Ed. Leon S. Roudiez, trans. Thomas Gora, Alice Jardine and Leon S. Roudiez. Oxford: Blackwell, 1980.

—— *Revolution in Poetic Language*. Intr. Leon S. Roudiez, trans. Margaret Waller. New York: Columbia University Press, 1984.

Krupat, Arnold. *Ethnocriticism: Ethnography, History, Literature*. Berkeley: University of California Press, 1992.

Lacan, Jacques. *Écrits: A Selection*. Trans. Alan Sheridan. London: Tavistock, 1977.

Lacan, Jacques, and the École Freudienne. *Feminine Sexuality*. Trans. Jacqueline Rose. New York and London: Norton, 1982.

Larson, Sidner. *Captured in the Middle: Tradition and Experience in Contemporary Native American Writing*. Seattle and London: University of Washington Press, 2000.

Leavis, F. R. *The Common Pursuit*. London: Chatto & Windus, 1952.

—— *Education and the University: A Sketch for an 'English School'*. 1943. London: Chatto & Windus, 1948.

—— *For Continuity*. Cambridge: Minority Press, 1933.

—— *The Great Tradition*. London: Chatto & Windus, 1948.

—— *New Bearings in English Poetry: A Study of the Contemporary Situation*. London: Chatto & Windus, 1942.

—— *Revaluation: Tradition and Development in English Poetry*. London: Chatto & Windus, 1936.

——, ed. *A Selection from Scrutiny*, vol. 1. Cambridge: Cambridge University Press, 1968.

Leavis, F. R., and Denys Thompson. *Culture and Environment: The Training of Critical Awareness*. London: Chatto & Windus, 1933.

Leavis, Q. D. *Fiction and the Reading Public*. London: Chatto & Windus, 1965. First publ. 1932.

Lemon, Lee T., and Marion J. Reis, eds., trans. and intr. *Russian Formalist Criticism*. Lincoln and London: University of Nebraska Press, 1965.

Lenin, Vladimir. *Lenin on Literature and Art*. Moscow: Progress Publishers, 1967.

Lentricchia, Frank. *After the New Criticism*. London: Methuen, 1980.

Lévi-Strauss, Claude. *Structural Anthropology*. Trans. Claire Jacobson and Brooke Grundfest Schoepf. Harmondsworth: Penguin, 1972.

Levine, Lawrence W. *Black Culture and Black Consciousness: Afro-American Folk Thought from Slavery to Freedom*. Oxford, London and New York: Oxford University Press, 1977.

—— *Highbrow/Lowbrow: The Emergence of Cultural Hierarchy in America*. Cambridge, Mass., and London: Harvard University Press, 1988.

—— *The Unpredictable Past: Explorations in American Cultural History*. New York and Oxford: Oxford University Press, 1993.

Levitt, Cyrill, Scott Davies and Neil McLaughlin, eds. *Mistaken Identities: The Second Wave of Controversy over 'Political Correctness'*. New York: Peter Lang, 1999.

Lewis, Wyndham. *The Art of Being Ruled*. London: Chatto & Windus, 1926.

—— *The Demon of Progress in the Arts*. London: Methuen, 1954.

—— *Time and Western Man*. London: Chatto & Windus, 1927.

Lipset, Seymour Martin. *Rebellion in the University: A History of Student Activism in America*. London: Routledge & Kegan Paul, 1972.

Lukács, Georg. *History and Class Consciousness*. Trans. Rodney Livingstone. London: Merlin Press, 1971.

—— *Writer and Critic*. Ed. and trans. Arthur Kahn. London: Merlin Press, 1978.

Lyotard, Jean-François. *The Lyotard Reader*. Ed. Andrew Benjamin. Oxford: Blackwell, 1989.

—— *Political Writings*. Trans. Bill Readings and Paul Geiman. Minneapolis: Minnesota, 1993.

—— *The Postmodern Condition: A Report on Knowledge*. Trans. Geoff Bennington and Brian Massumi. Minneapolis: University of Minnesota Press, 1984.

McHale, Brian. *Postmodernist Fiction*. London: Methuen, 1987.

Macherey, Pierre. *A Theory of Literary Production*. Trans. G. Wall. London: Routledge & Kegan Paul, 1978.

Macksey, Richard, and Eugenio Donato, eds. *The Languages of Criticism and the Sciences of Man: The Structuralist Controversy*. Baltimore: Johns Hopkins University Press, 1970.

McNay, Lois. *Foucault: A Critical Introduction*. Cambridge: Polity, 1994.

Magner, James E. *John Crowe Ransom: Critical Principles and Preoccupations*. The Hague: Mouton, 1971.

Mandel, Ernest. *Late Capitalism*. London: Verso, 1975.

Martin, Terry. *The Affirmative Action Empire: Nations and Nationalism in the Soviet Union, 1923–1939*. Ithaca and London: Cornell University Press, 2001.

Marx, Karl. *A Contribution to the Critique of Political Economy*. Trans. S. W. Ryazanskaya. London: Lawrence & Wishart, 1981.

—— *Early Writings*. Intr. Lucio Colletti, trans. Rodney Livingstone and Gregor Benton. Harmondsworth: Penguin, 1975.

Marx, Karl, and Friedrich Engels. *The German Ideology*. New York: Prometheus Books, 1998.

Marx-Scouras, Danielle. *The Cultural Politics of Tel Quel: Literature and the Left in the Wake of Engagement*. University Park, Pa.: Pennsylvania State University Press, 1996.

Mason, Peter. *Deconstructing America: Representations of the Other*. London and New York: Routledge, 1990.

Matthiessen, F. O. *American Renaissance: Art and Expression in the Age of Whitman*. New York: Oxford University Press, 1941.

Michaels, Walter Benn, and Donald E. Pease, eds. *The American Renaissance Reconsidered*. Baltimore and London: Johns Hopkins University Press, 1985.

Mihesuah, Devon A., ed. *Natives and Academics: Researching and Writing about American Indians*. Lincoln and London: University of Nebraska Press, 1998.

Mitchell, Juliet. *Psychoanalysis and Feminism*. Harmondsworth: Penguin, 1975. First publ. 1974.

—— *Women's Estate*. Harmondsworth: Penguin, 1971.

Morgan, Robin, ed. *Sisterhood Is Powerful: An Anthology of Writings from the Women's Liberation Movement*. New York: Random House, 1970.

Mulhern, Francis, ed. *Contemporary Marxist Literary Criticism*. London and New York: Longman, 1992.

—— *The Moment of 'Scrutiny'*. London: NLB, 1979.

Norris, Christopher. *Deconstruction and the Interests of Theory*. London: Pinter, 1988.

—— *Deconstruction: Theory and Practice*. London: Methuen, 1982.

—— *The Deconstructive Turn: Essays in the Rhetoric of Philosophy*. London: Methuen, 1983.

—— *Derrida*. London: Fontana, 1987.

—— *What's Wrong with Postmodernism? Critical Theory and the Ends of Philosophy*. New York and London: Harvester Wheatsheaf, 1990.

Ohmann, Richard. *English in America: A Radical View of the Profession*. Hanover, NH: University Press of New England, 1996. First publ. 1976.

O'Neill, William L. *Everyone Was Brave: The Rise and Fall of Feminism in America*. Chicago: Quadrangle, 1969.

Paddison, Max. *Adorno, Modernism and Mass Culture: Essays on Critical Theory and Music*. London: Kahn & Averill, 1996.

Pater, Walter. *Selected Writings of Walter Pater*. Ed. and intr. Harold Bloom. New York: New American Library, 1974.

Pease, Donald E. *Visionary Compacts: American Renaissance Writings in Cultural Context*. Madison and London: University of Wisconsin Press, 1987.

Pound, Ezra. *Literary Essays of Ezra Pound*. Ed. and intr. T. S. Eliot. London: Faber & Faber, 1954.

Ransom, John Crowe. *The New Criticism.* Norfolk, Conn.: New Directions, 1941.
—— *The World's Body.* New York and London: Scribner, 1938.
Reising, Russell. *The Unusable Past: Theory and the Study of American Literature.* New York and London: Methuen, 1986.
Reynolds, David S. *Beneath the American Renaissance: The Subversive Imagination in the Age of Emerson and Melville.* Cambridge, Mass., and London: Harvard University Press, 1988.
Richards, I. A. *Coleridge on Imagination.* 3rd edn. London: Routledge & Kegan Paul, 1962. First publ. 1934.
—— *Practical Criticism: A Study of Literary Judgement.* London: Kegan Paul, Trench, Trubner, 1929.
—— *Principles of Literary Criticism.* London: Kegan Paul, 1926. First publ. 1924.
—— *Science and Poetry.* London: Kegan Paul, Trench, Trubner, 1926.
Richardson, Diane, and Victoria Robinson, eds. *Introducing Women's Studies.* Basingstoke and London: Macmillan, 1993.
Rorty, Richard. *Achieving our Country: Leftist Thought in Twentieth-Century America.* Cambridge, Mass., and London: Harvard University Press, 1998.
Ross, Trevor. *The Making of the English Literary Canon: From the Middle Ages to the Late Eighteenth Century.* Montreal and Kingston: McGill-Queens University Press, 1998.
Rowbotham, Sheila. *Hidden from History: 300 Years of Women's Oppression and the Fight against It.* London: Pluto, 1977.
Salih, Sara. *Judith Butler.* London and New York: Routledge, 2002.
Sanders, Carol, ed. *The Cambridge Companion to Saussure.* Cambridge: Cambridge University Press, 2004.
Sauerberg, Lars Ole. *Versions of the Past – Visions of the Future: The Canonical in the Criticism of T. S. Eliot, F. R. Leavis, Northrop Frye and Harold Bloom.* Basingstoke and London: Macmillan, 1997.
Saussure, Ferdinand de. *Course in General Linguistics.* Intr. Jonathan Culler, ed. Charles Bally, Albert Sechehaye and Albert Reidlinger. Trans. Wade Baskin. London: Peter Owen, 1974.
Schlesinger, Arthur M., Jr. *The Disuniting of America: Reflections on a Multicultural America.* New York and London: Norton, 1992.
Sedgwick, Eve Kosofsky. *Between Men: English Literature and Male Homosocial Desire.* New York: Columbia University Press, 1985.
Showalter, Elaine. *A Literature of their Own: British Women Novelists from Brontë to Lessing.* Princeton: Princeton University Press, 1977.
Silliman, Ron, ed. *In the American Tree.* Orono, Me.: National Poetry Foundation, 1986.
Singh, Amrijit, and Peter Schmidt, eds. *Postcolonial Theory and the United States: Race, Ethnicity and Literature.* Jackson: University Press of Mississippi, 2000.
Small, Helen, ed. *The Public Intellectual.* Oxford: Blackwell, 2002.

Sollors, Werner, ed. *The Invention of Ethnicity*. New York and Oxford: Oxford University Press, 1989.

Song, Miri. *Choosing Ethnic Identity*. Cambridge: Polity, 2003.

Spengemann, William C. *A Mirror for Americanists: Reflections on the Idea of American Literature*. Hanover and London: University Press of New England, 1989.

Spiller, Hortense, ed. *Comparative American Identities: Race, Sex and Nationality in the Modern text*. New York and London: Routledge, 1991.

Spivak, Gayatri Chakravorty. *A Critique of Postcolonial Reason: Toward a History of the Vanishing Present*. Cambridge, Mass., and London: Harvard University Press, 1999.

—— *In Other Worlds: Essays in Cultural Politics*. New York and London: Routledge, 1988.

—— *Outside in the Teaching Machine*. New York and London: Routledge, 1993.

Steele, Tom. *The Emergence of Cultural Studies 1945–65: Cultural Politics, Adult Education and the English Question*. London: Lawrence & Wishart, 1997.

Stites, Richard. *Revolutionary Dreams: Utopian Vision and Experimental Life in the Russian Revolution*. New York and Oxford: Oxford University Press, 1989.

Tallis, Raymond. *Not Saussure: A Critique of Post-Saussurean Literary Theory*. Basingstoke: Macmillan, 1988.

Tate, Allen. *Essays of Four Decades*. London: Oxford University Press, 1970.

—— *The Man of Letters in the Modern World: Selected Essays 1928–1955*. London: Thames & Hudson, 1957.

Taylor, Charles K., Anthony Appiah, Jürgen Habermas, Stephen C. Rockefeller, Michael Walzer and Susan Wolf, *Multiculturalism: Examining the Politics of Recognition*. Ed. and intr. Amy Gutmann. Princeton, NJ: Princeton University Press, 1994.

Terry, Richard. *Poetry and the Making of the English Literary Past*. Oxford: Oxford University Press, 2001.

Trachtenberg, Alan. *The Incorporation of America: Culture and Society in the Guilded Age*. New York: Hill & Wang, 1982.

Trotsky, Leon. *Trotsky on Literature and Art*. Ed. and intr. Paul N. Siegel. New York: Pathfinder, 1972.

Turner, Graeme. *British Cultural Studies: An Introduction*. 3rd edn. London: Routledge, 2003. First publ. 1990.

'Twelve Southerners'. *I'll Take My Stand: The South and Agrarian Tradition*. Intr. Louis J. Rubin, Jr., brographical essays by Virginia Rock. New York: Harper, 1962.

Vizenor, Gerald. *Fugitive Poses: Native American Indian Scenes of Absence and Presence*. Lincoln and London: University of Nebraska Press, 1998.

Wandor, Micheline, ed. *The Body Politic: Writings from the Women's Liberation Movement in Britain 1969–1972*. London: Stage 1, 1972.

Washington, Peter. *Fraud: Literary Theory and the End of English*. London: Fontana, 1989.

Warren, Robert Penn. *Selected Essays*. New York: Random House, 1958.

Waters, Mary C. *Ethnic Options: Choosing Identities in America*. Berkeley, Los Angeles and London: University of California Press, 1990.

Widdowson, Peter, ed. *Re-Reading English*. London and New York: Methuen, 1982.

Wiggershaus, Rolf. *The Frankfurt School*. Trans. Michael Robertson. Cambridge: Polity, 1994.

Williams, Jeffrey, ed. *PC Wars: Politics and Theory in the Academy*. New York and London: Routledge, 1995.

Williams, Raymond. *Communications*. London: Chatto & Windus, 1966.

—— *Culture and Society*. Harmondsworth: Penguin, 1963.

—— *The English Novel from Dickens to Lawrence*. London: Hogarth, 1984. First publ. 1970.

—— *Keywords: A Vocabulary of Culture and Society*. Glasgow: Fontana/Croom Helm, 1976.

—— *The Long Revolution*. London: Chatto & Windus, 1961.

—— *Politics and Letters: Interviews with* New Left Review. London: NLB, 1979.

—— *The Politics of Modernism*. London: Verso, 1989.

—— *Problems in Materialism and Culture: Selected Essays*. London: Verso, 1980.

—— *Television: Technology and Cultural Form*. London: Fontana/Collins, 1974.

Wilson, Edmund. *Axel's Castle: A Study in the Imaginative Literature of 1870–1930*. London: Fontana, 1961. First publ. 1931.

Wilson, John K. *The Myth of Political Correctness: The Conservative Attack on Higher Education*. Durham, NC, and London: Duke University Press, 1995.

Wimsatt, William K. and Cleanth Brooks, eds. *Literary Criticism: A Short History*. London: Routledge & Kegan Paul, 1957.

Wood, James L. *Political Consciousness and Student Action*. Beverly Hills: Sage, 1974.

Woolf, Virginia. *The Essays of Virginia Woolf*. 4 vols. Ed. Andrew McNeillie. London: Hogarth, 1986–94.

—— *A Room of One's Own and Three Guineas*. Ed. and intr. Michèlle Barrett. London: Penguin, 1993.

Young, Robert. *White Mythologies: Writing History and the West*. London and New York: Routledge, 1990.

Young, Robert J. C. *Postcolonialism: A Historical Introduction*. Oxford: Blackwell, 2001.

Index